# SOCIAL WORK PRACTICE:
## *A Unitary Approach*

# SOCIAL WORK PRACTICE:
## *A Unitary Approach*

## HOWARD GOLDSTEIN

University of South Carolina Press
Columbia, South Carolina

FIRST PRINTING, June 1973
SECOND PRINTING, August 1973
THIRD PRINTING, March 1974

Published in Columbia, South Carolina, by the
University of South Carolina Press, 1973

*Manufactured in the United States of America*

**Library of Congress Cataloging in Publication Data**
Goldstein, Howard, 1922–
  Social work practice: a unitary approach
  Bibliography: pp. 276–81
  1. Social service.  2. Social service—History.
I. Title.
HV40.G64                361                73-4687
ISBN 0-87249-285-0

to my wife, Linda,
my brother, Herbert,
and "Harriet"

# CONTENTS

# INTRODUCTION

The profession of social work finds itself in a dilemma. Its years of maturation have been marked by first a one, then a two, and finally, a three method conception of practice which has tended to segment its knowledge and its clientele into categories labeled Individual, Group, and Community. Now, a plea for recognition of the fact that social work does have a common knowledge base is heard with increasing frequency. But this plea carries with it overtones of the question about what knowledge shall comprise this base. The issue, it seems to me, is not so much whether adequate knowledge is available, but how this knowledge can be systematized and ordered so as to afford the profession a coherent foundation for practice. There is no shortage of knowledge; the proliferation of research findings, the ascendance (and frequently, the decline) of schools and cults of practice and the significant theories, conceptualizations, and constructs generated by the social and behavioral sciences leave the practitioner, teacher, and learner in a quandary about what to select from this vast array of information and how it should be related and arranged. Gone are the days of naïve complacency when the teacher could plan his course or the practitioner could base his practice on a single theory or method. Now, both teacher and practitioner stand waist deep in at least a small sea of knowledge with an eye cast at the next incoming wave.

With due regard for the immensity of the task, it is the intent of this book to contribute to the need for ordering and systematizing pertinent knowledge and to affirm the reality of a common or unitary base for professional practice. In setting out to accomplish this intent, it was first necessary to determine the broad levels of knowledge that would be most applicable to the actualities of modern social work practice. Four levels were identified in an increasing order of specificity and utility: (1) general concepts, (2) functional concepts, (3) strategies, and (4) actions.

General concepts are of the highest order of abstraction. These serve to organize and expand perceptions and assist in the achievement of a broad base of understanding of certain phenomena in conceptual and hypothetical terms. Theories and concepts of personality, the social order, and deviancy would fit into this level of knowledge.

Functional concepts are of a more specific nature as they include knowledge for applications designed to achieve certain ends. These concepts provide comprehension of particular phenomena, and in the objectivity and logic that they afford, make these phenomena accessible to manipulation. Examples include aspects of communication theory and group dynamics.

Strategies are guides to the efficient and effective application of knowledge to given situations. In some measure, these are prescriptions for action in special circumstances. Strategy is also consonant with the notion of a repertoire of knowledge, technique, and skill applicable to a broad array of situations. Thus the strategy of study and evaluation defines an aspect of practice that is adaptable to all client units as well as its singular use in a specific case.

Finally, actions are the tactical operations within which explicit procedures are employed in relation to specific social units, problems or tasks within the purposes and constraints of a particular setting.

From these four levels of knowledge, the two intermediate categories, functional concepts and strategies, were selected as most pertinent to the organization of knowledge that would lead to an operational understanding of practice. Although reference to the broader theories, on one hand, and to the realities of practice, on the other, could not and should not be avoided, it is assumed that the reader will have access to the former and the opportunity to participate in the latter. The two levels also fit the objective of this book in another way. This objective is not to bestow upon the practitioner a set of methods or techniques, but to offer a knowledge support, a groundwork for practice upon which the individual practitioner can build his own mode and style of action in accord with his own predilections, skill, and personal attributes. For excellence in practice is construed here as an art that is evident in the unique fusion of ingenuity, versatility, knowledge, skill, and learning.

This book, then, is not addressed to the traditional methods of social work. Instead, it cuts across the previously staked out boundaries of Casework, Group Work, and Community Organization and Development to show that which is common to a unitary model of social work practice. This intent is achieved by a synthesis of concepts drawn from the behavioral and social sciences that best explain interpersonal and interactional processes, that are germane to practice with a broad array of social units and that are denotable and identifiable for application to the requirements of assessment, planning and action. As much as possible, reifications and rhetorical assumptions are resisted. This conceptual content is organized within three major frameworks: a social systems model which depicts the structure of practice and helps to locate and identify the salient problem or task and the key social units relevant to it; a social learning or problem-solving model which illustrates the logical and episodic nature of learning and change in social work processes; and a process model which captures the sequence and components of practice through the consideration of the variables of strategy, phase, and target in interaction.

The reader will detect a somewhat individual-oriented tone in some sections of this book. Certainly my long involvement in types of teaching and practice that dealt with personal, interpersonal, and group issues and problems may well influence this inclination toward the individual. One does tend to identify with the knowledge and experience with which he is most familiar. But the reason is more deliberate than accidental. A person-oriented construct underscores the belief that, irrespective of the design and objective, whether practice is aimed at grand schemes for social change or the resolution of a commonplace problem, social work practice is ultimately concerned with persons as distinct individuals—their plans, hopes, ideals, needs, and the way they go about living them out. The final measure of worth of the professional act can only be found in the meaning it holds for certain persons, individually or in association.

This book contains two major sections in accord with the selected levels of knowledge previously noted. Part One comprises the conceptual base of practice, and Part Two includes the strategies and negotiations of practice.

In the first chapter, the reader will find a concise overview of the orientation to practice that will be elaborated in subsequent chapters.

Presented here is a definition of a unitary approach to social work practice that includes its purposes, objectives, and operations.

Chapter Two acquaints the reader with an historical overview of the development of the theories, wisdom, and methods of practice. This is an inferential and theoretical history which attempts to show the beliefs and philosophies as well as the emergence and development of guiding theories and schools which influenced the evolution of present-day practice.

Chapter Three places major emphasis on the role, characteristics, and responsibilities of the social worker. Predicated on the belief that it is the combination of his influence and personal style that mediates the change process, considerable attention is given to the attributes and values that he brings to the change experience, to his sentient and affective characteristics, and to his professional role activities. In addition, his various professional roles are examined in depth.

Chapter Four studies the client as a social system and as an interactor within a set of social systems. The implications and values of this concept are considered as factors which influence how the practitioner comes to understand, plan, and intervene within the client system.

Chapter Five places the social worker and the client into a change system so as to gain an appreciation of its function and operation. A systems orientation illustrates the structure, function, and output of the change system, thereby taking into account the variables that affect its operation. Complementing this approach is the use of the concept of relationship which helps to explain the process, flow, and interchange between the members of the change system.

Chapter Six deals with the objectives of practice and the essential processes of the change endeavor. Here the concept and implications of goal setting and goal seeking are discussed in philosophic and functional terms. This is followed by the consideration of communication as the means by which change is negotiated. Finally, practice is conceptualized as a social learning and problem-solving enterprise within which its stages are defined and ordered.

With this knowledge as a foundation, it is then possible to study the strategies of practice as they are outlined in Part Two. Following a brief discussion of the rationale for the construction and use of a process model for the purposes of illustrating the logical and sequential components of practice, the practice experience is organized within the three major phases—the induction phase, the core phase and the ending phase. Within each phase, its characteristics and objectives are examined and the strategies of study and evaluation, intervention, and appraisal are elaborated in their application to various target systems— the individual, the family and small group, and the organization and community.

# PART ONE

# A CONCEPTUAL BASE FOR

# SOCIAL WORK PRACTICE

# 1

## AN OVERVIEW OF SOCIAL WORK PRACTICE

A profession may be known by the selective nature of what it does in response to specific needs, requirements, and sanctions of society. Although various professions may perform common functions, some core and composite of discernible actions comprise the property and substance of the individual professions. We may speak of the scope, intentions, or more abstract considerations of professional responsibility, but the final measure of a profession's identity lies in the explicit character of what it does in fulfillment of a societal need.

Professional actions that are discernible and denotable give the profession visibility and readily transmit to those persons requiring its services a more precise awareness of its function, scope and limitations. These actions also assist in the processes of recruitment of potential members as symbols of the types of performance with which the person might or might not identify. Finally, the observance of professional actions provides a realistic measure by which the profession can be held accountable to its stated objectives.

In addition to these practical implications, the concept of selective action serves to elucidate the specific characteristics and constitution of that profession. Action is, after all, the expression of certain preconditions which influence the nature, timing, and purpose of forms of behavior. When actions are viewed as the outcomes of professional intent they are indicative of the profession's authority of knowledge, its values and ethics, its specific objectives, and the manner in which these factors are translated into technical expertise.

There is, of course, the human element in professional action, the effect or influence of the attributes of those persons to whom are ascribed and who assume the responsibility for carrying out professional intent. The import of these attributes is probably in direct proportion to the extent to which the particular profession uses human resources more so than technological resources. Thus the biological and physical sciences or engineering might rely less on the personal characteristics of the members of their professions than would education, social work, and the allied helping professions. In these latter instances, and in social work in particular, knowledge, values, and techniques are lodged in the person. Their expression in professional performance is mediated by the personality and characteristics of the individual, who, in concert with like others, combine to form the body, the articulation, and the identity of the profession.

To restate, a profession may be defined by the denotable nature of the actions which comprise the execution of functions required and sanctioned by society. These selective actions form the outcome and objectives—they are the apex of an undergirding body of authoritative knowledge, a set of explicit ethics, values, and beliefs and an array of particular technical actions. The resulting actions are performed by sentient members of the profession and to some degree bear the stamp of personal attributes and styles of behavior.

SOCIAL WORK PRACTICE: ITS DEFINITION AND STRUCTURE

With these criteria in mind it is now possible to construct a definition of the practice of social work. Perhaps it is timely before proceeding to this task to state one obvious disadvantage that the profession of social work endures with regard to the attainment of visibility or understanding. The disadvantage lies in the semantic confusion of its title. Everything has a label, a descriptive term which enables us to "know" its purpose or substance. The more the label corresponds with the phenomenon, the more precise is our recognition of it. The term social work, particularly when compared with the more exact labels of other professions, emerges as ambiguous and nondescriptive, revealing only that it has something to do with human relations. It is precisely this nominal ambiguity which adds to the demand for explicitness in definition.

Social work is a form of *social intervention* which enhances, conserves, and augments the means by which persons, individually and/or collectively, can resolve disruptions in their social existence. The nature of the profession is governed by the combined recognition of the individual as a unique and active organism, the social environment as a dynamic force, and the effects of their reciprocal interaction.

The objective of social work is the *management of social learning,* a process which develops within the context and as a consequence of a purposeful human relationship comprising and involving the social worker and the individuals (singly or collectively) relevant to the objectives.

That which guides the process toward explicit goals and social change is the *influence* of the professional social worker which includes his technical, cognitive, affective, and personal resources derived from a system of knowledge, belief, and value.

Some time ago Samuel Butler, the English satirist and critic, said that "definitions are a kind of scratching and generally make a sore place more sore than it was before." The analogy is pertinent for although this definition does enclose and refine the particular character of the profession and its practice, it also demands further explication in terms that have meaning for its social and human design.

This definition proposes by its content that social work has its own substance and structure. To start with, the definition states that social work is made visible by *categorical professional actions,* congruent with its *purpose* and guided by a particular *social orientation.* Actions, purpose, and orientations are transmuted into the profession's *operational objectives* which are accomplished through particular *processes* and *mediums* and are transactionally guided by the *influential attributes* of the practitioner toward explicit goals and change. What follows, then, is the examination of each of these dimensions of the structure of professional practice.

## The Purpose of Social Work

In the expression of professional responsibility in a variety of settings, it may appear as if social work has various and perhaps even disparate aims. However, the central and distinguishing purpose of social work is its capability for providing the *means* and the *opportunity* by which persons can work out, find alternatives for, organize about, contend with, or, in otherwise autonomous ways, deal with conditions (internal, interpersonal, or environmental) which interfere with productive social living. This purpose is in accord with and in response to individual needs, individual means, individual ends, and individual experiences, expressed singly or collectively. The attainment of professional purpose is denoted in those changes that take place in the behavior of persons and in how this behavior is manifested in social and interactional environments. Although interim purposes may be directed toward emotional, attitudinal, and perceptual factors, social work is essentially concerned with how persons actively deal with their relationships and environment within their social existence. What needs to be understood is that social work provides a way, an access, a bridge, if you will, that persons may use to find a solution to or alternatives for a disruptive condition. The corollary to this statement is that social work does not solve problems or change conditions. Professional practice, in basic terms, is a means, not an end in itself.

In this regard, social work's involvement with and in the system requiring its services is time-limited. The ideal conclusion to which it strives is to depart from the system once a mutually determined degree of autonomy and competency is attained by that system.

Professional purpose derives from its own special authority of knowledge about the social context and meaning of human existence and from the sanctions given the profession by its own organization and by society. Social work can be conceived of as an expression of society's recognition of and concern with conditions which militate against salutary forms of social living by and for its members. The services of the profession, therefore, are not reserved only for those persons who may voluntarily seek them out and use them. In contrast, professional purpose may include self-initiated preventive attempts to identify those conditions which impair social living and aggressively engage those significant persons relevant to the condition in the process that effects change.

*Professional Actions: Social Intervention*

When the prior description of the profession's purposes is translated into behavioral forms of expression, a model of practice that is active, cognitive, and volitional logically follows.

As a means of more precisely clarifying what social work does do, it might be well to restate what it does not do. The actions of social work are not, in the final sense, unilateral. That is, professional practice requires some significant degree of involvement and active participation by persons related to the objectives. Social work practice is an interactional process, with or on behalf of persons relevant to the purpose, and it is carried out with the implicit or explicit sanctions of those persons.

The professional competence of social work is in the ability to responsibly and knowledgeably enter into and become a part of a complex system of human interaction to effect changes in existing patterns of cognition and behavior. This, then, defines the concept of social intervention; literally: the social worker enters into a system, thereby consciously altering its previous state and balance as a means of attaining explicit goals. In that the interventions primarily deal with human interaction, they are mainly social in nature as distinguished from technological, statutory, or physical.

The significance of the preceding statement is in the fact that the practitioner, in intervening in the particular social grouping, becomes a key member of that system. This presence is a force which changes the composition of the system and, therefore, its typical operational mode. The extent to which the system is subject to change corresponds to the extent to which the presence of the professional person is recognized and experienced by its members. The felt presence of the professional may therefore be considered as an indirect form of social intervention.

More direct forms of social intervention would emerge in ways which would deliberately aim to maximize for action discernible resources, motivations, and potentialities that are available within the system. These capacities can exist within a person, between persons, among groups of persons, within or between the structures of social institutions or communities of persons, or in the material resources in the social and physical environment.

Social intervention may take many forms and may be expressed within various types of human association. However, all interventive action is guided by four interrelated factors. These are *intentionality*— the immediate or long-range plan and aim related to specific outcomes; *cognition*—that knowledge and information needed for implementation of the intention; *strategy*—the means by which the intentions are carried out; and *interpersonal relations*—the abiding awareness of the immediate and anticipated meaning of the human association as it affects and is affected by the interventive process. These four factors are separable and denotable only in conceptual terms; within the interventive experience they coexist. Depending on the requirements of the experience, certain factors may take precedence but do not denigrate the presence of the others.

### Operational Characteristics of Social Work Practice

Having looked at the basic structure, the overriding principles which give the profession meaning and direction, let us move down the scale of abstraction. What follows is a transformation of the elements of practice into their broad operational characteristics.

*The Objectives of Practice*     The primary objective of practice is to provide a context in which the possibilities of improved social learning may be maximized. It is the learning of new knowledge and new patterns of behavior which disposes the relevant persons toward more effective means of functioning.

All human relationships are to some extent learning experiences. Whether transitory or extensive in duration, relationships provide the potential for expanding, deepening, or reaffirming awareness of self and others. The learning experience may be constructive or destructive in its effects; what is significant is that some change in perception and behavior derives out of human encounters. It can therefore be assumed that within the professional relationship learning takes place on the part of the professional person as well as the persons using the services.

The professional relationship differs significantly from most other forms of human relationships in that it *selectively* provides those conditions which can facilitate the most productive forms of learning on the part of the client. The term "selective" implies that conscious and deliberate behavior, thought, and planning characterize the professional relationship so as to sort out and include or exclude those conditions which would respectively enhance or impede successful learning. It can be assumed that the most effective relationships are devoid of those specific conditions which previously precluded effective problem solving.

The learning experience may take place on many levels simultaneously and may derive from a variety of forms of relationship. But irrespective of the problem, the number of individuals involved, or the frequency of contact, what evolves out of the experience is increased knowledge and new perceptions of self and others and of behavior and environment. In more precise terms, the participants in the experience may achieve the following: *substantive knowledge*—concrete information about objects, events, and situations; *psychological knowledge*—information about the self, motivations, needs, and past-present-future connections; and *social knowledge*—understanding of self in relation to others and the meaning and implications of the behavioral patterns of others. Although these three conditions prevail in all helping experiences, the nature of the task, the goal and the intent may thrust particular areas into prominence, but not to the exclusion of the others.

The means by which more effective learning can be facilitated are varied. They include social interventions which are deliberate and direct consequences of professional judgment; indirect interventions which obtain from the helping relationship, the setting, and behavior and attributes of the participants; and the unexpected opportunities which are typical of the human experience. The following are illustrations of the more direct forms of intervention:

1. *Augmentation of material resources*—providing for material needs, whether financial or otherwise, to remove conditions blocking learning and change.

2. *Didactic actions*—essentially information giving, instruction, and interpretation required to fill the knowledge gaps which impede understanding.

3. *Guidance and direction*—professional action to assist in resolution of conflict where two or more alternatives of action are confronted and a selective course must be taken.

4. *Rehearsal in thought and action*—the opportunity and security within which persons may think through and act upon new courses of action in advance of the actual experience.

5. *Observation*—inasmuch as the relationship, singular or multiple, is in itself a social experience, the opportunity is present for individuals to derive new learning from observing the ongoing patterns of human interaction.

6. *Experiential conditions*—similar to the preceding form of learning, these derive from actual participation in the process—learning by doing in its varied social forms.

No one optimal process of effective social learning characterizes the nature of social work practice. A variety of theories may guide the process and a range of techniques may be utilized in response to the requirements of the situation and the theoretical beliefs of the professional person.

*The Medium and Process of Social Work Practice*     The objectives of social work practice are implemented within and are characterized by the medium of the *relationship* between the professional and those persons associated with the objectives of the encounter. Inasmuch as the intentions of professional practice are carried out through reciprocal and responsive forms of human interaction, the processes by which they take place are referred to as *socialization*. The concepts of relationship and socialization require greater amplification.

"Relationship" is a somewhat amorphous concept which eludes definition in that it refers to a human phenomenon marked by affective and attitudinal characteristics. We may categorize the relationship by such labels as "good," "dependent," or "intense," but these do not capture its experiential meaning. Its pivotal significance is in its potentiality for providing a climate for change, growth, and confirmation. Perhaps a major measure of the depth and meaning of any relationship is the extent to which it authenticates those who are part of it.

In this regard, the professional relationship differs little from other social relationships. What distinguishes the professional relationship is the presence of deliberate, purposeful actions which enable the association to evolve into a favorable context, a dynamic system within which learning and change can be effected. As a mainstay of practice, the relationship, in either dyads or groups, is a major element. Consideration of the characteristics which abet or impede evolvement, as well as its developmental and maintenance requirements, may be coincidental with or may even precede concern with the problem or task at hand.

Relationships are not solely the property of two-person systems. Humans are capable of and are most frequently involved in more than one set of relationships at the same time. Groups, then, can be characterized as networks of multiple, concurrent relationships.

The primary characteristics of the professional relationship, therefore, include the relative absence (or a striving for the removal) of conditions which would ordinarily impede growth and learning; a degree of consistency and constancy which enables the participants to depend on its quality and continuity; and an overriding sense of purpose and direction.

In addition, the relationship is, in itself, a socializing force which impels its members toward order and change. Persons in relation tend to move toward some measure of congruence as they increasingly commit themselves to the worth and meaning of the association. The assumption of new roles and ways of acting derives from the cues and promptings that are part of and permeate the transactions that take place. A few illustrations of socializing forces might include the values, norms, and expectations of the social worker; the methods he uses; and the persuasive elements in communication. Learning evolves out of exposure to these and other interpersonal expectations for performance. Change accrues through reinforcement and reward for the accomplishment of the performance. To this point, I have not differentiated between the social worker and the other participants in the socialization experience. While the person in authority, the social worker in this instance, would tend to govern socialization, he, too, changes and accommodates to the social pressures of the relationship and modifies his role accordingly.

*The Social Orientation of Social Work*   The purposes and functions of social work are guided by a view of man in his social and environmental context. Thus we simultaneously attempt to understand the individual, the social and physical setting, and the interaction between them.

The attempt to understand man may be made through the use of numerous theories and concepts, each partial, explaining some aspect of human existence. We may know persons in interpersonal terms; or as bearers of specific intrapsychic states; or as persons in concert with other persons combining to form organizational, neighborhood, or community bodies; or as economic or political beings; or in other terms. But underlying any and all of the selected theories there needs to be some set of principles about human and social behavior which tend to govern our expectations and actions relative to the way persons can manage their lives, work out their problems, and accomplish their tasks. These are, in essence, philosophical considerations: the question is whether we tend to see man as one whose actions are determined by forces within or external to himself or, taking into account the limitations and constraints of his condition, as a person free to make his own choices and act. Practice based on the former perception would aim first at the reduction or removal of those forces which are believed to cause or interfere with how persons manage their lives. Practice based on the latter would be directed to strengthening or developing capabilities to deal with or resolve problems of living or to accomplish certain tasks. This is not to say that each orientation excludes reference to the other in practice. However, it is the fundamental belief as to whether man is determined by or determines his own existence that tends to predispose the nature of practice more towards one approach than to the other, whether the intent of practice is social action, organizational change, or the resolution of interpersonal difficulties.

It is the principle of autonomous action that represents our view here, a principle which complements an actional and volitional practice previously described. The person, then, is seen as a unique being who may also share common human characteristics but who translates them into action in his own style and manner. He can be known only in an *holistic* sense—how he goes about his business of living—rather than in a *molecular* sense which fragments mind and body, thought and action, and past and present. As a consequence of his autonomy, he is capable of spontaneous expression and can actively integrate and deal with stimuli coming from internal and external sources. The significance of these conditions lies in the resultant ability to continue to advance to higher orders of performance, to perceive the self differently, and to strive toward objective goals.

The individual learns how to act and be in the long process of socialization that is a consequence of his lengthy period of dependence on his social environment—his family, community, and culture. Behavior, then, is neither fixed nor permanent. It is subject to unlearning, relearning, or new learning.

The individual understands his reality through the apprehension of the meaning of symbols and orders reality through a process of valuing. He is capable of making interpretations of symbols which are internally, externally, culturally, or situationally derived and of making judgments based on the hierarchical values which he ascribes to objects, events, or situations. As a consequence, behavior is purposefully and directionally based on what is deemed valuable, and it is influenced by what is interpreted and known.

The social tendencies of man come from both survival needs and affiliative needs. He is cast into relation with his world in his interdependence with the providers of physical, affectional, and protective resources. As a reasonable degree of physical and personal security is attained, the individual is able to seek out fulfillment of those affiliative needs which, through his relationship with significant persons or groups of persons, confirm and authenticate him as a person. Hence, one seeks interaction to attain a response that has meaning for his being.

In the realities of daily living, persons are involved in multiple social environments. This involvement is an active process in which the individual both influences and is influenced by these environments and milieus. These include the socio-cultural (culture, nationality, ethnic group); socio-psychological (family and kinship groups); and the societal (socio-economic structures and institutions). Persons, therefore, are versatile in their behaviors and responses as behavior is reactive to and varies with the individual's self-expectations, the expectations of others, and the interpretation of the situation by the individual within each type of environment. The repertoire of learned behavior which distinguishes persons therefore needs to be seen in its varied forms as they meet the diverse requirements of specific social situations. In sum, we can know persons only in relation to their numerous social roles.

As individuals aggregate with other persons, groups evolve. That which distinguishes a group from a collectivity of persons is the mutually purposeful actions of the individuals who comprise the group and who share interdependent interpretations, values, and goals. Affiliation with a group is therefore contingent on the ability to change, put aside, or exchange certain personal values and goals for the benefits accruing from interdependence with the group. It is this capacity to diversify behavior that makes it possible for the individual to enter into and become an active, contributing, and responsive member of various social groups.

In addition to his involvement with others in groups, the individual is, concomitantly, a member of human society—particularly as we understand society as consisting of acting people. This would include singular individuals, groups of individuals, and individuals comprising the institutions and organizations which serve or act on the behalf of particular constituencies of individuals. Persons, then, are members of both smaller and larger systems in a number of simultaneous relationships. As citizens, acting individually or in concert, they can be viewed as participants in productive or regressive activities, as recipients of the system's benefits, or as victims of its malaise. While persons may be consumers of services and commodities, they are also capable of altering the existing structure and function of the social institutions that provide these benefits.

*Recapitulation*

The preceding demonstrates how the basic structure of social work practice is a complex of three interlocking variables—the profession's definitive *purposes,* implemented by forms of *social intervention,* and guided by a *social and behavioral orientation* to the human experience. Each element of the complex is related and responsive to as well as influential upon all others. The observation of practice from any one of the three vantage points should reveal the nature of the other two.

The socio-behavioral orientation is congruent with the social purposes and functions of the professional. Social work is distinguished by its basic concern with the social well-being of persons perceived simultaneously as unique individuals and as active, responsive members of various social systems. Ultimately, behavior becomes the valid key to understanding as it is indicative of what has been learned, how it characterizes the individual, and what it implies as it is used to meet diverse social experiences and requirements.

Although the individual may be regarded as a distinct unit from an objective point of view and for objective purposes, in the actuality of the human experience he is not encountered as an entity. The association between the professional person and the client creates a social configuration which calls forth specific forms of behavior learned and used in other social situations with other persons. In addition, this human contact draws into it other significant persons and systems of each of the participants (for example, the conditions in the setting in which the social worker operates and the relevant others and groups of others of which the client is a part or represents). These affiliations cannot be disregarded as they are variables which affect the immediate relationships. Hence, a characteristic of social work practice is its concern with and capability for entrance into the various forms of human association that are related to the problem or task.

### The Social Worker: Characteristics and Influence

The introduction of the characteristics of the professional in this sequence is by design inasmuch as the foregoing principles become vital and eloquent only as they are expressed in the intentions and actions of the social worker.

Social work is most frequently practiced in circumstances which are critical and which reflect the vicissitudes and complexities of human behavior, both individually and collectively. The particular ingenuity that the practitioner brings to these human encounters is the ability to bring order to or reorder the situation, to give meaning and purpose to and make viable what was formerly discontinuous, diffuse, or conflicted. The intent now is to attend to the characteristics that contribute to this ability and that distinguish the social worker in his professional role and responsibilities as a prelude to later elaboration.

It has been established that the medium for social work practice is generally some form of human association that differs from other social relationships in its purposive, goal-seeking properties. Although goal attainment is a collaborative endeavor requiring the involvement and participation of significant persons, the responsibility for the effectiveness of the endeavor rests with the competence of the social worker. This competence includes the ability to develop new relationships, to become a pivotal member of existing relationships, to manage the distinctive courses of human conduct and interaction, and to direct these relationships toward the attainment of explicit goals.

It is this capability to facilitate, to persuade, and to manage the forces and events within the medium of the professional relationship or sets of relationships that establishes the social worker's role of influence. Influence in this instance connotes the power to bring about an effect without the employment of force or command. One source of this influence is the authority of knowledge and skill. However, the value of this authority and its effectiveness is contingent on the extent to which the right to be influential is granted or ascribed to the social worker by the other participants. The authoritative role must be recognized, valued, and experienced before it can achieve its potential.

To recapitulate, the social worker enters into an experience between humans in which he facilitates and sustains a relationship or network of relationships (as in a group) as a medium for change. That the relationships may be a growth-producing, learning experience does not differentiate it from other productive human encounters. That it is purposive and goal-directed gives the experience its professional mark. Within the relationship, the social worker consciously enhances his position of interpersonal influence in the endeavor to maximize the capabilities for learning through the management of the variables upon which learning and change are contingent. Thus the practice of social work is not a benevolent type of botany, a nurturing of natural growth culminating in spontaneous flowering. It is, instead, active, volitional, and cogent.

Influence is not used capriciously; instead, it is governed by two factors. The first is *normative* controls—those preconditions of knowledge, values, and principles assimilated by the social worker which guide professional conduct. The second is *operational* controls—the requisite aptitudes and capabilities which provide the substance of professional practice.

*Normative Characteristics*   A viable knowledge of and identification with the essential values, principles, and sanctions of the profession will insure the probability that modes of practice will complement the purposes and objectives of the profession. In addition, professional identity carries with it the responsibility and the ability to critically evaluate whether the intent and structure of the profession is consonant with the profession's place in society in response to changing social needs and problems. In sum, meaningful professional identification serves to clarify the intermediating role of the practitioner in his responsibilities to his clients and to society.

A proclivity for the exploration of the metaphysical and philosophical questions related to professional intent and activity serves to preclude tendencies for practice to become mechanistic and dehumanzied. Because the hub of professional practice is the many forms of human experience that tend to transcend purely rational considerations, the ethics and morals of intervention, what constitutes the "good life," the optimal values that professional actions aim for, the relative meanings of adaptation, conformity and individuality, and many other issues are open to question, questions that cannot be fully answered by scientific knowledge.

An awareness and appreciation that behavior is purposive, adaptive and, at times, survival-oriented assures the presence of regard for individual needs. Although judgments relative to the usefulness, causality, or morality of behavior may be made by the social worker, the significance of the behavior for the individual or other relevant persons will determine the mode, timing, and sequence of interventive influence.

The inadvertent or heedless imposition of preconceived goals or values is precluded by an understanding of the processes and means of human change. Change occurs as persons, individually or in concert, learn or relearn through gaining new knowledge, finding alternatives, and altering problem-solving behaviors in accord with their own unique styles, attributes, and value systems.

Judiciousness in interventive actions is further strengthened by the discernment of the implications of changes in behavior, subtle or overt, immediate or long-range, for persons relevant to but outside of the professional encounter.

*Operational Characteristics*   The competence to enter into and to enhance the worth of the relationship as the medium for practice first requires substantial clarity about one's professional self-image, the authority of knowledge and skill, and the intentions and purposes of professional intervention. These factors are translated into the ability to study, understand, and participate in the transactional dynamics between persons, within groups, and in larger systems of society.

The competence to meet the diverse and differential requirements of practice with the array of persons, social situations, and social problems encountered requires the availability of a repertoire of systems of social intervention which can be drawn from in response to professional intent. The practice of social work is not governed by the constraints of a single theory. Instead, the acquisition of a variety of theories and concepts which explain the various dimensions of personality, group and family dynamics, and the workings of organizations and communities provides the social worker with the freedom and flexibility to select and use them as they are applicable to the task.

Within the transactional processes, competence requires the availability of a variety of methods and techniques—those subsumed under structuring, modulating, clarifying, and guiding, for example—to achieve the objectives of practice. Their effectiveness rests on the ability to acquire and transmit pertinent information with a minimum of ambiguity, with a sense of timing, and with an awareness of opportunity, all in response to the requirements of the change experience.

This overview of the factors which, in combination, characterize the social work role cannot be completed without some acknowledgment of the transcendent meaning of the personality of the social worker. The adroitness with which he can integrate these characteristics into forms that are spontaneous, expressive, and creative determines the extent to which the professional encounter becomes an enriching human experience. It is the composite of values, life experiences, exposure to particular events, literature, relationships, and the like which, when expressed in the personal style of the social worker, provide the colorations, sentiments, and features of a distinctive practice. His intuitiveness, sensitivity, and warmth give the experience depth and richness. Competent practice, therefore, will express the unique style of the social worker—notably, professional behavior that is spontaneous rather than ritualized, an authentic responsiveness to the human condition, and a blending of professional skill with personal attributes. Who the social worker is, then, is as significant as what he knows and what he does.

## Definition of Social Work Terms

To preserve clarity and to avoid the risks of ambiguity in the chapters to follow, the following are brief definitions of terms common to social work practice.

STRUCTURE OF PRACTICE: The felt influence of those interrelated factors which serve to organize, guide, and direct the social work process. Felt influence refers to only those factors or conditions which directly impinge upon and are experienced by the participants. They include (1) the characteristics of the physical setting; (2) the policies, directives, or conditions for service set by the organization providing service; (3) length and frequency of professional contacts; (4) the assumed and ascribed roles of the participants, i.e., the expected forms of behavior; and (5) the theories, orientations, and philosophies which guide the substance and direction of practice.

FUNCTION OF PRACTICE: The purpose, aims, or intent of the change process. These may include (1) the function and purpose of the setting—the social problems for and with which the organization providing service is designed and sanctioned to deal; (2) perception of professional self—how the social worker believes he can and should help and how he sees himself in relation to the client system; (3) the specific purposes of the professional encounter; (4) the desired outcomes—what is expected to be achieved; and (5) the focus—the specific aspects of the social problem needing attention.

CONTENT: The substance of the encounter as it is perceived by the participants. Included may be (1) the essence of the problem or issue under consideration; (2) communications, verbal and nonverbal; (3) the nature of transactions, interchanges, and negotiations; and (4) the latent content, the affect, values, intentions, and attitudes.

CLIENT: A generic term applied to the person or persons who use social work services. The client may be an individual or collectivity of individuals (family, group, organizational, or community substructure) either meeting with the social worker or benefiting from services indirectly through the participation of other relevant persons. The term *target* of service may also be used to define the person or groups of persons in actual contact with the social worker irrespective of whether they are or are not the client.

MODALITY OF PRACTICE: The form of human association within which practice is implemented. Dyadic relationships and small or large group associations are the usual forms. The former is carried out in interviews; the latter in group meetings.

STRATEGY: The overall plan, a systematic approach to the problem that guides specific interventions.

METHOD: Systematic procedures in an orderly arrangement. Methods include, but are not limited to, such activities as clarification, guidance, exploration, and persuasion.

TECHNIQUE:  The specific means by which aims are implemented. Included are interviewing, conducting group meetings, screening, program formation, data collection and study, and report writing and recording for accountability.

SKILL:  The unique aptitudes and capabilities that are typical of the social worker.

PRACTICE VARIABLES:  The broad array of conditions which affect the particular practice experience in its nature, timing, and patterns of interaction and coloration. Variables may include the elements of personality of the participants, attitudes, motivations, affect and moods, and events that occur in or out of the relationship which bear on the change process.

# 2

## SOCIAL WORK PRACTICE THEORY:
## AN HISTORICAL PERSPECTIVE

Because social work is a social phenomenon, a response to specific societal conditions and needs, an understanding and appreciation of its substance requires an historical and developmental point of view. The term "social" is indicative of motility and evolution, of a dynamic based on interactional change. A social profession, particularly, is in a constant state of evolvement and change. To the extent that the profession is watchful and responsive, the protean nature of society will shape its character and function. Simultaneously, its internal mutability—the endeavors within the profession to examine, refine, and make its structure more viable—also effects change. In sum, a profession that continues to fulfill its objectives in society, that does not become rigidly fixed, is constantly in a process of transition. Therefore, an understanding of a profession can be achieved only through viewing it at some point in time, as it is, and retrospectively, as it has been.

Other purposes are also served by an historical appreciation. For one, heritage and history are consummate. The professional, though an acquaintance with the beginnings and the evolution of his profession, may thereby achieve a greater identity with its roots, spirit, and substance. Perhaps the most meaningful realization is the knowledge that where the profession is now in its nature and function is, at once, a culmination of what has come before and a preparation for what is yet to follow. An historical perspective dilutes the tendency to perceive the current state as static and encourages the valuing of what is as well as the vision of what can yet be. Thus doctrinaire and ideological rigidity can be averted and replaced by objective and innovative thought.

How should the development of a social profession be pursued? At least two methods suggest themselves. The events can be examined with greater emphasis on their linear and molecular characteristics. That is, the specific series of events which comprise the whole may be elucidated with regard to their individual meanings and their relation to preceding and succeeding conditions. Or, the phenomena may be studied in organismic terms in an attempt to achieve a perspective on the dynamic whole. In this instance, the particular events are also subject to examination, but with more direct reference to their interrelations and effect on the emergence of structure and form. The former tends to be a fact-gathering process in seriatim, an accumulation of data which informs and clarifies *how* the phenomenon came to be. The latter is an inferential process in which facts, as they are interpreted, provide meaning about *what* the phenomenon is.

For our purposes, the historical overview that follows will tend towards the inferential and theoretic mode of examination. One reason for this choice is the availability of excellent, factual historical material in social work literature (*Encyclopedia of Social Work,* 1971; Kohs, 1966; Klein, 1968). The second and major reason has to do with the issues in practice that will be dealt with in this book. The profession's theoretical stance needs to be viewed as an outgrowth of particular trends and patterns derived from the profession's attempts to explicate the knowledge base of practice. As will be seen, these patterns and trends were often covert, were at times fortuitous, and were not too often planned or sequential. An inferential approach, although admittedly colored by a personal view and selectivity, can yield more critical and prognostic impressions.

Before proceeding to the historical overview, some guiding comments are in order to encourage a clearer perspective. It is important to note, for instance, that practice throughout most of the profession's development was characterized by social casework in the one-to-one relationship. Although the earlier development of practice with groups and communities will be considered, it is necessary to keep in mind that this elaboration of group work occured somewhat outside the nominal profession of social work. As will be seen, it was not until the 1940s that formal acknowledgment was given to group work as a "method" of social work. Similarly, community organization was an adjunctive activity for many years and did not receive formal acknowledgment and definition until the 1940s. Social work, then, was essentially identified with the casework method during a major portion of its development.

Social work is an American product. It is a profession that evolved out of the industrialization of the United States and its consequences, particularly the kinds of social disorganization which resulted from the dichotomization of society into two main classes, the very affluent and the very poor. Also, the character and direction of the profession's evolution was shaped at its outset by the fact that it grew within the domain of public responsibility in contrast with the private philanthropy typical of British social work.

Still another influence on the emergence of the profession came from the attributes of those persons who assumed leadership and who, through their thoughts, writings, and actions, contributed to its form and development. Many had suffered misfortunes in their own lives. There is no doubt that their beliefs and philosophies about helping the unfortunate and deprived enriched the quality of professionalism. These humanistic views can best be summed up in the following words of Octavia Hill written in 1869:

By knowledge of character more is meant than whether a man is a drunkard or a woman is dishonest; it means knowledge of the passions, hopes and history of people . . . what is the little scheme they have made of their lives, or would make if they had the encouragement . . . how to move, touch and teach them. Our memories and our hopes are more true factors of our lives than we often remember. [1913, p. 258]

*The Antecedents*

Well before the emergence of social work and providing the foundations for its development, ideas about human nature and human behavior were gradually undergoing some significant changes. A marked shift from ethical philosophy and mysticism to scientific study of human behavior was in process (Bruno, 1957). Comte had introduced his positivistic social philosophy in the early nineteenth century, and it provided a frame of reference for knowledge that could be obtained from the observation of the existence of phenomena. Darwin had begun to develop his logic relative to the origin of the species, and though his ideas were not fully accepted, his methodology for viewing development in a causal, orderly fashion influenced modes of thinking and observing. It was therefore possible to begin to conceive of human problems in terms of their causes. Hence, if one is aware of the causes of particular conditions, then ways of eliminating these causes can be sought. The significance of this new philosophical and theoretical orientation was that it served to counter and subsequently reduce the prevailing notions of "sin" and "fate," of moral weakness, and of the "bad seed." The unfortunate, the poor and the degraded, then, no longer needed to be seen as victims of fate or as carriers of inherent inferiority; instead, they could be understood as victims of conditions external to themselves. The philanthropists and social thinkers of the middle and latter nineteenth century could then proceed, on this more scientific basis, with their intentions of creating a better society by alleviating and eliminating the ills of poverty, sickness, and crime.

Causality and positivism profoundly affected the character of practice and the stance of the profession in society. Causality became the mainstay of professional thinking about problems and conditions and prevailed until recent years when other theorists began to question whether true causes could be fully or usefully understood or revealed because of the complex nature of man.

Gouldner refers to how positivistic theory later evolved into functional theory and became institutionalized by the middle class, industrialized society (1970). Middle class attachment to and encouragement of this theory was based on the belief that it did not threaten the existing structures or demand radical changes in the future. Social work, in its emergence as an extension of the middle class and its view of society, underscored this theory by its tendency to work within existing structures and institutions and by urging adaptation rather than change. The mission of professional practice became its concern, with the consequences and residue of the system's defects rather than with the system itself.

*The Foundations, 1870 to 1900*

The beginning of an organized, formal approach to coping with society's problems came with the formation of the National Conference of Charities and Correction. It was the forerunner of what is now the National Conference on Social Welfare and was formed some thirty years before the emergence of what could be called the profession of social work. The National Conference was the first association of individuals concerned with welfare, its institutions, and their problems. Its initial purpose was the attainment of communication among those committed to a more humanitarian and effective administration of social progress with regard to the problems of poverty, social degradation, and crime. Comprised mainly of volunteers, the organization was formed by representatives of the state boards of charities in Massachusetts, Connecticut, New York, and Wisconsin. It is significant that it first convened under the auspices of the American Social Science Association. But early in its development, in 1879, it split away from the association, and in doing so, it left behind the possibility of assuming a more scientific base for its considerations and concerns (Bruno, 1957). While the American Social Science Association was concerned with scientific inquiry into the sources, the nature, and the conditions of human problems, the National Conference stressed as its aim the practical ways of meeting the exigencies of existing problems. The National Conference in a sense turned its back on the pleas for research and theory building and on the possibility of beginning to consider the tentative social theories that were emerging. Left without a theoretical frame of reference for understanding human and social conditions, the early practitioners were, from the first, compelled to develop methods of practice on a trial-and-error basis in order to get the job done and to gain public approval and recognition for their efforts. As will be seen, a "doing" rather than a "thinking" orientation became typical of the profession's approach to problems.

The formal expression of these methods was incorporated into the structure of the Charity Organization Society first formed in 1887 at Buffalo, New York. The society originated in a reaction to the existing uncoordinated and unintelligent giving and was designed to eliminate waste, to substitute work for alms, and to study the individual as a case of dependency. Study was based on the idea that the recipient of aid was an individual rather than a member of a dependent class (Bruno, 1957). By 1892, Charity Organization Societies were operating in ninety-two communities. The consensual aim of COS was the sympathetic study of the individual in his social environment. However, the pressures and demands on the volunteers who were to carry out this task blocked the achievement of this aim and reduced their function to determining eligibility for financial aid.

During this same period there was a proliferation of other forms of specialized services. In 1889, for example, Chicago passed a juvenile court law as a result of the influence of various women's clubs, children's agencies, and social settlements.

Early preparation for work with the residue of society was fragmentary. Infrequently, a few universities gave courses on the relationship of sociology to charitable work. Here the attempt was made to link principles about social interaction with data about the recipients of charity. A few early writers assumed that the discipline of sociology was the proper education for social workers and a means of recruiting the people necessary for enlarging the fields. This trend was resisted because it was believed that the theoretical approach of sociology was not useful to the vocational nature of the task.

However, for practical reasons education was endorsed. Anna L. Dawes, in 1893, stressed that people in the charitable field needed to impart to their successors what they had learned so as to avoid repetitive mistakes. Four years later, Mary Richmond encouraged this notion and defined the conditions under which such a school could be established. She believed that the common elements of "charity work" could be taught at a school that emphasized practical rather than academic means of achieving the goal. These ideas implanted the roots of subsequent education for social work as they stressed that classroom instruction should only parallel field experience in which students could observe and be taught by supervisors who were affiliated with the agencies. Method was to be taught in the field by the supervisor while classes were designed to deal with general principles. Despite some resistance based on the belief that the salary of the agents was much too low to justify time in school, a summer training course was started at the end of the century and subsequently developed into the New York School of Philanthropy. Its stated aim was the improvement of the investigatory personnel of the charity organizations (Bruno, 1957).

*The Emergence of the Profession, 1900 to World War I*

During this period social work came into its own in terms of the fundamentals of title, function, purpose, and education. Because the label which identifies social work is considerably less descriptive than those of other professions—for example, law, medicine, psychology, and education—it would be interesting to know the derivation of its titles. The origins of the term "social work" are vague. "Casework," however, appears to have emerged fortuitously. It first appeared in a paper read at the National Conference in the late 1890s in a sentence that stated, in part, "work with cases." The term did not appear again in the proceedings of the National Conference until 1909. But by 1911 it had become accepted and defined as a technique and had entered literate history (Bruno, 1957).

The value of the casework method became more widely appreciated by persons in related fields. Its utility was demonstrated in work with the ill by Richard Cabot and Ida Canon. Casework was used in work with unmarried mothers in Boston, in protective services with children, and in other areas of social welfare. Some beginning attempts were made to define casework. Karl de Schweinitz called it "the art of helping." Mary Richmond spoke of it as the use of common sense in uncommon situations. Zilpha Smith referred to taking pains to know the applicant.

The notion of causality was pervasive in the content of social work practice in its beginnings. It was assumed that if adequate knowledge could be attained about the individual, then some form of action would logically follow. This was, however, a simplistic equation: if a problem was caused by unemployment, then work was needed; if the problem was illness, then medical help was required. Thus the weight of professional activity was on the collection of "facts" in order to establish a cause-cure relationship. And with these actions came the aura of the social worker as the investigator.

Quite apart from the domain of social work, this period witnessed the emergence of group work as still another way of dealing with human problems. What came to be known as group work derived from a diversity of sources which recognized the values of collective interaction. These sources included the labor movement's concern with the working conditions and the adult education of its members; brotherhoods and nationality groups in settlement houses; youth agencies and recreation movements; and specific organizations—settlement houses, the Young Men's Christian and Hebrew associations, and the Scouts. But the real core of group work was in the settlement movement which began with the Hull House, created by Jane Addams as a consequence of her experience with groups at Toynbee Hall in London. It was in the settlement movement that the most experimental and realistic work with groups was attempted (Bruno, 1957). In contrast with the methodological and goal-oriented nature of early casework, group work was considered an activity, a means by which numbers of people could meet to find outlets for or to develop conditions in their lives. In a few instances groups were employed for more specific uses—in small classes of tubercular patients, with foster parents in casework agencies, and with recreation groups in mental hospitals. However, group work was, in the main, an opportunistic program with no acknowledged set of methods. Improvised in local neighborhoods with activities devised to meet local needs, with some leanings toward reform and political effort, group work was interested in action, not theory. Since the strength of the settlement influence resided in the efforts of the people using groups, settlements did not, for some time, make any direct theoretical or practical contribution to the professional development of social work. An index of the absence of concrete formulations about its practice is evident in the fact that group work activity was represented in papers and reports in the National Conference only eight times in the organization's first thirty years (Bruno, 1957).

The beginnings of community organization as a systematic approach to problems were similarly informal and unstructured. Early interest in community work was found primarily among those social welfare workers who were concerned with social conditions in American society. Their interests were in labor conditions, the causes of poverty and the means of its alleviation, and the use of police power to rearrange economic relationships (Lurie, 1965). These were the first few reformers who were concerned with social action and who recognized the source of human misfortune within the ills of society.

Education for social work became a reality. The first school expanded its program to a full academic year, and by 1910 the program had increased to two years. Other schools were opened during this time in Boston, Philadelphia, Baltimore, Chicago, and St. Louis, organized most frequently by practicing social workers in the respective communities. These schools were essentially training institutions designed to prepare social workers for the specifics of practice. The association of the schools with the universities in which they were located was tenuous as each school wanted to develop its own curriculum and program unfettered by academic requirements. In addition, each school developed its own program in accord with its perception of the social work task. A minority did attempt to distinguish between education and training, noting that the former implied the acquisition of knowledge, whereas the latter meant the attainment of experience under leadership. In large part, the distinction was not observed. Education was conceived of as the teaching of orderly methods of helping in the field apprenticeship programs, whereas class work was used primarily to develop habits of mind and to discuss the generalities of work in the field (American Association of Social Workers, 1929).

In 1915 education for social work did begin to assume a more definitive position. It was at this point that the profession began to turn toward denotable methods and techniques for a symbol of identity. This tendency resulted from the impact of Abraham Flexner's address to the National Conference in that year. In his paper he stated that the criteria for professionalism included intellectual operations with individual responsibility, a basis for science and learning, a progression towards practical ends, an educationally communicable technique, a tendency toward self-organization, and increasing altruism. Apart from bringing community resources and clients together, he could not identify any specific technique or method; hence, he did not consider social work a profession. Social workers accepted his statements at face value and set themselves to the task of refining their field's own particular methods. The timing of his address, two years in advance of Mary Richmond's book, was another adventitious factor which served to cement the foundations of social work into methodological forms which emphasized technique rather than knowledge and theory.

Richmond's *Social Diagnosis* was acclaimed at once as meeting the most exacting professional and scholarly standards. Its effect on the field of social work was dramatic; the book immediately became the symbol of what social work did, overshadowing all other techniques. Richmond, however, was troubled about the wholehearted acceptance of her work without regard to its limitations. She stated, "I have spent 25 years of my life in an attempt to get social casework accepted as a valid process of social work. Now I shall spend the rest of my life trying to demonstrate to social caseworkers that there is more to social work than social casework" (Bruno, 1957).

The major achievement of *Social Diagnosis* was its creation of a framework for the diagnostic activities of the caseworker. Richmond set forth a set of principles which served to define the parameters of casework practice and the specific responsibilities of the social worker within them. Social casework was defined operationally as consisting of specific processes which developed the personality through adjustments consciously effected, individual by individual, between men and their social environment (Richmond, 1922). Diagnosis was described as "the attempt to make as exact a definition as possible of the situation and the personality of a human being in some social need." Although Richmond sought a categorical understanding of the individual, she also stressed the significance of the client's relationship with others and to the social institutions of his community. However, despite her profound awareness of the individual as one who interacts with and responds to other persons and the social environment, the available sources of knowledge did not provide the means for studying this phenomenon. Using a somewhat legalistic orientation, she spoke of the collection of evidence, the development of inference from the comparison of the various pieces of evidence, and the attainment of a diagnosis from the interpretation of the meaning of these inferences. Although she started from a legal framework, Richmond succeeded in setting the groundwork for the procedures of study, diagnosis, and treatment that became the model for social work practice.

Richmond elevated the importance of interviewing, formerly carried out in mechanistic ways. She spoke to influences which she saw affected the nature of the interview, including the origin of the request, the setting, the kind of task at hand, and what was known about the client. To these she added the qualitative conditions which would enhance the value of the interview. Although she did not refer to the import of the relationship in explicit terms, she did require that the client receive a "fair and patient hearing," that there should be privacy and time, and that recognition should be given to the client's endeavors to do something about the problem as well as to his hopes and plans. In short, Richmond stressed the importance of differential understanding, individualization, and the client's ability to assume responsibility for his condition. Transcending the methodological importance of Richmond's work was the direction she offered towards a more humanistic "doing with" in contrast with the former investigatory "doing for."

Richmond's work contained two major ideas. The first and most explicit presented an organized way of understanding the individual through a systematic collection of information which, if sufficient, would reveal a problem's ultimate cause and therefore the obvious cure. In her succinct style she presented the methodological steps which comprised effective practice. But on a more implicit level, a somewhat visionary quality was evident. As has been noted, she encouraged an expanded view of the individual as a social being. She admonished the profession's tendency to become too specialized. The following statement reveals her recognition that social work is an essentially generic process that is carried out in specialized ways:

In essentials, the methods and aims of social casework should be the same in every type of service. . . . Some procedures, of course, were peculiar to one group of cases and some to another, according to the special disability under treatment. But the things that are most needed to be said about case work were the things that were common to all. The division of social work into departments and specialties was both a convenience and a necessity; fundamental resemblance remained, however. [Richmond, 1917, p. 5]

In addition, she emphasized the overriding importance of the family in work with individuals. She stressed that the family has a history of its own apart from the histories of those who compose it. It is the conception of the main drift of family life that discriminates between what is significant and insignificant. She introduced to the profession the ideas of family cohesion, the influence of hidden tendencies, and the sustaining importance of the family with regard to affection, admiration, training, and social development.

However, it was Richmond's methodological and procedural ideas which captured the interest of the young profession, combined with her emphasis on the individual as an entity somewhat divorced from his social environment. This interest was probably a result of the profession's hunger for a set of rules and methods which could be used and which would provide some identity. In addition, the prior accent on the practical, day-to-day application of methods could be verified and reinforced by Richmond's writings. What was once loosely assumed about practice could now be more fully defined and crystallized. And finally, these ideas tended to substantiate the existing educational orientation with its emphasis on apprenticeship learning.

Thus Richmond's visionary ideas were bypassed in favor of those that were performable. As a result of this choice and the other factors during this period, there emerged the orientation and the educational philosophy which served to characterize social work practice in the succeeding years.

*World War I to 1930*

Two conditions outside of the profession further shaped the scope, direction, and methods of professional practice. These were the opportunity to treat the problems of World War I servicemen and their families and the emergence and acceptance of Freudian theory.

As a consequence of the wartime opportunities, the profession found that its services were applicable to other classes in society apart from the poor. Increasingly, then, social work turned away from its primary concern with the problems of the poor and the unfortunate. Services became more restricted to those persons whose economic needs were cared for elsewhere—those families and individuals who could articulate their problems, who could seek help on their own, and who had the time to do so. The subsequent growth of family agencies and child guidance clinics further provided the settings and the impetus for work with this population.

As social work was expanded and broadened, its practice became more definitive and sophisticated. The experience of working with patients in the war period strengthened an enthusiasm for psychiatry, which provided what was needed to understand the inner person. Rhetorical Freudian psychology was a welcomed substitute for the sterile laboratory psychology that emphasized intelligence tests, diagnosis, and classification. The richness and coherence of Freudian thought replaced rational and intellectual orientations with a need-basis of behavior founded on longitudinal derivations.

This new knowledge dovetailed with and substantiated the prior acceptance and acclamation of Richmond's book. While *Social Diagnosis* organized the procedures in helping, psychoanalytic theory provided their rationale and theory structure. Quickly, the profession made a radical shift from the consideration of environmental factors to the preoccupation with the intrapsychic. Freudian theory overshadowed all other approaches to social problems and orientations about behavior. By the mid-1920s casework teaching staffs at universities taught psychoanalytic principles as a basis for casework practice. It was not uncommon for both faculty and students to undergo psychoanalytic therapy as part of their training. The outlets for this type of practice were expanded by the development of child guidance clinics and veterans' programs and by the emergence of the psychiatric social work specialization. A training program for psychiatric social workers was established at Smith College, and its members later formed their own association, the American Association of Psychiatric Social Workers. Their shift away from the usual range and modes of social work practice was made as they identified themselves with psychiatric practice.

The result of these influences was a major change in the role of the professional. In accord with Freudian technique, the social worker departed from the stance of a doer, a provider of concrete services, to that of a passive observer. Prior manipulative approaches were disclaimed. The concept of a detached professional attitude emerged along with the admonition that practitioners should keep their feelings and activities in abeyance. Thus practice of this type would have to limit services to those clients who could respond to and use a less active approach, to those whose problems did not require immediate action.

Group work, as it was practiced during this period, continued along the course previously set in its aim for the highest fulfillment for the individual through democratic participation (Konopka, 1963). In its emphasis on learning by participation, group work reflected the philosophy of John Dewey, although quite indirectly. It remained more or less an activity, insisted on its informal participatory functions, and chose not to identify with or draw from emerging theories as did casework in its wholehearted grasp of psychoanalytic principles. Thus the fascinating progression of theories, building one upon the other during the first third of the century, had little influence on the development of group work practice. Casework, as a result of the individualistic constraints of psychoanalytic theory, was also isolated from the newer formulations about group life.

These ideas were already evident in the late nineteenth century when Durkheim isolated the phenomenon of group structure as a "collective representation" and observed that each group had its own identity. A short time later, Simmel advanced the notion of dynamics within groups. He noted that groups had a continuity which depended on the character of interaction within the groups, the extent to which their members felt that they belonged to them, and the degree to which each group maintained its equilibrium. The capacity for group interaction, the inclusion of group experience as part of human nature, was then stressed by Cooley. He rooted the origins of group experience in the family, where the possibility of knowing and feeling with others' experiences and roles evolves out of vicarious interactions.

These concepts culminated in Lewin's field theory, borrowed from the discipline of physics. In his discussion of the "life space" of persons, he disclosed the immediate and profound significance of the dynamics of individuals in interaction within groups. He noted that any change in behaviors within the field of human experience changed the entire field and affected the individuals comprising that field. However, these and other constructs and theories that burgeoned by the 1920s were ignored by group workers who, in their concern with environmental and social conditions, saw groups as informal bodies.

In a very general sense, Dewey's principles also guided community social work during this period. It emphasized the democratic processes within the small community and aimed at some reconstruction through the involvement of both citizens and experts at the grass roots level. Fragments of knowledge and theory from contemporary sociological and social-psychological ideas did intrude into practice. For the most part, community organization tended to resemble an implicit philosophy rather than a definable methodology. This philosophy was strengthened and articulated by Lindeman, a professor at the New York School of Social Work. He brought to social work the wealth of the humanities, a belief in the inquiring mind, and an awareness of ethical goals and values (Kohs, 1966). He spoke of unity being achieved through a creative use of diversities, of the need to see means as consistent with ends in the achievement of any democratic purpose, and of genuine consent as a vital ingredient in a democratic way of life. Only brief mention can be made here about the importance of his contribution within the profession to the encouragement of social action in its concern with human beings.

Education for professional practice continued to be dominated by the casework method, with virtually negligible recognition of work with groups or communities. Casework remained the only avenue to practice that contained some educational content that could be communicated. Yet this knowledge lacked organizing principles and concepts, and as a result, the inductive method of teaching and learning became firmly entrenched. Case records were the major means of instruction. Although case records were a valuable aid in helping students learn by the indirect observation of other practitioners (ostensibly more skilled) and in finding how to draw transferable generalizations from specific human events, this mode of teaching had certain limitations. The range of concepts that could be taught was inevitably restricted to the kinds of cases at hand. The validity of the content presented was, in addition, questionable because it was, in the final analysis, inferentially construed by the recorder. Finally, what was notably absent was a frame of reference within which the derived concepts could be organized.

Fragmentation of learning also resulted from the profession's splitting into specializations, in part a response to the widening array of settings in which social work was practiced. Consonant with these needs, schools of social work opened departments in such fields as family welfare, educational guidance, and hospital and psychiatric social work.

Paralleling these developments was the halting emergence of a professional organization, a body that would provide communication, identification, and a set of standards. The first movements toward organization came with the formation of local social work clubs designed to provide employed social workers with the opportunity for contact and discussion. These clubs encouraged the formation of the American Association of Social Workers, finally organized in 1929. Prior efforts to organize had failed because it had not been possible to achieve any agreement about what constituted a social worker. Eligibility for membership in the association was at first based on what the social worker did rather than on what a social worker was as a professional. The issue was finally settled in 1929 when the association required the completion of education in a recognized school of social work as a condition for membership. But by this requirement, membership would tend to be restricted to caseworkers, the typical professional produced by graduate education.

Concurrently, other professional organizations were being formed, reflecting the growth of specialization in the field. These were the American Association of Hospital Social Workers, the American Association of Visiting Teachers (school social workers), and as has been mentioned, the American Association of Psychiatric Social Workers.

The decade following World War I, then, can be characterized as one in which the profession, having defined itself in terms of its method and function, moved toward expansion of its purpose and theory. However, the carte blanche adoption of Freudian psychology produced several ramifications. For one, little more was done in the direction of theory building or the construction of a set of principles that the profession could claim as its own beyond those that Richmond presented as a framework for practice. Her urgings for the consideration of persons as social beings were displaced by a more intense focus on persons' psyches. The role of the social worker became more explicit and circumscribed, and the possibility for aggressive entry into the broader aspects of the client's life system was blocked. The profession turned away from its concern with the poor in its proliferation of services and specializations. In part, this was a natural consequence of a profession painfully coming into its own.

*1930 to 1940*

The Great Depression forced some qualitative changes in the way that practice had become formulated. The depletion of funds caused the closing of some specialized agencies; and psychiatric social workers, who had defined their purpose apart from the mainstream of social work, returned to the administration of financial aid for the unemployed.

The financial disaster that enveloped the nation also forced the profession to reconsider the importance of politics and economics.

As regards practice theory, new influences were beginning to be felt. These ideas were to become more fully articulated in the following decade, and included those first advanced by Jesse Taft and Virginia Robinson in their respective books, *The Dynamics of Therapy in a Controlled Relationship* (1935) and *A Changing Psychology in Social Case Work* (1930). Here the significance and the immediacy of an active relationship as a means for change was stressed in contrast with the Freudian tenets of passive receptivity to permit the emergence of repressed feelings. In their thinking, the helping process was not contained in a medical model but was instead a collaborative experience between the social worker and the client in interaction. This approach, which was soon to become elaborated in the Functional school of social work, introduced a new element into the principles of practice—that "cure" did not result from the eradication of causal factors but from the experience of the helping relationship itself. The emergence of these ideas cannot be linked to a progression of developments within the field. Instead, these, too, were fortuitous happenings, consequences of Taft's analytic experience with Otto Rank, from whose theories these ideas were selectively borrowed. Nonetheless, the appearance of this more interactional orientation at a point at which economic conditions were fostering a greater degree of social awareness was timely.

These changes in casework thinking were accompanied by the attempts of group workers and community organizers to clarify their methods and objectives. Group work began to receive at least tentative acceptance as a method of practice. Before 1930 the National Conference on Social Welfare had little representation from group work practitioners; by 1935 the National Conference had established a section on group work. It was in the same year that the editors of the *Social Work Yearbook* introduced the heading "Social Group Work," listing it as a major division of social work in a brief article. A professional orientation began to permeate this once informal activity and precipitated a beginning awareness by group workers of being part of a profession.

Within the field's literature, some broad and general definitions of the nature of group work began to appear. Newstetter, in his speech, "What is Social Group Work?" defined it as an educational process. He emphasized the development of the social adjustment of individuals through voluntary association and the use of this association as a means of furthering socially desirable ends. This formulation introduced still another way of perceiving practice; namely, it stressed the educational purpose in contrast with the medical conception of therapeutic cure. A second concept offered by group workers and evident in Newstetter's statement was *duality*, the purpose of practice serving two distinct ends. One was the traditional aim of achieving a certain desired outcome. The other, however, introduced the significance of the association between the participants in the change endeavor as a source of growth. Although starting from a different set of premises, these concepts were consonant with the relational focus of Taft and Robinson, that significant learning derived from the immediate experience of the client-social worker interaction.

This beginning change in the orientation of practice was indicative of the start of a common base for practice. In the pragmatics of their practices, community workers had also stressed the importance of the association between the practitioner and the social unit, who together were working toward particular ends. Stated in terms of democratic action, their attention was directed toward the enhancement of participation in the process as well as movement toward problem resolution. That these changes occurred concurrently with the emergence of interactional theories in the social and behavioral sciences may be more than coincidental; however, social work literature of that period does not reveal any impact of that knowledge.

Similarities between casework and group work became evident in the mid-1930s in other ways. The profession recognized that both fields needed to study their common objectives since both were concerned with the well-being of individuals. In 1935 the National Conference did give some consideration to ideas about the integration of group work and casework, primarily along the lines of the operational problems of overlapping services. Two years later joint committees were working together to study common relationships, and this endeavor was followed by reports of cooperative work between the two groups in settlements and family services. These actions anticipated the recognition of common theoretical structures within the two methods based primarily on the acknowledgment of similarities of functions.

The exigencies of economic strife during this time added still another social dimension to the conception of professional responsibility. The necessity for some form of social action to meet the needs of a society in turmoil became manifest. However, the growth of social intentions far outstripped the development of a methodology to implement them. Using the National Conference reports as an indicator of trends, of the sixty papers presented relative to social reforms from 1924 to 1946, only six dealt with specific techniques of action (Bruno, 1957). In 1932 the American Association of Social Workers enunciated the "economic objectives of social work" which included adequate relief, programs for public works, social insurance to replace public assistance, and taxes on land, income and inheritance.

This kind of program orientation was typical of a community organization practice which lacked the structured means for action. But by the end of the decade some needed definitions of community practice had been proposed as a foundation for its technical processes. The Lane Report in 1939 defined community organization as a field of practice comparable to casework and group work (group work was now becoming enough of an entity to warrant comparison). The report viewed community work as both a process and a field carried on inside and outside the area of social work, but as a rule not offering direct help to specific clientele. Its objectives were (1) fact finding for planning and action; (2) initiating, developing, and modifying social work services and programs; (3) setting standards; and (4) promoting coordination between organizations, groups, and individuals. The ambiguities in the perception of community organization are apparent. It was akin to, yet separate from social work. It had as its objectives the welfare of individuals yet did not provide direct access to them. It was described as a field of service and a process without revealing the nature of its technology.

The development of community work was also hampered by the absence of graduate education for direct practice. In these and the ensuing years, much of what could be called community work was done primarily by a special breed of caseworkers and, to a lesser extent, by group workers who were interested in involving themselves and developing programs that comprised community organization.

The Thirties, then, were turbulent years for the profession as they were for the nation as a whole as it played its part in dealing with the economic and social cataclysm that was the Great Depression. Internal changes were beginning to take place which would ultimately alter the thinking and practice of the profession. The slower and more controlled search for cause and cure in practice began to give way to concern with the more immediate behaviors and needs of clients. This shift was supported not only by pressing reality problems typical of the times but by the emerging formulations that stressed the significance of the professional relationship as a source of change. Social action came into the purview of the profession's responsibilities. Although casework continued to retain its singular prominence, social work as a profession expaned its scope and potency by the inclusion and the development of the group work and community organization methods. And as the latter two matured and moved towards explication of their purposes and processes, the commonalities of professional practice began to take shape. In sum, social work was becoming, once again, a social profession.

*1940 to 1950*

The movement towards greater explication of knowledge and technology continued in this decade. Casework was in the forefront of this endeavor, as the burgeoning of its literature shows. For the most part, these efforts were reexaminations and reformulations of what was already known about practice rather than attempts at the kind of theory building which would offer a broader base for knowledge. While these empirical approaches did classify and refine methods and techniques, they also detracted from the building of a frame of reference that would make practice more coherent.

Some part of the impetus for this elaboration stemmed from the emergence of two diverse forms of practice contained in what were now called the Functional (Rankian) and Diagnostic (Freudian) schools. Added to the fact that the profession had not yet arrived at a consensus about what a curriculum for professional education should include, preparation for practice was further split as some graduate schools taught casework according to Freudian principles, others taught a Rankian approach, and a few presented both.

The two schools were representative of two distinct philosophical and psychological views of man. The Diagnostic school, with its origins in Richmond's formulations of social work and subsequently enlarged and structured by Freudian theory, contained a deterministic interpretation of behavior. The individual was seen in linear terms; his present condition was determined by causal events in early life which, to be resolved and to free possibilities for current adjustment, needed to be uncovered and understood. Insight in some form was necessary before one could begin to master his present existence. The Functional school, in contrast, was based on a psychology of growth and a philosophy not unlike existentialism. Potentialities for change were not believed to be significantly determined by prior events. Given the opportunity, within a structured and socially productive relationship, the individual could work out his own changes. In the Diagnostic school the center of change was in the social worker who diagnosed the problem, prescribed, and carried out a treatment plan. In the Functional school, the center of change was the client, while the social worker acted as a helper and facilitator present within the relationship to enhance growth potential latent within the client.

Because of the residual influences of the two schools on modern-day practice, it is worthwhile to sort out briefly the two distinct formulations of practice and their premises. The Diagnostic school created a practice model of study, diagnosis, and treatment in accord with traditional medical principles of treatment and cure. Study sought to collect relevant facts about the possible conditions or causes of the problem. Diagnosis comprised the arrangement of these facts into a dynamic whole which explained the nature of the problem and which prescribed particular modes and goals of treatment. Study, diagnosis, and treatment were at first conceived of as linear processes; treatment could not be undertaken until the major facts were in and a diagnosis had been made. It was recognized by many that treatment could not wait because of the pressing needs of the client. But most important, it was seen that treatment did, in fact, begin with the first contact with the client. Rooted in premises about the overriding significance of intrapsychic forces, treatment was directed towards resolution of inner conflicts and distortions. As ego psychology grew in importance and meaning, the emphasis was shifted to the ego as a mediator of these inner forces in relation to the outer environment. However, the prevailing theory did not include premises that would explain the interactional or reciprocal nature of man's relations with his social environment. Hence, man tended to be understood as a reactor rather than as one who could influence or modify his environment.

The Functional school assumed that the individual could best be understood by how his personality was manifested in the immediate circumstances and that the person was too unique and complex to be diagnosed in relation to past events. Thus practice was organized around specific concepts that illuminated the character of persons within the immediate arena of treatment. These concepts included, first of all,

agency function (from which the name was derived), the boundaries
and limits of services that could be offered in accord with the setting's
purposes. It was surmised that the deliberate application of these limitations at the outset of treatment would confront the client with a chal-
lenge to his "will," to his motivation and capacity for decisive action.
The concept of will supplanted that of ego and was used to determine
whether the client had sufficient strength to continue to work on his
problem. A time structure was also imposed and had dual implications.
First, it was believed that what could be understood or achieved needed
to be contained within temporal boundaries. Second, awareness by the
client of temporal limitations would arouse anxiety leading to the motivation to change.

A major contribution by the Functionalists that has persisted was the
introduction and expansion of the concepts of relationship. The two,
together, magnified and made viable the transactional ebb and flow of
what was taking place between the client and the social worker. How the
client presented himself and acted within the relationship provided critical understanding of the characteristic ways in which he dealt with loss
of control, anxiety, intimacy, and the like. The differentiation between
projection and reality in these factors was achieved by the social worker's use of his own experience, warmth, and concern. Thus it was the
dynamics of the immediate relationship which supported the impetus for
growth and change (Kasius, ed., 1950).

The growing fissures between the two schools affected both agency
practices and graduate training programs. However, as both schools
diligently spelled out their respective theoretical positions, they were
able to move towards rapprochement and the eventual diffusion of differences, abetted by the infusion of new knowledge from other sources.
The development of ego psychology altered the purely intrapsychic orientation of classical psychoanalytic thought and gave the Diagnostic
school a more useful social and interactional viewpoint. The Functional
school, already attuned to relational concepts, was ready to assimilate
some socio-behavioral concepts coming from the social sciences. And
as practices and concepts were tested, each school drew from the other.
Functionalists acknowledged the importance of and incorporated some
ideas about study and diagnosis. The Diagnostic school found the concepts of relationship and process valuable for its purposes.

It is probable that what also contributed to the dissolution of the respective schools after relatively short lives was the absence of an ex-

plicit commitment to and articulation of the philosophical conception of man that undergirded each of them. Practice that is based mainly on a set of pragmatic methods and necessarily incomplete theories is flimsy and subject to change when new approaches come along. The rational-deterministic and the experiential-positivistic philosophies of the Diagnostic and Functional schools, respectively, were not enunciated as were their methods and systems. This absence reflected the tendency of the profession to emphasize its technical and idiographic characteristics, its methodological heritage, rather than a guiding social philosophy which would do more than merely express some ideal notions about man and society.

The events in casework tended to overshadow the struggle by group workers and community organizers to determine their identities and what comprised the content of their methods. Group work in the early forties was not yet fully identified with the profession and was perceived as a method to be used in an array of educational experiences, some exclusive of social work. But by 1946, Grace Coyle had developed the first social work course in group work at Western Reserve University. She noted that casework, group work, and community organization did have a common factor based on the understanding of human relationships. She saw group work falling into the scope of social work because the underlying approaches and philosophies were the same.

The maturation of community organization took the form of a debate that continued over this decade. In 1942, Helen Witmer stated that the activities of community organization belonged to other institutions as well as to social work, that it was different than casework and group work, and that it was, in reality, auxiliary to social work. This assertion urged other writers on to the task of demonstrating that community organization was, in fact, comparable and related to other social work methods. Arlene Johnson wrote in 1945 that the community worker becomes a professional social worker when he helps people in a community discover the common problems that may interfere with the desirable norms of living and assists them in doing something about these problems (Lurie, ed., 1965).

Johnson's ideas countered the notion that community organization was mainly a set of intentions and programs. She identified the target that was shared with casework—the well-being of individuals. She stressed the generic base of the three methods as comprising the knowledge derived from psychology, psychiatry, and sociology, all of which offered the understanding of individual, group, and collective behavior. By defining the community as a group of people having common interests, actually or potentially realized, Johnson established the commonality of the three methods.

McMillan, also in 1945, corroborated this view of community organization as being akin to casework and group work. He defined it as a method of helping people find ways to give expression to their inherent desires to improve the environment in which they and their fellows must carry on their lives. He referred to the social workers' efforts to stimulate people to use their powers for the cooperative improvement of group life and to assist in developing the process through which required technical services could be applied. Two years later, Kenneth Pray also designated the facilitative efforts of community organization as a means of helping individuals adjust in their constructive use of social relationships.

As can be seen in these efforts at definition, community organization was not directed toward change in the existing structures or institutions. Instead, it was viewed as a means for sustaining the existing processes for dealing with problems of social relationship and adjustment. Its function was to work with potentials that were believed to exist within persons rather than to rework or change pernicious conditions. Emphasis was on group structure and function as a way of enhancing the participation of groups of individuals in their adjustive efforts. Although we can question the belief of these writers that people merely need the assistance of a skilled person to bring into the open latent attributes for social change, their explication of the importance of group processes was an important contribution to the clarification of the community organization method and its tie with group work.

Much of what was happening in the profession's maturation was reflected in the literature of social work during this decade. World War II had its effects on the profession, and many of its members made immense contributions to the lives of persons displaced by the debacle. As will be seen, the war experience brought about changes in practice that became formalized in the years to follow. Although casework retained its primacy, the emergence and recession of factions within it left in their wake many changes in the principles which governed practice. While group work and community organization objectified their positions as social work methods, the scope of the profession broadened to include the needs of persons in larger systems. In this regard, some thinkers began to question the artificiality of the separation between the methods as they tentatively identified the generic base supporting them and their common concern with the welfare of people in both individual and collective terms.

### 1950 to 1960

This decade was of major importance in the development of the profession. It was a time in which substantial clarity emerged about the many dimensions of professional activity and thought—its structure, its definition of aims and purposes, the nature of its practice, and by implication, its philosophy. During this period many of the disparate elements of social work coalesced into what could more reasonably be called a profession.

Early in the 1950s the Hollis-Taylor Report (*Social Work Education in the United States,* 1951) was completed. The report advocated a generic curriculum of education, a master's course lasting two years which, in its academic structure, modified the profession's former apprenticeship style of education. Curriculum content was ordered in three major areas: (1) social welfare policies and services, (2) human growth and development, and (3) the three methods. The report generated considerable interest in the introduction of a totally generic educational plan and the question of whether the specialized training of social workers in one of the methods would produce a superior type of social worker than would a broad, generic approach. The absence of criteria for adequate education or competent practice precluded the attainment of a definitive answer to this question. A middle ground was finally taken that expressed the need for the profession to begin to reconcile its generic principles with the requirements of specialized practice.

As graduate schools redesigned their curricula to meet these standards, it became possible to think of professional education in more universal terms. A broader educational base supplanted the former narrow concern with technical ability. As a result, agencies in which students were trained were asked to give up the immediate gains involved in students' contributions to the practicalities of daily practice for the long-term gains of education for the profession.

This development in education was no less striking than was the creation of a professional organization that represented the entirety of the profession. In 1955 the National Association of Social Workers came into being as a result of the efforts of the Temporary Inter-Association Council of Social Work (TIAC), which represented the seven existing professional organizations. The TIAC plan reflected the compromises required to unite seven previously autonomous organizations and provided for a second analysis of the single organization after five years of experience.

These two events provided the profession with a backdrop against which it could reevaluate its content and purposes in relation to its social responsibilities.

Although they were inconclusive, the written and spoken reflections on the theories and aims of practice during this time indicated that persons in their social environment were the central concern of social work rather than the method used to treat them. Casework thinkers spoke to the significance of the social components of practice. That casework served individuals in a society and that the intent of the caseworker was to help persons derive greater benefits from social living and from their institutions became emerging themes in casework literature.

Group work practice moved from many directions toward the centrality of its position within the profession. Both the literature about and the use of group methods proliferated during this period. In addition to its former functions relative to democratic participation, education, and role development, practice with groups now included therapeutic aims as a consequence of its use for this end in World War II. Thus group work shared common aims with casework. Similarly, the value of the group for social action brought group practice into the realm of community organization.

The assimilation of concepts from sociology, anthropology, and social psychology permitted group workers to use the group experience more deliberately and planfully. The former dual purpose of groups was refined to gaining a deeper understanding of individual members as social beings and to using the group as a mediating force between the individual and his society.

Community organizers were engaged in similar endeavors to define their function, and in doing so, they also borrowed from the social sciences. However, certain conditions militated against the attainment of a cohesive and communicable structure of community practice at that time. First, the theory and knowledge content of community practice was both limited and diffuse. This meagerness was apparent in its literature and in the educational content of preparation for practice. By this time the community method had become a part of curriculum, but many schools offered only a few courses that were frequently ancillary to the general program. In addition, community organizers erroneously tried to follow the model used by casework and group work by attempting to define practice in relation to the size of the social unit served rather than in terms of the social problem requiring its services. The diverse interpretations of what a community was made the success of this attempt doubtful.

The basic premises of community social work were also obstacles in the path of purpose and method formulation. At that point in time, community organization still pursued its intent to improve adaptation to social conditions within the community with less regard for the causes that contributed to the condition. Again, this approach was in accord with the casework and group work models which tended to be reactive rather than aggressive forms of practice. Casework was limited to clients who voluntarily sought help, and group work assumed an enabling rather than an assertive role. Thus community organization found itself restricted to a practice that dealt with the residue of social problems or the planning for and coordination of existing services.

An awareness that social work did not have even a rough framework within which elements of practice could be ordered impelled the profession to produce the document, "A Working Definition of Social Work Practice," in 1958. The responsibility for this effort was assumed by the Committee on Social Work Practice of the National Association of Social Workers. It was designed as a foundation for their ongoing study of practice.

The document described practice as a constellation of value, purpose, sanction, knowledge, and method which, in their configuration, distinguished social work practice from the practice of other professions. Values were said to include concern with the individual as a unique being who nonetheless is in interdependence with other individuals in society, as well as concern with the social responsibilities of individuals and society. According to the document the purpose of practice is to assist individuals and groups to identify and resolve or ameliorate social problems and to identify potential problems. Sanctions derive from governmental agencies, voluntary agencies, and the organized profession. Knowledge as a guide for practice includes cognizance of human development and behavior: communication processes; the processes and influences of groups, culture, interactional systems, and the community; the broad character of social services; and the social worker himself. Methods encompass casework, group work, and community organization and are defined as a conscious and disciplined use of self in relationship with an individual or group to facilitate change in the individual, the social environment, or both. Method also refers to the evaluative and technical components of practice.

The "Working Definition" proves to be a valid indicator of the profession's ideas about itself at that time and provides some observations about its state. The document strikes one as vaguely general and not particularly ambitious with regard to establishing the relevance and domain of social work practice. Its generality discourages argumentation; its lack of definitiveness precludes the refinement of its concepts. That it was just the first attempt of the profession to define its practice is of less importance than the way in which it reveals the paucity of available conceptual content. The global nature of the document tends to reveal the profession's leanings toward a greater concern with the practical rather than the theoretical aspects of practice.

But the "Working Definition" did underscore two major views of practice which were indicative of where the profession was heading. First, it strengthened the appreciation of the individual as a social being rather than as an entity. Second, it implied that individuals, their relationships with one another, and their involvement with society formed an inextricable whole. Thus practice with any segment needed to take into account all other parts and pointed to the question of the efficacy of a methods approach that was aimed at singular units. In addition, the document presented social work practice in a unitary form; specializations in practice were seen as variations of how the universal components of practice were applied.

Despite its ambiguities and generalizations, the "Working Definition" did reveal that the profession was catching up with itself. Some new and vigorous trends were appearing, perhaps wandering and uncertain, yet demonstrating the potential for effectiveness. The limitations of the former apprenticeship orientation in education were recognized as an obstacle to the transmission of a conceptual foundation for professional activity. And within these conceptualizations it was becoming apparent that social work was no longer solely identified with casework methods, that the separate methods orientation was questionable.

*1960 to 1970*

This decade built on the major efforts of the fifties and witnessed an evolving maturation and expansion of practice. If theory development did not keep pace, then at least there was a growing consensus that theory building should become an important aim of the profession.

The growth of the profession was immense in its many dimensions. Eleven new graduate schools of social work had opened and had been accredited by 1969, many in the western and southern states, thereby expanding the opportunity for professional education to the nation as a whole. In addition, nine other graduate schools were in operation and working toward accreditation. Enrollment in graduate training over the ten-year period more than doubled in the master's program from less than 5,000 in 1959 to almost 12,000 in 1969. Although a minor part of professional education, the gradual growth of doctoral programs in social work could be attributed to the accretion of professional knowledge and educational content.

As a consequence of the expansion and refinement of services in both public and private sectors, social work services, traditional and innovative, proliferated. The Economic Opportunity Act, the broadening of social insurance and public welfare services, the expansion in the type and quantity of family services, the increasing availability of mental hygiene clinics and day treatment centers, community action, and poverty programs were a few of the projects and settings in which the profession assumed a major role.

From among these many trends and events it should be possible to sort out a number of factors which influenced how theory and practice were developing. An eminent one among them was the beginning introduction of a social systems concept in which individuals, groups, and larger systems could be understood in their interdependence, a concept which tended to supplant the previous monadic orientation. Another factor, related to the first, was the return of social work to a family orientation based on the conceptual means for understanding the family as a viable system. In other respects, the new systems approach made it apparent that one could not conceive of change in any one social unit without reference to the implications for the related units or persons. So the ramifications of practice were now seen to extend beyond the confines of the immediate social worker-client configuration.

These movements reflected the development of a frame of reference which made patterns of interaction and interdependence visible and accessible to intervention. Concepts borrowed from the social sciences helped to expand perceptions of interpersonal behavior. More important, this conceptual base offered the profession a vocabulary that was more precise, translatable, and communicable.

The newer family orientation to practice had the effect of further equivocating the assumed differences between the practice methods. Some persistence about maintaining this separation was indicated in such euphemisms as "casework with families" or "casework with groups."

In more specific terms, casework had already shifted to the theoretical base of ego psychology. Increasingly, but still exploratively, caseworkers began to use concepts from the social sciences for interpersonal conceptions of behavior. In contrast to the monadic, intrapsychic view of behavior, the individual could be seen in the context of a family or group structure and could be understood in relation to the determinants of culture, class, and socio-economic conditions. With the rise of the Economic Opportunity programs, casework completed a full circle in its return to an interest in the poor and the culture of poverty. The previous concept of a client as a person who voluntarily sought help and who could identify the existence of a problem was enlarged to include unmotivated and hard-to-reach persons. Focus, then, was shifted to the preventive aspects of practice as the concept of crisis intervention and its implications were accepted (Perlman, 1965).

In contrast with the extension and broadening of the theoretical base and range of casework services, group work and community organization moved toward a tightening up and clarification of their constitutions. With the availability of comprehensive theories of group dynamics, there was an increase in literature that spoke to the need for group work to begin to formulate its practice by specifying the "hows" and "whys" of professional performance. The structure of the group became an area of interest. Group services could be seen as a model as well as a process, thereby illuminating the matter of boundaries and function. In short, group workers were coming to recognize that the group experience was not merely a random, informal event and that it was instead a microcosm of social living within which its members and processes were subject to explication and comprehension.

The scope of group work practice grew as it continued to move beyond its former educational and recreational boundaries and included in its domain restoration and rehabilitation. Group workers, forming their groups for therapeutic purposes, found that they needed to use the same knowledge base comprising personality and behavior theories as did caseworkers. Furthermore, they were serving the same clientele as did the caseworkers—the poor, the alienated, and the delinquent.

The confluence of community organization practice and theory with the mainstream of social work was coincident with these changes. In 1962 this movement was articulated in the statement of the Committee on Community Organization of the National Association of Social Workers which formulated the specific purposes of community practice. The consistency of its values with those of the profession was first reaffirmed. The purpose of practice was stated in dual terms—the strengthening of community capability for problem solving and the achievement of specific goals. As will be noted, this duality of purpose tended to unify all forms of professional activity. The committee saw the community and those elements which comprised the target of service as the "client-system." And in accord with the growing definition of the social worker's role, the community practitioner was construed as one using a problem-solving approach rooted in the techniques of study, structuring, and conciliation. Added to the responsibility for organizational work with communities were those of community development and planning. Planning, coordination of services, and financing in work with existing community structures became increasingly active, assertive, and goal seeking. The focus of community workers, formerly restricted to community leaders, now widened to include the indigenous citizens who might also be the recipients of social welfare services. This shift was part of the intention to develop new institutional structures as well as to change the old. With the infusion of federal and state funds into the local communities, there was a change from the coordination role in the distribution of funds to a more active role in planning and implementing new programs and organizations that could utilize these funds more effectively.

Greater congruence with the profession's objectives also resulted from the recognition that community practice shared common technical and theoretical approaches. Inasmuch as the modality for providing services was frequently the group, community workers became aware of the need for knowledge about theories of group and individual dynamics and the attendant skills and techniques.

A major product of this period, reflecting the concern with the generic aspects of education and practice, was the thirteen-volume *Social Work Curriculum Study* (Boehm, dir., 1959). This significant work was conceived and executed by the Council on Social Work Education with the participation of the National Association of Social Workers. It may be noted parenthetically that by the 1960s the association had reestablished its purposes to advance research, to improve practice and education, and to set standards and criteria for professional practice and performance. In these purposes, the mutuality of the professional organization and the council was strengthened. The study contained the general objectives and guides for curriculum development and the explication of the major intentions of education. In large part, the study could be thought of as a pioneering effort. In addition to its practical purposes it also served the valuable function of bringing to light other issues requiring study—e.g., clarification of the purposes of field instruction, what distinguishes social work as a professional entity, and the need for more definitive knowledge (Witte, 1959).

These many indices of the profession's growth and maturation were mirrored in the changes that were taking place in the content of graduate education. After some years of testing the basic curriculum, some graduate schools found that the stable educational base provided a point of departure for experimentation and innovation. Two trends became apparent. With the emergence of both common and specific knowledge bases of practice, group work and community organization and development became integral parts of the curriculum, thereby further diluting the former identification of social work with the casework method. But in still another direction, many schools were moving toward teaching some form of generic or integrated practice in either the first year or both years of the master's program. Some schools retained the three-methods approach to teaching but required that students in one specialty take courses in the others to achieve some acquaintance with the range of the profession's methods. Other schools attempted to integrate the three methods into one or two courses that identified both the common and the unique characteristics of each. By the end of the decade a few schools were striving toward the development of a unitary concept of practice, one that identified the common core of principles, concepts, and skills that were basic to any specialization (Pincus and Minahan, 1970).

*Review and Summary*

As was noted at the outset, the history of the practice, as it is presented here, is essentially theoretical and inferential. The objectives are to accent those selected conditions which influenced and shaped the way in which professional practice and theory developed and took form. Many other important forces were omitted in the process of selection. Certainly, little enough attention was given to the contributions of particular personalities in social work whose lives and work, expressed in practice and in literature, served to enrich the profession. Little reference was made to the Great Depression and the major wars that punctuated this era. The work of the early social reformers and the later mass of social legislation including the Social Security acts were not included. Neither were the more subtle, yet still profound alterations in the character of American political, social, and economic systems. While these omissions may well strike some as arbitrary, our purpose was to capture the essence and the flow of the evolvement of theory, knowledge, and practice in order to give the reader a more incisive understanding of the state of the profession and the progressions that underlie the theoretical structure of this book.

The origins of social work as regards intentional theory development were not unlike the origins of other professions. The apprenticeship approach was also characteristic of the beginnings of medicine, law, and pharmacy, for example. In these cases, neophytes worked with experienced professionals or "read" to prepare for eventual confirmation of professional skill by a licensing body.

However, social work more resistantly and belatedly moved toward a type of professionalization that was based on the learning of a knowledge and theory foundation. Various conditions delayed this important aspect of the profession's maturation. At first social work regarded itself as a vocation. Because of its quite practical operations, this perception was not entirely erroneous. However, this predisposition tended to persist even when the need for academic preparation became apparent. Schools of social work were, for too many years, training centers, each operating independently. The vocational orientation was sustained by the reliance on field instruction as the mainstay for learning, while classroom content was either secondary or ancillary. Although the balance between class and field learning has shifted somewhat during the past two decades, the complementariness between the two remains.

It is still not uncommon for schools to place beginning students in the field with little more than a basic orientation experience, a plan that is a vestige of the apprenticeship approach that denies the importance of academic preparation for actual practice.

The ascription of value to the profession's services by elements of society and its social welfare institutions resulted in the specialization of practice. This tended to fragment the growing nucleus of social work knowledge. Competency in practice was seen as skill in narrow areas of specialization. As a result, practitioners departed from the core and commonality of social work and refined their own knowledge, skills, professional identifications, and associations.

In addition to these trends in practice and education, four factors influenced the paths toward theory development. First, the profession was inclined to borrow theories from other disciplines and professions in a somewhat random fashion. The major instance was the total embrace of Freudian psychology, which had little relevance to the profession's former interest in the poor and the alienated. The adoption of Rankian psychology was even more adventitious. This leads one to puzzle over the question of why other prevalent theories—Jungian, Adlerian, or for that matter, behaviorist—were not selected. In any case, the nature of the theories that were adopted did not necessarily correspond with the profession's identity and purpose.

The second factor was the essentially empirical and circular process of study in which the profession chose to examine and construct its knowledge base. The need for formulations and principles of practice impelled the profession to study the pragmatics of what practitioners did in implementing professional responsibility. What resulted was a set of loose, abstract, and discontinuous findings, mainly a form of practice wisdom rather than theory. This wisdom was then fed back into the field and at a later point was reexamined. Absent were organizing principles, a frame of reference that the profession could identify as its own.

The third factor was an adjunct to the first two, the apathy about or the reluctance to use research methods as a tool for examining and validating practice and theory. At earlier points in the profession's development the lack of research activity could be attributed to the absence of a research culture within the helping professions. But after mid-century, when more sophisticated research techniques were valued and found useful, the profession tended to turn its efforts more toward studies of client populations and service programs and less toward the study of the content of practice.

The fourth barrier in the path of theory development has been and still is the relative absence of explicit discourse on the philosophies which undergird the profession's beliefs and concepts about human behavior and about the social and societal relations which guide and influence practice. The term "explicit" is used advisedly, for in implicit terms, the value and ethical base is ineluctably embedded in ideas about man's uniqueness and the significance of his place and role in society. In this regard, a paradox is evident: social work, as much or perhaps even more than any other social profession, is concerned with and responsive to ontological and ideological issues in man's existence. Yet only negligible attempts have been made to examine the questions that are intrinsic in the various concepts and goals of the profession. As we look back into the history of the profession, we can see that the philosophical character of practice has been at some times positivistic, at other points deterministic or pragmatic, and lately somewhat existential. The issue is not the relative merit of each orientation but the way in which a more precise understanding of the implications of the philosophical underpinnings would give substance and meaning to the form and intent of specific practice formulations.

The consequences of these four factors are still residual in the profession's identity and modes of theory building. What has emerged is the model of a profession that has a valued and effective body of services and purposes but, like a cell without a nucleus, does not contain a substantial interior. Various theories have passed through the core of social work, parts of which were assimilated into the periphery of practice. Some content was randomly fed back into the core, which accumulated a mass of practice wisdom that was hardly sufficient to give the profession a substantial and communicable internal knowledge structure.

Despite these constraints, the look backward shows that there has been an evolving cohesiveness of ideas, a gradual unification of common concepts which has tended to give the profession its gestalt. Paradoxically, much of the unification of thinking resulted from each method's endeavor to explicate the unique and separate qualities of its technique and theory. These fortuitous consequences have altered the face of the profession from that of a limited, singular approach to the amelioration of certain human problems to that of a diverse, creative, and expansive discipline possessing the potentiality for meeting a whole complexity of human needs through a variety of services and an array of stratagems. In contrast with the profession's disparate beginnings, the following concepts illustrate the emerging concurrence and unity that gives the profession its own identity.

1. COMMON VALUES AND OBJECTIVES:   Irrespective of the setting or the specific aims or intentions, social work is concerned with social meanings of human existence. The theoretical polarity which separates persons from their society or vice versa is no longer tenable. Thus practice needs to be based on the conception of man in his relationships and ties with the groups and systems which comprise social life and society as inseparable and in constant and reciprocal interaction.

2. DUALITY:   The process of problem solving as well as the outcome have significant meaning for the participants in the experience. What persons learn about their engagement in the process is as important as what they gain out of the end results.

3. THE GROUP:   Knowledge about the dynamics and processes of groups appears to be evolving into a structure that unifies social work knowledge. Group concepts illuminate the understanding of the individual as an entity as well as his roles within an interacting social system.

4. THEORY DEVELOPMENT:   The profession has come to recognize the need for greater sophistication in theory development in the realm of educational preparation and practice.

5. A SOCIAL PROBLEM APPROACH TO PRACTICE:   The trends indicate an increasing concern with social problem definition and the assessment of where, within the configuration, the determined type of intervention is required in contrast with the idea of a practice that is guided by the size of the social unit and the problem or pathology it presents.

6. AN EDUCATIONAL, PROBLEM-SOLVING APPROACH:   This concept alludes to a common base of practice which, irrespective of the intent or purpose, conceives of social work as a means of providing new ways of perceiving and learning, new knowledge, access to a broader and more useful range of alternatives for action, and the opportunity to find more productive types of social living.

7. A SOCIAL AND BEHAVIORAL SCIENCE FOUNDATION FOR PRACTICE: The preceding trends are indicative of the profession's tendency either to augment or supplant previous theories that are rhetorical or circum-

scribed in relation to what they intend to explain with theories and concepts that more accurately denote aspects of human behavior, social interaction, and the human community. While at present the selection and application of this knowledge is fragmentary and discontinuous, there is much evidence that the profession is attempting to synthesize these pieces of knowledge into one or many wholes. In so doing, the effectiveness, accountability, and communicability of professional practice will be greatly enhanced.

# 3

## THE SOCIAL WORKER:
## CHARACTERISTICS AND ROLE

The plan of this chapter is to examine the characteristics that, in combination, form the image of the social worker. Following a survey of research on professional attributes, consideration will be given to the major interlocking variables which effect the professional image—the observing self that the social worker brings to his practice, his sentient attributes, and his professional role. The last will be defined in relation to the norms that govern professional behavior. The three main properties of the professional role—status, values, and intention—will be discussed, which in turn will lead to an amplification of each characteristic and its relation to specific role activities.

In the initial overview of social work practice, the characteristics that the social worker brought to the professional setting and the influence that he provided in managing the processes leading to social adjustment and social change were considered essential and fundamental. The ingenuity with which he approached his responsibilities and the extent to which his flexibility, creativity, and skills and knowledge precluded a mechanistic stance were seen to offer the possibility for both change and growth. It was suggested that knowledge, skill, and purpose were inseparable from personal and professional attitudes and values. To repeat, who the social worker *is* is no less significant than what he *does*.

This conclusion is both obvious and logical. The term "practice" connotes the action of certain humans in their implementation of professional intent. However, until quite recently little attention has been directed to the personal-professional configuration as it affects practice.

A study of the literature of social work covering the period from 1890 to 1966 produced almost sixty behavioral and personality characteristics used to identify what was desirable in the helping person (Coleman, 1967). The majority were qualitative characteristics, neither clearly definable nor exclusive to social work. Some examples are the ability to identify with the client; to feel appropriately; to express warmth and empathy; and to be objective, analytical, responsive, self-aware, and op-

56

timistic. Writers either admonished or exhorted the social worker to control his feelings, to be diplomatic or good mannered. While the desirability of these attributes is not questioned, the extent to which they can be objectified, understood, or communicated and therefore extracted from the realm of good intentions is limited. Beyond these generalities some recent attempts have been made to sort out practitioner variables in more reliable terms.

*Empirical Studies*

As will be seen, the bulk of research relative to the attributes of the practitioner has been within the context of dyadic relationships, either in casework or in psychotherapy. These findings are pertinent to the other modalities and purposes of practice, whether in groups, for social action, or in other nontherapeutic endeavors. Essentially, the findings have to do with persons in relation. Irrespective of the size or intensity of the practice relationship, certain relationship variables prevail, primarily those that reflect the personal characteristics of the helping person. As a sidelight, it is interesting to note that in many instances these research findings were serendipitous, a spin-off of the original search for other, seemingly more significant variables.

This last point is evident in three studies, two by Reid reported in 1967 and one by Schmidt in 1969. In a content analysis of 121 taped interviews of thirty families by seven caseworkers, Reid sought to determine the categorical nature of casework interventions. He found, instead, that the patterned style of the social worker accounted for the major differences and provided the greatest variation in how service was implemented. Thus such categorical factors as diagnostic classification, frequency, and length were of less significance than the style of the worker. In an experimental and simulated study of the use of insight-oriented techniques as they are related to the degree of ego disturbance, Reid also found that the treatment approach of the social worker was characteristic of his style quite irrespective of his client's degree of ego disturbance. Schmidt's findings were similar. In her study of the practice of thirty-six social workers and their clients to determine the presence of the use, perception, and communication of professional purpose, two distinct patterns of practice were found. The first stressed focus, planning, and direction; the second stressed a psychoanalytic orientation. Schmidt hypothesized that these two patterns were more clearly related to the style and personality of the social worker than to the purpose of practice in specific situations.

These conclusions about the importance of the personal style of the social worker are congruent with the findings derived from a study of thirty family caseworkers in typical practice situations (Goldstein, 1970). The study was designed to elicit the theoretical base that guided practice. What emerged were two patterns of practice representative of the workers' styles which were used flexibly but consistently, regardless of the nature of the problem or the objectives of service.

Mullen's study, reported in 1969, was in accord with the preceding assumptions. In a content analysis of eighty-seven family counseling interviews by six social workers, he studied four variables—the casework method used; phases of treatment; diagnosis; and the social worker's style. It was the last variable that accounted for the significant amount of variation. Mullen concluded that technical behavior is significantly influenced by the social worker's personal qualities. As a consequence, the social worker is seen more as a *person* exerting *personal* influence rather than as an expert applying techniques, a particular instance of a human relationship.

A few other studies have been directed toward the consideration of specific attributes and dispositions. Taber and Vattano (1970), in their empirical study of the clinical and social action orientations of social workers, found that a dichotomy did not exist between the two, affirming the prior assumption about the thread of commonality and continuity that pervades all forms of social work practice. Their analysis of 800 responses to a questionnaire sent to a nationwide sample of social workers revealed that clinical and social orientations are not mutually exclusive, that the controversy is, in reality, an artifact of existing practice theory. Social workers appeared to share a common perception of social work practice irrespective of where they practiced on the so-called clinical-social action continuum.

The variable of empathic functioning has received the attention of researchers as a personal attribute that affects practice. Three studies produced very similar conclusions. Plotnick's study (1965) of the intraceptive tendencies of 129 first-year social work students revealed that therapeutic understanding is not necessarily related to knowledge about the patient. One type of clinical ability is the use of empathy in an automatic fashion in carrying on a successful interpersonal relationship. Studies by Lide (1966) and Zanger (1968) showed that empathic understanding assured psychological comprehension of alien internal lives and external worlds and the detection of affect.

Research by the allied disciplines of psychology and psychiatry has produced similar conclusions. Strupp and Bergin studied some 2,500 references in their review of research in psychotherapy (1969). They, too, suggested that their findings about psychotherapy have relevance for practice with groups, families, and communities because these techniques have as their purpose the attainment of impact on individuals. Hence, principles of individual change emerging from systematic psychotherapy research may well provide the foundations upon which effective group techniques can be built. The major trends and findings detected by the authors include an understanding of psychotherapy as an elaborate and sophisticated teaching process involving the transmittal of the culture's basic values and the personality of the therapist as the major therapeutic agents regardless of objectives or procedures. The variable of the therapist's personality includes the attributes of warmth, acceptance, and empathy; his style and values; and lastly, his theoretical orientation.

In another study the nature of the professional role was considered from the point of view of the patient (Strupp, Fox, and Lessler, 1969). This study of patients' reactions to their therapists demonstrated the immense importance of the relationship. A direct correlation was found between success in therapy and the patient's rating of the therapist as warm, attentive, interested, and respectful.

All of these studies, in themselves evidence of increasing interest in the characteristics of the practitioner, amply demonstrate that the social worker is not merely a manipulator of techniques. However, we should evaluate these findings cautiously and in relation to what they measure because they too easily may be interpreted as evidence that technical prowess and skill are not essential. This would be a most erroneous assumption and a product of the limitations of these studies. In much of this research the presence of technical ability was accepted as a given; in some instances the studies set out to find how these skills were used selectively. Further, no attempts were made to correlate technical ability and personal attributes. What these findings point to is the concept of style—the composite of characteristics, both personal *and* technical, in responsive interaction which finds expression in the manner of practice that is generally typical of the social worker's behavior.

THE CHARACTERISTICS OF THE SOCIAL WORKER

The concept of style is valuable in that it directs us toward an appreciation of this interplay of personal and technical factors which, as noted, comprise professional behavior. These are the attributes that are common to all practitioners as well as those uniquely reflective of the person.

Three major variables will be considered as a means of investigating and delineating these personal/professional forces which affect the change experience. The three are, of course, arbitrary divisions, separated for analysis. Their major importance lies in the extent to which the three are integrated into a functional whole. A brief definition of these variables follows as a prelude to a more intensive analysis.

THE OBSERVING SELF: This concept includes an understanding of the individual in terms of how he views his world and constructs his reality. It is based on constitutional and intellectual factors combined with life experiences and learning. The latter takes into account the product of significant relationships, personal experiences, and education, as well as cultural and socio-economic influences. Together these influences result in attitudes, habitudes, values, perceptions, and behaviors that are idiosyncratic to the person.

SENTIENT CHARACTERISTICS: The affective and responsive attributes which distinguish the individual in the way he perceives, feels, relates, and responds to his social reality; in short, his capacity for awareness.

ROLE CHARACTERISTICS: The position and status in the change system and the attitudes and behaviors that result from one's self-conception, from the perception of the expectations of others in the system as to performance, and from the requirements of the system itself.

The triangular diagram illustrates the interrelationship of the three characteristics and their expression in the professional schema.

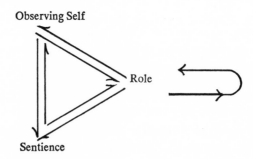

Any one characteristic may be considered as an entity and in its recipro-cal relations with the other two. Sentient characteristics, the extent to which one is empathic, for example, affect and are affected by the role one is in at a particular time and by how the immediate world is perceived. In reciprocal terms, how one sees his world and enacts his role is affected by what is sensed at that point. Consider, for instance, the social worker who, at the moment, is acutely aware (sentience) of the undercurrent of feeling going on in his group. He will feel more certain about his responsive actions (role) as these actions are defined by how he interprets the phenomenon (observing self).

But it is necessary to complicate this matter further, for these three variables do not operate in a circular state within a closed system. Consider again what happens if the same social worker acts prematurely and his well-chosen comment is met with negative silence. This re-action will bear on his role, perception, and feelings about the event. The point is that humans are responsive and open to their environment and react to it with some form of behavior.

Behavior is more than an active state because it has two dimensions: *strategy*—what is intended, its purpose and objectives; and *action*—the manifest performance of what was intended. To some extent, both strategy and action are perceived and responded to by the other sentient beings whose responses might validate or denigrate all or some part of the behavior. It is important to note here that the concept of behavior is not restricted to motor activity but also includes speech, gestures, body posture, and other means by which humans communicate. Action, then, is based on what is intended, is met with reaction, and some form of information is channeled back to the actor, where it minutely or gravely alters the original perception, role, and feeling.

What this diagram illustrates and introduces is a *communicational feedback system*. This concept is useful in explaining the circular change of events that results from an ongoing exchange of information (be-havior). Feedback serves to regulate stability, the steady state of organisms in relation. The concept more accurately and realistically explains the dynamics of human interaction than does a determinstic theory with its conception of behavior as being a consequence of pre-existing conditions that direct action in rather inevitable and static terms (Watzlawick, Beavin, and Jackson, 1967).

Returning to our social worker and his group, we see feedback in operation as he ponders the meaning of the response by the members.

He questions whether he misread the group's state of being, whether he chose the wrong words or failed to reach the group, or whether his behavior was untimely. Whatever answer he decides on includes how he perceives the event, how he understands what is taking place, and how he believes he should now act. These perceptions then determine what he does next, which in turn evokes another response from the group, ad infinitum. The extent to which the participants in this process use the feedback accurately and openly gives this system stability and continuity.

Thus when we speak of the need for the social worker to be objective, we are not referring to a detached appraisal of some event. What is referred to is the ability to make prior judgments plus an accessibility to the feedback that is experienced and may alter these judgments. With this in mind, let us now examine the three characteristics in more specific terms.

## The Observing Self

Refining the previous definition of this concept, what will be considered here are those components of the personality which impinge directly on the dynamics of practice. These are the more cognitive aspects, those that affect how the individual selectively sees and understands his immediate world. The intent here will be to identify rather than to define these factors.

*Constitutional Factors*   Frequently overlooked conditions that influence practice are the configurations of intellectual and physiological factors which distinguish individual behavior. To cite only a few examples, the quality of the intelligence of the worker has much to do with how he deals with the abstractions and metaphors of human interaction. Levels of energy and the neurological structure affect the degree of animation, vitality, or equanimity that flows into interaction. Thus the social worker brings with him intellectual and physical predispositions which filter and color his role behavior and attitudes.

*Life Experiences*   In some measure, behavior is a result of the cumulative effect of prior life experiences as they are perceived and interpreted by the individual. That is, what really happened is of less significance than how the person estimates the event and uses it to explain his view of the world.

Ellenberger colorfully and dramatically illustrates the many conditions that affect the professional's style in his remarkable depiction of the advent of dynamic psychiatry (1970). His biographies of notable psychologists describe the events, encounters, and fortuitous conditions in their lives and practices. He refers to social forces—not only friends and families, but colleagues, peers, critics, and adversaries—who enriched the psychologists' sensitivity and understanding. He notes that the books one comes upon, relationships with patients, the times within which one lives, the issues of the day, the happenings in other fields, and even the discovery of an abandoned idea all feed into the growth of the professional. He adds, finally, that it is impossible to ascertain in a man's thought what is truly his and what he has assimilated from events and persons around him. Practice, then, is distinctively colored by the range, expansiveness, and richness of one's life and is affected to some degree by the perceptions that derive from these experiences.

*Educational Experience*    It is only possible to speculate on the impact of one's professional preparation for practice beyond the level of knowledge and skill one is expected to assimilate. The nature of professional education thrusts the student into an array of personal experiences which, by their potency, may directly or indirectly demand some restructuring or reexamination of formerly held perceptions. The richness, breadth, and range of his educational opportunities certainly have the effect of deepening and enlarging his understanding of the social world. In his encounters with teachers and members of other professions, the student may come upon models of professionalism that may guide his own maturation. Peer relationships are still another source affecting growth because the other students with whom he associates may be living through the same tensions and apprehensions, thereby providing vicarious awareness of feelings and attitudes.

In a recent study that sought to find out what motivated persons to select one of the helping professions as a career choice, the respondents most frequently pointed to the experiential qualities of their training as being more significant than the intellectual (Henry, Sims, and Spray, 1971). They believed that the most important aspects of their training derived from their work experience, contact with patients, the field work setting, and contact with colleagues and practitioners rather than from formal training, their courses, the faculty, or their readings.

*Philosophy: A Personal Art*    If we reduce practice in any and all of its modes to its basic form we find it is a social experience between humans that it purposefully directed toward some change—personal, relational, interactional, or institutional. Hence, we need to consider the significance of those moral, ethical, and metaphysical factors that are embedded in the person of the practitioner and that ultimately shape and order his practice. London refers to three explicit elements of any therapeutic system: (1) a theory of personality which addresses itself to the nature of man and behavior; (2) a superordinate moral code, usually a social philosophy, which addresses the organization of society and the relationship of individuals to it; and (3) a body of therapeutic techniques which is a deliberate means of manipulating or influencing behavior (1964). The first and third elements are mainly derivative: knowledge of personality and social organization and technology can be taught and learned.

The philosophical element, however, is for the most part intrinsic to the person and comprises the basic attitudes, beliefs, and values—the "self," if you will—that the person as a professional brings to his practice. It is doubtful, for example, that the profession's Code of Ethics is really taught to the neophyte social worker. The words and terms illustrate, order, and conceptualize what should be felt beliefs. Actually, some set of attitudes about conduct with and toward other humans can be expected to preexist, probably having influenced the choice of the profession as a life work in the first place. The learner comes to his educational preparation with a rich abundance of beliefs and values about the "good life," the optimal goals in living, the meaning of reality, what is desired and ought to be, and how humans should interact most productively. These basic beliefs are usually unstructured, unquestioned, and unarticulated; persons rarely find it necessary to voice or test out what they essentially believe. But irrespective of their abeyant nature, the practitioner's value and metaphysical systems do find expression in his practice. As has been demonstrated, the total character of the practitioner is a significant force.

Thus it is essential that the social philosophy of both the profession and the professional be brought into cognition. There are at least three premises underlying this need. First and most obvious, awareness of one's philosophical stance would more clearly identify the essential aims and directions of practice and would lend meaning and substance to the theories and techniques selected. The practitioner could not delude himself into believing that his actions are not guided, in part, by his own values and goals. In addition, this clarity would reveal the presence of congruence and/or discrepancy between the beliefs of the professional and those of the profession, the sanctioning body, and the client system itself. Hence, feelings of being at one or at odds with critical systems take on substance and lend themselves to conscious deliberation, if not to resolution.

Second, the practitioner's beliefs and values are eloquent factors in his relationship with the client system. As an influencing and managing force, the social worker brings to the change system his knowledge, encourages learning, directs perceptions, and supports certain actions—all of these selective, value laden, preferential pursuits. While these actions are based on expertise, knowledge, and skill and are modulated by the feedback that he perceives, they are ultimately performed with some orientation to what he believes about optimal living. In short, what the practitioner aims for in terms of desirable outcomes cannot help but be affected by his own view of life and is no less significant than how and through what means he carries out these intentions.

The third premise has to do with how the social worker is perceived by those who use his services. The studies previously reviewed disclosed the many ways in which he is seen by his clients—as a role model; as a value bearer; and as a warm, understanding, and empathic individual. Thus the social worker displays many roles: as an existential being—how he deals with his own values and choices, what he stands for, and how he manages his own life; as an ethical being—how he carries out his professional identification with and commitment to the basic precepts of professional practice; as a value transmitter—what he selects from the multifarious conditions in living as supreme and significant; and as a moral agent—a carrier of the code of the dominant culture who, despite his capacity for acceptance and understanding, cannot be divorced entirely from the attitudes and standards of his own culture. These roles, emergent or recessive at various times, also bear on how the client perceives and uses the experience.

To recapitulate, the social worker brings to an encounter between human beings that is concerned with some aspect of social living a readiness to provide the professional influence that is necessary to bring about some valued change. Readiness comprises his armamentarium of knowledge and technical ability. But how these are put into action is bound by his personal style—the composite of temperament and constitution, the consequences of life experiences, and the substance of his own philosophy and values. Inasmuch as one's values and character are inevitably present in any meaningful human interaction, they cannot be subordinated or denied. These factors must be made explicit and subject to the needs of the process in order to become purposeful rather than subtle influences.

## Sentient Characteristics

What we now come to are those personal attributes that have to do with the capability for feeling and sensing, for "knowing" in internal ways the inner state of others at times without the benefit of specific clues. Sentience complements cognition; sentient reactions are subliminal whereas cognition is supraliminal. Together they form a continuum, the breadth of realization and awareness that are indicative of one's capacity to apprehend the range of feelings and behaviors in a human encounter. Sentience adds the dimensions of color and texture, the vital meaning of what usually might be perceived in ordinary or literal terms.

The definition of particular sentient attributes which follows will not include reference to such typical terms as warmth, caring, and interest, which are frequently used to characterize positive reactions. These terms do not lend themselves to explication; they are essentially ambiguous generalizations about affect. However they exist in the professional relationship, we can accept their presence as a necessary given. Instead, we will consider two orders of sentient characteristics: the responsive— those internal reactions that add to knowing and understanding; and the interpersonal—the understanding that arises out of meaningful relationships between persons. The former includes the facility for *sensitivity, empathy,* and *intuition;* the latter, the capability for *acceptance* and *commitment.*

## Responsive Sentient Characteristics

SENSITIVITY   By definition, sensitivity is the ability to know and therefore to predict what another individual will feel, say, or do. H. C. Smith, in his incisive study of the phenomenon (1966), differentiates sensitivity from projection, identification, or sympathy—those processes which relate the state of another to the characteristics of one's self. Sensitivity is a more direct awareness, an insight into the inner state of others. Smith's review of the studies on sensitivity demonstrates that it is not an ability that can be taught. When the sensitivity of trained psychologists was compared to that of physical scientists, artists, general employees, graduate students, and others according to selected criteria, there was no indication that training had increased the sensitivity of the psychologists.

However, sensitivity may be enhanced since its presence and intensity depend on particular capabilities. These include judging habits (how one is able to discriminate and appraise another's performance and characteristics); the ability to observe and make inferences; the ability to transpose one's self imaginatively into the feelings, thinking, and acting of another; the ability to make judgments based on one's familiarity with the groups to which the other belongs; and the ability to avoid stereotypes and perceive specifics, thereby increasing the possibility of making differentiations between persons.

Training, then, should be aimed at improving the accuracy and range of these abilities. Professional education should include opportunities for testing and validating perceptions and for determining what accounts for discrepancies between perceptions and realities. Expanding the awareness of persons as social beings would make it possible to understand them in their various social roles, thereby blocking the tendency to stereotype or to simplify perceptions into categorical or clinical shorthand entities.

According to Smith, research reveals that the traits of highly sensitive people are indicative of their ability to relate freely. In addition, highly sensitive people have both superior intelligence and intellectual efficiency, a high degree of affiliation and independence, a readiness for change, an openness to new experiences, a sense of social responsibility, and tolerance. In sum, sensitive people tend to be those who have learned the most from their relationships with others within which there was a desire to understand.

Sensitivity and the related attributes to follow obviously are not restricted to any one level, type, or modality of social work practice. Whether the social worker finds himself before a group of citizens with whom he is to work to improve housing conditions, with a group of teen-agers planning an excursion, or with an individual needing to work on some personal problems, the cogency of his relationships and the efficacy of his technical actions are intertwined with the extent to which he can sensitively know the other and, therefore, predict.

EMPATHY    Due to the growing evidence that the successful outcome of a helping experience is significantly related to the presence of empathic understanding, empathy, as a personal attribute, has been subjected to considerable inquiry. Carl Rogers defines empathy as the perceiving of the internal frame of reference of another with accuracy, and with the emotional components which pertain thereto, as if one were the other person without ever losing the "as if" condition. [1966, p. 409]

R. L. Katz goes a step further in delineating the stages of empathic involvement (1963). With the relaxation of conscious controls, one can become absorbed in contemplating the other person and his experiences, a process leading to *incorporation*—the taking of the other person's experience into one's self in some nonrational way. The separation between the persons is what he refers to as *reverberation*—the paradoxical awareness of the identity of the other while at the same time experiencing one's self. This is followed by a state of *detachment*—a deliberate withdrawal from subjective involvement so as to use methods of reason and scrutiny for objective analysis.

As the previous studies indicated, empathic understanding provides access to factors within the person which would ordinarily seem to be foreign to the observer. While sensitivity makes for knowing the other, empathy puts one into the feelings and experiences of the other. Not unlike intuition, empathy jumps the gap of apparent absence of concrete information and makes known what is out of conscious reach.

But probably the most significant aspect of the empathic response is the gift that it offers to the other. It is an expression of the placing of credence on what the other feels and experiences. Transcending the value of the knowledge that empathy provides, its presence conveys to the other a validation of that part of the inner self that is so often held in abeyance out of the fear of denigration or ridicule.

This is not to say that empathic understanding is without its risks. Expressed too early in the development of a relationship between the social worker and a client or between group members where trust has not yet been established and isolation is a necessary protection, empathy may stir feelings of transparency and vulnerability. In addition, the practitioner's seeming empathic understanding needs to be validated to determine if it does, indeed, correspond with the reality of the other's state of being.

INTUITION   Although intuitionism has been the object of considerable attention by many who have searched for the meaning of this inner experience, study of this phenomenon has produced few empirical findings and little agreement about its meaning. Some writers view intuition as a source of absolute truth, while others see it as certain nonsense.

Bruner believes intuition is a thought process that complements analytic thinking (1960). Where analytic thinking proceeds a step at a time, intuitive thinking involves maneuvers based seemingly on an implicit perception of the total problem. He sees intuitive thought as resting on familiarity with a domain of structural knowledge which makes it possible for the thinker to leap about and employ shortcuts in achieving immediate apprehension or cognition, to grasp meaning without explicit reliance on analytic apparatus.

In contrast, Henri Bergson, in his philosophic discourse on the subject (1912), sees intuitionism as the sole means by which basic reality can be known. Prime reality is ordinarily not accessible to human understanding because it is a perpetual happening involving change, evolution, and interaction. It is the analytic intellect which "makes sense" out of reality by artificially categorizing pieces of reality for the practical management of human affairs. But in prime reality, all events, objects, and processes are inseparable. Understanding of the truth of reality can be achieved only by freeing one's self from the restraints of reason and logic and by letting one's self into the experiential appreciation of the event. The product of this experience is a distinctly personal set of symbols that, through the sympathetic interaction with intelligence, can be transformed into analytic constructs. Thus Bruner sees intuition as a complement of analytic reason, while Bergson believes that analysis is only the means by which we can explain what we experience in a nonrational involvement in the flow of reality.

Within the field of psychology, Jung has offered a "grand theory" of intuitionism (in Westcott, 1968). He lists the four mental functions constitutionally present in all individuals—thinking, feeling, sensation, and intuition. Thinking and feeling are rational functions, the former involving judgments, deductions, inferences, and cognitions; and the latter including pleasant and unpleasant, pro and con reactions. Sensation and intuition are irrational because they involve no use of judgment. Sensation operates through the reception of sense data from the internal or external world as truth. Intuition, likewise nonjudgmental, is the perception of possibilities, of implications, and of objects as a totality at the expense of details. Jung goes on to say that these four functions, combined with other orienting attitudes, levels of consciousness, environmental demands, and constitutional factors, give each individual a propensity for the use and development of one or the other functions. In his terms, intuitionism is not only a cognate function but also a personality characteristic which, he adds, gradually becomes lost as we move from the primitive understanding of the child through the differentiating and constricting processes of socialization.

Westcott, after a review of the various conceptualizations of intuition, states that "intuition can be said to occur when the individual reaches a conclusion on the basis of less explicit information than is ordinarily required to reach that conclusion" (p. 41). His definition is at a purely behavioral level and represents elements which are potentially measurable. This behavioral formulation provides a sound basis for understanding the sentient characteristics described thus far. Whether we consider the source of these perceptions and awarenesses as innate, learned, socialized, or mystical, it is how they are manifested behaviorally in relations with others that interests us. Sentience, whether it increases knowing and predictability, enables us to feel with another, or captures the true meaning of a particular event, does serve to transcend the obvious and validates the inner being of others. In sum, sentience expands the circumscribed parameters of human experience that rationality, by itself, creates.

### Interpersonal Sentient Characteristics

ACCEPTANCE AND INDIVIDUALIZATION   The second order of sentient characteristics derives from the particular nature of interpersonal and relational experiences. A common term in social work jargon is "acceptance" which, in its simplistic usage, tends to suggest approval of the other person no matter how unpleasant or uncongenial his actions may be. I would not ascribe to this hortatory notion inasmuch as acceptance is not a facility which can be universalized, willed, or turned on merely because it is the professional thing to do. Acceptance is, instead, a differentiating process that demands a profound awareness of the values, needs, and purposes of the other person. Acceptance that is willed, that is applied so as to conform to the rules of the game is necessarily shallow and tends to be, more realistically, toleration or a "putting up with" for the sake of the desired ends.

The equivalents of acceptance are "knowing" and "individuation." These terms make the point that one cannot accept another unless he knows that other as a distinct individual and not as a member of a class or in the way he is similar to other persons. But "knowing" is a complex and difficult process that is never final and is often impeded by the social restraints that are employed so as not to reveal any more about one's self than what appears to be "appropriate."

How we come to know another depends on the selectivity of our perceptions. We sort out of another's reality those factors which make the most sense and fit into our own peculiar cognitive and emotional frameworks and value systems. We tend to carry with us a set of stereotypes about persons and groups which may be quite useful in enabling us quickly to grasp the meaning of casual encounters in daily living. But these stereotypes may also block understanding and therefore acceptance in those relationships that require greater discernment. Still another impediment is the inherent difficulty of taking in another's reality and experience. Here we are forced to deal with a relatively limited number of symbols which only approximate the other's reality. Words, gestures, or reports cannot fully convey the nature of the inner experience. Thus the observer is forced to make his own interpretation, the accuracy of which is dependent on how similar his range of experience is to the other's or the extent to which he can call upon his sentient faculties.

We not infrequently find that we are reacting to the other with feelings of aversion or repulsion. These negative feelings, perhaps to even a greater extent than the positive, demand a disciplined consideration, for contained within these reactions may be the key to or the symbol of the essential problem or issue with which the practitioner will need to deal. It is not uncommon for even the experienced social worker to "transfer a case," exclude a member from a group, or bring a project to a premature end because of reactions of antipathy to the behaviors of certain persons. This is not to say that all practitioners can successfully relate and respond to all persons or groups; but by the same token, reflexive action that does not take into account the meaning and source of negative reactions deprives the social worker of valuable understanding and the client system of a productive learning experience. After all, the persons who come to the attention of the professional frequently are having some difficulty in their social relations and would therefore be expected to transfer their maladaptive ways of coping and relating to the professional relationship or group. In this regard, it is the social worker's ability to read his own feelings that provides a means of understanding, a gauge of what is taking place in an interpersonal exchange. What may appear to be negative and disturbing behavior may, as it is understood, be indicative of messages that cannot find proper expression or maneuvers that provide the other with a sense of protection and security. Thus the adaptive meanings of the behavior of so-called resistant clients, of the retiring or over-dominating group member, or of the officious administrator may deepen understandings that enlarge the alternatives for professional action and enhance acceptance.

Acceptance of persons evolves rather than occurs and can be conceptualized in the following three-stage learning process:

STAGE ONE: INTRODUCTION. The level of acceptance at the point of introduction and immediately following is based essentially on social norms and amenities, on the expected behaviors of persons in their designated roles. Hence, behaviors would tend to conform with and be responsive to the understanding of what is appropriate for the professional and client roles. If the introduction is successful, there is then a search for common grounds for acceptance.

STAGE TWO: IDENTIFICATION. Acceptance at this stage is generally based on areas that the participants have in common. These might include similar views of the world; common values, purposes, and experiences; or a kindred cultural heritage. These similarities provide a sense of identification, a feeling of oneness and security. Acceptance that remains at this level creates relationships that are qualified by the requirement that these initial identifications must be sustained. As a result, boundaries for behavior, inquiry and action are fixed, and movement is constrained. In many instances where the professional objective is of a more planful or practical nature—for example, arriving at a consensus for action, referring to other resources, or providing needed information—this level of acceptance is sufficient and workable.

STAGE THREE: DIFFERENTIATION. At this stage, acceptance is not qualified by any restraints and indicates that the unique and peculiar characteristics of the other are subject to awareness without undue risk or vulnerability. Differentiation connotes the willingness to accept the range of patterns that might otherwise be labeled positive or negative, constructive or destructive, mature or immature. This acceptance does not suppose a blanket endorsement or approbation of these behaviors; instead, it conveys an awareness of the person as a being in his own right, as one whose behaviors can be understood in the way they allow for adaptation if not for survival.

In summary, the stages of acceptance are essentially conative, risk-taking functions which have as their intent the apprehension and appreciation of the individuality and dignity of persons. First, risk is involved in the willingness to face the possibility of having to reevaluate what we thought we knew about human behavior as we face each new relationship and permit it to unfold. It may be necessary to rethink or discard the frameworks, biases, or theories used to order our perceptions of persons and their ways of relating. Second, risk is attached to permitting one's self to relate to others on a level that is devoid of the usual social norms and constraints. Finally, acceptance itself produces no quick cures and may instead stir anxieties and apprehensions that may need attention. For any person, and particularly for one whose distress reflects alienation or failures in prior relationships, the offer of acceptance, given without a requirement of repayment or reward, creates a new learning experience that can be fraught with ambiguity or fear.

COMMITMENT AND CONCERN     In the discussion of sensitivity, empathy and intuition, emphasis was placed on the movement toward an awareness of the other beyond his categorical attributes. This intent embodies a willingness, a desire to unleash the restraints of rational understanding by the perceiver's placement of trust in his own senses and reliance on an internal wisdom about people and events accumulated through his own life experiences. The meaning of this sentience lies in its vision and in the way it offers to the other the experience of being known beyond conditions of role, status, and performance.

The consequence of knowing—as differentiated from having knowledge about—is an emerging acceptance of the other that is not a conditional exercise or a categorical ordering. Acceptance provides accessibility, a pre-condition for the emergence of relationships that are free of constraining obligation and conformity. Acceptance conveys the impression that "I am here, I am available without risk of disconfirmation to your self."

Unfortunately, relationships of all kinds—parental, marital, and social, as well as professional—often do not unfold beyond the attainment of that affinity. We open, but do not enter. It is only in our commitment with the other that we obtrude and make known our involvement.

I hasten to differentiate between commitment and dedication. The latter suggest a perhaps unrequested giving of one's self, a unilateral offering that may be without regard for who or where the other is, or a fulfilling of one's need to give. While dedication requires the preposition "to," commitment demands "with."

Commitment may be defined as an involvement with another or others that is unqualified by conditions of personal security or safety, and as a volitional wish to help without the need for recompense or rewards that prove worth, add to self-esteem, or preserve the status of the giver. Manifestations of commitment include constancy, follow-through, and the preservation (not merely the awareness) of the other's dignity and individuality. It requires a simultaneous responsibility and accountability to one's self, to the other, and to the professional system.

All of these sentient attributes usually have been considered characteristic of the one-to-one or psychotherapeutic relationship. The very nature of the revelations of self that are inherent in these processes is dependent on the extent to which the client can experience the security of acceptance and commitment. These last conditions provide the experiential base for relationship, the unyielding bedrock for trust and risk taking.

These attributes are no less significant for the seemingly less intense experiences that are found in the multiple relationships in groups or in the more planful or intellectual processes that are part of social action, social change, or other task-oriented approaches. With regard to group leadership, the sentient characteristics of the social worker serve, first of all, as a model, as a symbol of the norms of human interaction that are desirable for the development of group cohesion and interaction. The willingness of the social worker to go beyond the acting out of usual social roles in order to extend his acceptance and commitment provides a demonstrable but unspoken set of guidelines and expectations for the group's members. In addition, the leader's security and self-responsibility may provide the impetus for the members to transcend usual security-oriented, self-protective patterns. Involvement beyond typical behavioral norms shows a belief in the value of relationships and illuminates the basic human intent of any group's purposes.

Similarly, sentient attributes are essential to the actional processes relevant to social change, community work, organizational restructuring, and the like. On the surface, these endeavors may appear to be a set of operations based on facts and hard knowledge and aimed at somewhat concrete, perhaps quantitative ends. I would suggest that if the participants are fully identified with their purposes and goals, something deeply personal is attached to the change that is sought, including some basic and closely held beliefs about human relations. Hence, the social worker in this instance is not merely fulfilling a task or an assignment; he is also pursuing the achievement of ends that are related to a set of values and beliefs about what is possible and desirable in some aspect of the human condition. To deny these beliefs would be to deprecate the passion and vigor that can animate systematic operations. These sentient characteristics—the presence of vision, empathic understanding of others involved in or related to the task, and an unyielding commitment—strengthen the charismatic qualities of the leader and lend to the task a richness that enhances the methodological processes. Facts, data, and knowledge must be fashioned against the ground of human belief and motivation, for facts alone, no matter how conclusive, do little to change existing structures.

## Role Characteristics

The significance attached to the facets of the professional image presented thus far could well leave the reader with at least vague feelings of ambiguity. The attributes of self and sentience are (1) not peculiarly professional attributes; and (2) do not denote professional intent, purpose, or objectives. While these attributes add human texture and quality to the helping process, they do not, in themselves, encompass the entirety of the professional character. They are, in the end, contained within the structure of the *professional role*. For our purposes, role may be defined as those recurrent behaviors, normative obligations, and responsibilities which delineate status and position and determine the behaviors that are directed toward and responsive to a particular social situation.

Role, as a product of interaction between persons, is comprised of three components: *role conception*—how a person in a particular social situation believes he is expected to perform; *role expectations*—how others actually do expect the occupant of a particular position to perform; and *role performance*—the real behavior of that person in a given position (Thomas and Feldman, 1967). Where congruence between the three components exists, there is continuity and smoothness in social interaction.

A role, then, whether social or professional, comprises psychological processes on one hand (one's perceptions and feelings about his own status and the status of others in relation), and the influence of the social and institutional controls of society on the other. The latter are internalized norms for behavior derived from learning about the expectations of the social environment.

With this definition in mind, the following discussion will be restricted to consideration of the social worker's role performance and the influential actions and responsibilities that the social worker brings to the change experience in order to round out and complete the explication of the professional image. At a later point and in relation to the transactional processes of the social worker-client system, the other aspects of role will be discussed as part of the interactional process. So as to animate the concept of role, let us first look at a hypothetical but typical practice situation.

A childless couple comes to a social agency which offers adoption services to make application for the adoption of a child. After a brief wait in the reception area, a social worker greets them and requests that the couple follow him to his comfortably furnished office. After pointing to some chairs, the social worker returns to his place behind his desk. On the wall behind him hang his diplomas and certificates of professional affiliations. He apologizes for their wait and refers to some phone calls he had to make. The three then talk a bit about traffic, the weather, and other small talk. The social worker then engages the couple in a preliminary discussion about their plans and wishes and tells them about some of the basic procedures and operations of his agency. He determines from the content of their discussion that they do seem to meet the initial requirements, conveys this information, and goes over some forms that they will need to complete to provide the factual and personal information that will be required for further evaluation of their request. Another appointment is arranged for their return.

Having received the information and studied its content, the social worker, in the next interview, reviews this with the couple and talks with them further about their wishes, intentions, and motivations. After a time, he refers to the agency's use of a group to enhance the application process. He asks the couple to join with eight other couples also applying to adopt in a group that is now being formed. He notes that the group will meet at a specific hour for four consecutive meetings and that they, with the others, will have the opportunity to discuss some of the processes and concerns that they hold in common about adding a child to their family. Although both husband and wife express a little uncertainty, they comply with the social worker's request.

At the first group meeting, the social worker initiates the discussion by expanding on the procedures and problems relative to adoption and what will be expected of them as applicants. He then universalizes some of the feelings about adopting a child, noting that it is not infrequent or unexpected for a couple to have fears or apprehensions about the idea of adding a child to the family. After a brief pause, two of the group members speak up in rapid succession. The first refers to the experience of some friends who had applied for adoption in another community and the particular procedures they had to follow. The second hesitantly speaks with some feeling about the discussion she and her husband had the previous evening regarding some important changes that a new child would require in their living situation. After briefly acknowledging the comments of the first speaker, the social worker responds to the second by asking the group if others were experiencing similar questions. Some others respond affirmatively, and gradually the entire group becomes involved in a discussion of some practical and emotional factors relative to adoption and child rearing.

For our purposes we can leave our hypothetical group at this point in their deliberations. The illustration, although it is not a particularly noteworthy or critical event, does depict typical processes in the usual practice experience whether that experience has to do with personal and emotional problems, concrete services, or the pursuit of a particular organizational or community task. While the content may differ, the role functions and performance are similar.

Three major processes which distinguish the social work role are revealed by this example. They are (1) status clarification, (2) elaboration of significant values, and (3) specification of intentions. The three processes develop out of the social worker's *perception of his purpose* and expectations as they are implemented in his *professional function* and are governed by a set of *norms* or rules which guide the boundaries of behavior.

*Status Clarification*    The first process which defines the social worker's role is one in which his weight and position are elaborated by direct and indirect means. The social worker comes to the actual encounter with his clients already granted specific powers of action and decision by the community, by statutory sanction, by his profession, or by the social welfare organization that employs him. In the case cited, he has been specifically delegated the authority to make certain determinations about this couple in terms of their suitability as adoptive parents. In addition, his education and experience give him a special competence to make evaluations and to intervene in the situation he is confronting. In sum, the social worker carries with him certain sanctions and warrants that place him in a decisive and authoritative position.

This influence is manifested at the very outset of his association with his clients as he assumes direction for the processes to follow. His office, its decor, and the trappings of professional insignia lend further credence to his authority and further symbolize his superordinate position. In this instance, where the clients require a service that they believe can be granted by the social worker and that cannot be achieved through their own resources, further prestige and power is ascribed to him.

We have, then, the beginnings of an imbalanced relationship comprising persons in a subordinate position who require something that only the other can offer and for which they cannot bargain, and the social worker in a superordinate position who carries prestige and is in the position to evaluate and either grant or deny the request of the others. There are still other examples which would illustrate how the practitioner's status is maintained (his statement of requirements and the authoritative information he provides), but what has been mentioned is sufficient to demonstrate how the *role of power and authority* emerges out of these status-clarifying processes.

*Value Elaboration*     The second set of processes affecting the social work role have to do with the choices and exchange of values that are part of the interactional experience. Prior to and continuing from the outset of their relations with the social worker, our hypothetical clients are confronted with a number of choices about actions and outcomes that have value content. That is, these choices stir feelings about what is and what is not preferable and desirable. For example, this couple values the idea of adopting a child more than they disvalue the procedures that they are required to endure in order to achieve the desired outcome. Once the couple makes contact with the adoption agency and the specific social worker, they are faced with additional value choices imposed by the institutional nature of the setting, its policies, and the requirements they have to meet for eligibility. They need to decide which is most preferable—to continue with the program, go elsewhere if that is possible, or drop the idea of adoption entirely. The association with the social worker then involves an exposure to his values, which are conveyed both implicitly and explicitly. His willingness to discuss and further explore the possibility of adoption confirms their values about adopting a child. His probing and questioning stirs some consideration of their potential value as parents and evokes some thoughts about what they, as parents, have to offer a child. The request to fill out forms elicits some thoughts about the importance of certain of their life experiences and their meanings as well as about what would be preferable to include to enhance their value as potential parents in the social worker's eyes. The social worker makes known the kinds of patterns and behaviors that he or his setting deems desirable—compliance with the number of interviews and group meetings they are to attend, how they are to act within them in broad terms, the value of giving and sharing personal information, and other adaptations that may be more subtle. These processes are indicative of the *socializing role* of the social worker, for intrinsic to the professional encounter are transactional currents within which the social worker manages and directs the attention of his clients towards those actions and attitudes which are deemed preferable if certain ends and goals are to be achieved.

*Specification of Intention*   The processes here that contribute to the particular social work role involve the deliberate and intentional activities of the social worker that represent his function, task, and aims.

Again, the illustration affords us many examples of strategic activity that is direct and indirect. With regard to the latter, in the initial interview the social worker engages the couple in a genial conversation and then directs the discussion toward consideration of more personal and purposeful content. Here he implicitly provides a model of interaction that instructs the pair about the ways they are to interact in order to accomplish the stated purpose. Although these actions are part of the socializing role in that they provide order and direction, they are also edifying.

In more direct ways, he asks the couple to participate in a group which conveys to them how experiential learning can take place. The social worker takes charge of the group and first provides the substantive data that the members need to learn and understand as part of the adoption procedure. When confronted with alternatives for discussion, he selects the ambivalent comments which direct the group's attention to the importance of their own feelings. His encouragement of the pursuit of this theme proposes that learning about one's self can be achieved through (1) awareness of feelings and motivations (psychological learning), and (2) awareness of others' ways of coping (social learning). We can assume that this process will continue in various forms and on various levels of emphasis on the psychological, social, and substantive aspects of adoption in response to the concerns and needs of the participants. Here, then, the social worker performs a *teaching role* as the means by which he implements professional purpose and intent.

*Professional and Operational Norms*  Before going on to a more expansive description of the three aspects of social work role performance, it is first timely to examine the normative factors which underlie and guide role assumption and role behavior. R. C. Carson, in his study of interpersonal behavior (1969), defines norms as the behavioral rules whose acceptance is shared in some degree by the participants. The presence of norms is mutually advantageous in that they allow the enactment of contracts between persons concerning how they are expected to behave with one another. In addition, they facilitate the progress of increasingly complex relationships, particularly those in which the distribution of power is unequal. Norms permit the development of procedural patterns of interaction and interdependence which can be anticipated, thereby reducing anxiety. Norms may be pragmatic; for example, they may determine who sits where, who speaks first, or the penalties for absence or lateness. They may also affect such abstract issues as the principles about integrity, propriety, ethics, morality, and justice that are to be followed. For the present we will consider these last principles, already introduced in the earlier overview of social work practice, as rules which guide the social worker in his enactment of the professional role.

Norms become instrumental as they are internalized in the person of the social worker and become extensions of the principles which are reflective of him as a whole person. That is to say, one whose field of operations is in the realm of human relationships cannot markedly disjoin the values, morals, and ethics that guide his personal conduct from those that guide his professional behavior.

Hence, how the social worker carries out his role is governed by his principles about the dignity and worth not only of his clients but also of others who are affected by what he accomplishes with his clients. Whether the problem he is dealing with is pedestrian or exceptional, how he manages his practice is contingent upon his wish to understand the exigencies of the values, aspirations, and life views of the persons related to the problem. He seeks to understand the weight and meaning of these factors in the life systems and life styles of these persons. Dignity is not merely a state that we assign to another; it is derivative, arising from what we come to know and appreciate about the other's beliefs and ways of being.

Similarly, the professional is governed by his regard for the implications of change that reach beyond the immediate system. He is, first of all, aware of the adaptive or survival meanings of the behavior of his clients, whether they are individuals, groups, or larger systems. He is also responsive to the consequences of actual or anticipated change for others related to the client system when he recognizes that any alteration in existing adaptive patterns—whether personal, interpersonal, intergroup, or organizational—imposes on relevant others the need to accommodate to that change.

Norms are also linked with the typical and personal modes by which the social worker develops and maintains affinity with his clients. The potential depth and quality of a relationship is contingent, in part, on the personal investment, adroitness, and openness that the practitioner gives to it. In any change setting as with any form of human association, it is the distinctly personal manner with which the practitioner engages the others that vitalizes and strengthens the problem-solving endeavor. Investment refers to the social worker's volition and intent to enter into relation in a way that transcends the usual social conventions and to assume assertive responsibility for his part of the human experience. Adroitness is the facility for flexibility and responsiveness in relation to the emergence of the undetermined and unforeseen, the ability to move with the flow and change in an interpersonal event and to discard ritual. Openness adverts to the freedom with which the practitioner presents himself as an affective, effective, and perhaps fallible human being in ways that are appropriate to the nature of the particular relationship.

Norms bear on the social worker's professional acumen, which supports his technical ability. He is not merely a bearer of technical devices; based on the assimilation of knowledge and experience, his technology is rooted in his perceptions and beliefs about growth-producing interpersonal experiences and behaviors. Let us briefly look at some major sources of technical competence.

Technique is tied to a theory base. As has been stated, effective practice requires a theoretical frame of reference which serves to organize information and observations, to make sense out of the phenomena, and to provide sound assumptions that permit the devising of strategies for interventions that are not random or adventitious. Theory includes the rubric of workable knowledge about intra- and interpersonal functioning of individuals—singly, in families, or in groups—as well as about the larger systems of society to which persons are related. Theory also includes philosophic considerations of social ideals, beliefs, and values. But in the final analysis, theory is a value experience rather than a rote accumulation of facts or unquestioned knowledge. It is essentially a set of beliefs and explanations about persons and the social structure which, to be effective and useful, should in some way be congruent with the informed and basic beliefs of the theory holder. I would assume that the theories that the social worker ultimately finds useful for his practice are those that are more sophisticated elaborations of what he previously believed about human living. That is, education and experience expose the person to numerous theories and concepts out of which he sorts those that tend to validate prior, less conscious assumptions and ideas. I say this uncritically; theory that has to do with the human condition should be connected with one's essential beliefs rather than remaining an extraneous piece of learning in which there is no investment.

Technical ability also derives out of the application of knowledge to practice when this knowledge is evaluated in terms of its usefulness and value in the array of problems and situations encountered in practice. Thus the social worker should be able to draw from a repertoire of techniques, with his selection based on his understanding of the particular conditions he is dealing with—communication problems, group conflict, the absence of needed information, depression, dependence, or specific community problems. It is this repertoire, rather than a narrow set of methods, that provides the acuity and flexibility necessary for an assertive and responsive practice.

These, then, are broad professional norms which undergird and guide role performance. As will be seen, there are other norms that derive out of the nature of the specific interactional experience and provide the rules for it. The awareness of these norms gives substance to the following description of roles which identify professional purpose and function and which are the components of the total professional role.

THE ROLES OF THE SOCIAL WORKER

## The Role of Authority

Until quite recently, the profession has given little attention to the conception of the social worker as a dominant force, as one who accrues and employs some degree of power and authority within the change relationship. Apart from Studt's considerations of authority factors in the field of corrections (1954, 1959), few references appeared in the bulk of social work literature. The neglect of this concept has been due to the lack of a framework which could organize the patterns of ascendancy of control growing out of the transactional shifts in balance within interpersonal relationships. Of late, the social sciences have contributed to the construction of such a framework.

In addition, it has been the tendency of social workers to disclaim the role of authority and the idea that any degree of power was used in practice. Various rationales softened the concept of an authoritarian role despite the fact that much of social work practice was within the realm of concrete services in which the practitioner's prerogative of providing or withholding that which was requested placed him in an inherently powerful position. The adoption of classical psychoanalytic theory by the profession also tended to diffuse the role of authority because its basic tenets of neutrality and minimal intervention militated against the intrusion of what might be seen as a forceful or assertive image. Those social workers who practiced with groups or communities leaned toward a fairly literal construction of democratic principles and rights. Equality, cooperation, and the recognition of others' rights were valued precepts; any manifestation of power and control would therefore be seen as the antithesis of these principles and as an abuse or manipulation of others' rights. Little reference was made to the fact that democratic participation is not spontaneous and that in the most democratic group, authority is a natural product of the participation and interaction that takes place within it.

R. M. MacIver defines power and authority as similar phenomena except for the matter of consent (1947). He considers power as the capacity to control the behavior of others either directly by fiat or indirectly by manipulative means. Authority is differentiated as an established right to determine policies or pronounce judgment on pertinent issues, but it includes the committed consent of the other who is responsive or subject to that authority. Power, in and of itself, has no legitimacy. It is a latent force which has to be clothed in authority in order to obtain a legitimate quality. For authority to be effective, it has to be sanctioned for the promotion of collective goals. Authority, then, derives from two sources: the institutional, in which authority is granted or delegated by some sanctioning body; and the psychological, in which it is ascribed by one who recognizes and accepts that authority.

We have already considered some major sources of institutional authority in the forms of the sanctions and the statutory frames which legitimize the profession's right to provide service to segments of the general public. Sanction is also articulated in the specialized nature of services provided by particular social agencies, for they are the authoritative expressions of the community's will and intent in response to certain social problems. The logical corollary of this sanction is the authority to act on behalf of the community, to intervene into those social conditions that fall within the domain of professional competence, or to act on behalf of a client system as a member of the community.

The derivations of psychological authority are somewhat more complex in that authority and power are the sequelae of the imbalance that characterizes practice relationships irrespective of their size. P. M. Blau sees power arising out of exchange transactions between persons when one person has the competence, the commodities, or the services that the other needs (1964). What results is what he terms a "power-dependence relationship." In contrast is an equal or symmetrical relationship in which the members are comparable to the extent that each is dependent on the behavior of the other. In this case, power is either absent or the presence of counter-power resulting from interdependence tends to dilute the tension. But when persons require what another has to offer that cannot be obtained elsewhere—whether one is seeking the adoption of a child, financial assistance, help with a personal problem, or professional services to assist in a social action enterprise—the relationship cannot be equalized. The seeker cannot reciprocate or supply the provider with any reward that would restore balance, for the practitioner's needs are of no relevance to the task. Even the payment of fees for the services does not restore balance since control still remains with the provider. The seeker has limited alternatives: he can attempt coercion; he can resign himself to do without these services or commodities; he can attempt to alter his value system and minimize the importance of his needs; or should he decide to continue, he can place himself in a position that grants authority to the provider. In this last instance psychological authority is also enhanced by other conditions, among which the most important are the practitioner's competence and knowledge as they are effectively demonstrated. In addition, the seeker is subtly encouraged to grant authority by the prestige factors that he observes—the quality of the surroundings and decor, degrees and certificates, and whatever charismatic attributes the social worker conveys. Finally, the myths that are associated with titles, terms, or the change process itself contribute to the aura of authority and power.

J. W. Thibaut and H. H. Kelly, in their study of groups (1959), found that three forms of control accrue to one whose power lies in his superordinate position—contact control, fate control, and behavior control. Contact control alludes to the power of one to keep the other in relationship. When the social worker says, "We [the social worker and a client system of any size] will need to meet a few more times" or "once a week," he is setting the conditions for a relationship. Even if the statement is voiced more permissively ("If *you* wish to continue, I will arrange weekly meetings"), there is still an implicit requirement that may be stated as follows: "To get what you require, you will have to enter into association with me under certain conditions and for certain periods of time."

Fate control exists where the rewards one desires depend on the choices or whims of another. This is not to say that the social worker controls the destiny of the members of the client system. But many existential issues are influenced by the practitioner, particularly by his choices for action based on how he evaluates the problem and what outcomes he anticipates. Whimsicality cannot be excluded; very human choices can be made on the basis of momentary impressions, new ideas garnered from a recently read and appealing book, or how the practitioner feels at a given moment. In any event, the decisions and choices of the social worker do affect the subsequent sequence and direction of events. Decisions to accept or reject the presenting symptom in terms of importance, the involvement of another member of a family in the treatment of a marital problem, the inclusion or exclusion of a group member, or the selection of data for presentation to a policy-making body are obvious examples of how at least the immediate life experiences of others can be influenced by the control of the social worker.

Behavior control is the power one has to influence changes in the behavior of another, usually through varying his own behavior. In a sense, this control points to a major intent of the social worker—the deliberate development of the influence and leverage needed to bring about changes in the ways clients behaviorally deal with problems. Examples are numerous, particularly in the imbalanced relationship in which the subordinate may seek cues and direction for the behavior that he believes is expected. The social worker employs direct means of behavior control in the form of guidance, direction, interpretation, and information giving; and indirect means by symbols that convey reward, approbation, or reinforcement.

The preceding discussion may seem to be more indicative of practice situations in which prospective clients voluntarily seek assistance and are therefore more prepared to assume the subordinate role. Are these issues of authority, power, and control pertinent to the involuntary situations in which the target of service may not only be indifferent to the proffered services but might well actively resist them? Increasingly, much of social work is directed toward those social problems which are distinguished not only by their chronic, debilitating properties, but also by the barriers to change that result from the apathy or hostility of their victims. While the question of power and authority in the case of voluntary clients is one important issue among many, it is the preponderant issue that precedes all else in the practitioner's attempts to engage the involuntary, or what has also been termed the "resistant" or "unmotivated" or "hard-to-reach" client with the available services. It is elemental that nothing can be achieved until authority has been granted and influence is attained.

Depending on the task or goal, the social worker approaches those persons related to the problem either as a power figure or as an authority figure. The social worker is a power figure when he is acting on behalf of the social welfare community and its statutory provisions for purposes of social control—for example, as a child protective services worker, as a probation or parole officer, or as a member of an institution. The social worker is an authority figure when he is acting on behalf of the social welfare community and its institutionalized systems of skill, resources, and knowledge designed to ameliorate pernicious social conditions—for example, with the intent to organize residents of decaying neighborhoods; to work with youth groups; or to offer services to the poor, the ill, and the aging. In the first case, the social worker carries delegated power—the right and ability to bring about change through forms of direct control. In the second, the social worker carries delegated authority—the right and ability to bring about change by the employment of special skills, competences, and resources.

The primary importance of the concepts of power and authority resides in how they are accepted and helpfully used by the social worker. To attempt to abdicate his status or pretend that a state of equality exists would only serve to reinforce persistent suspicions and doubts, particularly those of persons who are resisting professional services. The task of the social worker in acknowledging the implications of his status is to bring into the open the feelings, distortions, and misapprehension held by potential clients which impede their use of his competence, control, and services. As the social worker strives to reduce ambiguity, stereotyping, and dissonance, the following may accrue: (1) appreciation of the similarities or differences in the respective value systems—therefore, the possibility of working toward a common ground for action; (2) possible alternative paths or procedures toward goal attainment—therefore, a broadening of possibilities and the inclusion of the client's ideas and plans; (3) greater clarity about what should go into problem solving—therefore, some sharing in the knowledge about readiness and the areas and the levels of the problems that can be worked on; and (4) a recognition of the possible benefits and how they are to be distributed.

Let us make a final comment about these specific role characteristics. It is important to stress that no value judgment is attached to the presence of power and authority in the social worker's role performance. They are neither good nor bad, desirable nor undesirable. Instead, these conditions need to be understood as natural phenomena, as the products of the imbalanced, unequal relationship that is typical of practice. Awareness of the impact and meaning of these states will increase the social worker's appreciation of how the seeker or recipient of his services feels in the less powerful, one-down, and unreciprocating role. The practitioner's awareness of his own status in the relationship, whether dyadic or group, will effect a less capricious and more judicious and timely use of his interventive capabilities.

*The Socializing Role*

The earlier statement that the socialization process in social work practice is tied to values, valuing, and value experiences raises a number of questions. What is socialization, and how does it fit into the social work purpose and objectives? What is meant by values; are they of a specific order, or are they found in some hierarchical order? What are the issues in the exchange of values between the social worker and the client system?

Young's brief definition will suffice as a starting point. Socialization is "the interactional process by which the individual is taught his place in the social order" (in Hinsie and Campbell, eds., 1960, p. 681). It is the means by which the person acquires the ways—the behaviors, norms, attitudes, and primarily the guiding values—of a social group of which he is a part through his interactions with persons or groups of persons to whom he ascribes importance and with whom he interacts.

Socialization begins with the first learnings by the child of parental and familial attitudes about what is "good" or "bad," in short, the behaviors that are preferable according to the dominant values. Continuing throughout one's life, every entry into what is believed to be a new social situation requires some measure of socialization if one wants or has to be part of that situation. Entry into school, the formation of friendship groups, assimilation into neighborhoods, employment, or dealings with organizations and bureaucracies are common examples.

Certain institutions in society are formed and persist primarily to serve the purposes of socialization (Levine, 1969). These may be such "developmental" socialization systems as schools, colleges, or universities or such "resocialization" systems as mental hospitals or prisons where the formal purpose is to make up for some deficiency in earlier socialization. The social worker, as an agent of the social welfare institution, is intricately involved with all dimensions of socialization. He is active in the developmental programs—schools, community centers, various group services, and child care—and in resocialization programs —mental hospitals and clinics, child guidance, and public welfare. But it must be noted that the profession is increasingly concerned with a kind of "socialization of the socializing institutions" in terms of the motives, efficacy, intent, and practices of those organizations which presume to represent the social order of society. The profession's commitment to the social well-being of persons demands the continuous examination of existing policies, programs, and services of institutions and their impact on special populations in functional, ethical, and value terms.

With this introduction to the concept of socialization we can now consider the value factors that infuse the social worker's role in socialization. Values, value transmission, and value exchange are issues that only recently have come forward as being significant for practice. First of all, theoretical structures about value systems were late in developing. The study of the importance of human values has traditionally been within the domain of certain philosophers who recognized that one's values revealed one's aspirations, appetites, and motivations— one's essential character. Within the professional practice, there was little question that the presence and expression of the practitioner's values was undesirable. His values represented an intrusive element at best and an offense at worst. Proscriptions about "disclosing one's values" were frequent, and as the historical overview reveals, the notions about "transference," the importance of detachment, and the "enabling" role tended to inhibit value expression. Some ideas about "professionalism" separated the social worker from his own natural and human responses. I recall the seemingly serious discussions that continued endlessly around the question of whether a social worker should accept a cup of coffee offered by a client and the devious means that were devised to deal with a client's simple questions about the social worker's life. "Are you married?" was often met with the rejoinder, "What makes you ask that question?" This technique gave the impression of incisive inquiry, but it really served to forestall an honest and direct answer that might reveal something about the social worker's value system.

A cursory look at any human encounter will show the paradox, if not the absurdity of a conception of interpersonal exchange that does not include reference to its implicit and explicit value communications. Our first tentative impressions of another, even the decision to continue or terminate the association, are based on value symbols—the commonality of interests, neatness, vocabulary, and the like. And if the association continues, it is marked by the search for and exchange of the beliefs, preferences, and strivings which define one's values.

Social work practice has as its purpose the resolution of value conflicts. The social worker faces people who, by simple definition, are struggling or need to know that they are struggling with a value dilemma. Whether the problem is related to policy or organizational change, family conflict, group cohesion, parent-child difficulties, or anxiety about personal choices, some complex of opposing values is in operation. And even the contemplation of a change in these conditions stirs a value conflict about whether one should give up what is painful but predictable for that which is uncertain and untested.

In accord with our interest in the components of the social work role, let us now survey the sources and implications of the practitioner's values for the socializing process in practice.

*The Social Worker's Value System*

The social worker is a value-laden individual in his own right. Through periods of maturation and education; within a particular culture; in his relationships with important others; in his decisions about religious affiliations, political leanings, and economic planning; in his aesthetic choices in dress, art, music, and decoration, he has indicated substantial preferences and value choices which work for him and which make for a fairly predictable and characteristic set of life styles. He therefore carries with him well-formulated beliefs and perhaps some biases about essential roles, relations, economics, tastes, theology, and the like. Although these beliefs and preferences need not narrowly direct his professional actions, they will color his perceptions, touch on his affective reactions, and influence his feelings about the value systems of his clientele. More important, these values are conveyed to his clients in the various ways that he presents himself as a human being in interaction.

The social worker's education for the profession should have the function of making these values more explicit. It is doubtful that they would be altered markedly in his learning, for I would question the depth and profundity of the self of the student whose lifetime of values could be significantly changed by his relatively brief exposure to graduate education. But the intensity of the experience should bring his significant values to the fore, where he can subject them to personal observation and can determine their validity and meaning for himself as one who enters the life experiences of others. He can also determine how they influence his style of practice and the evolving nature of his relationships with his clients.

The social worker is a member of a community. Not only is he sanctioned by that community to practice, but to some extent he has a personal and vested interest in its welfare, continuity, development, and improvement. His concern with its structure and institutions—its schools, economics, and welfare organizations—affects how he responds to the values of other community members as clients and to the community itself.

He is most frequently a member of a bureaucratic system in which he conducts his practice. That system's policies, rules, regulations, and expectations are in themselves value formulations which set preferential boundaries, methods, and services. They include the criteria that have to be met in order to benefit from the organization's services and the conditions requisite for continuing once eligibility is bestowed. In carrying out his professional responsibilities, the social worker is a translator of these values to the clientele of the organization, and not infrequently, is a regulator to assure adherence.

Simultaneously, the social worker is a member of and, we can assume, identifies with his professional organization. Beyond its formal and structural characteristics is its value system comprising its ethics for performance; its social mission; and its criteria for competence, admission, and membership. The social worker acts as a valued and valuing member in that he subscribes to these conditions and brings to his practice the major aims, the code of conduct, and the social orientation of his organization.

Finally, he brings to the practice experience his own system of professional actions, the configuration of the preceding value sources and conditions as they blend with the following socializing components of the professional role.

### The Social Worker's Professional Values

VALUED THEORIES: We have previously considered the possibility that the theories and concepts that the social worker selects, tests, and finds useful are congruent with his own beliefs about the nature, dynamics and transactions of persons, groups and society—that they are, in a sense, more formal elaborations of his basic values about person-to-person and person-to-society relations.

As these conceptions guide how the social worker will act in the context of practice, they will, by the same token, direct the client system into a socializing process which cues behavior and governs what needs to be learned. For example, causal or deterministic theories will encourage clients to delve into developmental and historical events in their lives so as to gain knowledge about the past significant experiences that bear on the present. Group encounter ideas will direct persons to interact, to strive for openness of expression, and to learn about themselves in terms of how they affect or are responded to by others. The particular explanation of the nature of a community would cause its members to see themselves as, say, active elements of a political substructure, victims of its economy, or representatives of its symbolic processes. Similarly, how the client system comes to understand the problem with which it is grappling depends on the valued theory that is used to define the problem. Although similar ends might well be achieved irrespective of the theories that are used to point the way, the expected behaviors and learnings along the pathways of change could vary greatly.

VALUED INTERPERSONAL BEHAVIORS: The social worker carries with him into his professional relationships certain beliefs about how persons should act in relation to one another. In his authoritative role, the social worker sets the tone and manages the ways in which relationships develop and assume a particular tenor, all in accord with his values. His own behavior, balanced against the state of the client system, provides a model for interpersonal conduct. Thus whether he subscribes to either more or less self-revealing or active approaches to practice, his actions will eventually evoke complementary responses on the part of the others in relation.

VALUED LEARNINGS: Although each practice experience with a particular social problem or social unit merits appreciation of its unique characteristics, that it is a human experience marks it as more or less comparable to previous encounters. Therefore, the extent and nature of the practitioner's prior professional experiences will encourage the use of certain approaches or methods which seem useful in enhancing or accelerating the processes of socialization and change. The group leader, for example, who found that his activity at the outset tended to achieve a more workable cohesion in a shorter period of time would tend to use this behavior with succeeding groups.

VALUED MODELS OF PROFESSIONAL PRESENCE: The degree of abstraction and the absence of precise guidelines that characterize social work practice could dispose the learning and developing practitioner to turn to real persons—teachers, supervisors, and colleagues—as exemplars of professional behavior. This tendency is also evident in the emergence of "schools" of practice which are frequently reflections of the charismatic as well as the theoretic attributes of major figures. As a result, these valued stances, ways of relating and acting borrowed from others as a model, become active socializing influences.

*Specific Socializing Influences*

These valued professional factors become transformed into influential behaviors and conditions which give order and sequence to the desired patterns of socialization. They are conveyed to the client system in three ways: (1) *directly* through those actions which are more or less deliberate and purposeful; (2) *indirectly* through actions which are more covert or oblique; and (3) *symbolically* through the factors which surround the experience.

*Direct Influences*

STRUCTURING: In any setting of practice, some amount of patterning is necessary in order to give the process a sense of order and continuity. Structuring includes but is not limited to setting times for appointments and meetings, seeing that temporal factors are adhered to, specifying what information is required, determining membership and programs, and the like. In any event, the recipients of service are required to accommodate to certain requirements and to alter certain patterns in order to adapt to the structure and boundaries of service.

SELECTION AND FOCUS: From the welter of information generated by the social worker-client system, some selection of significant information must be made that is relevant to the purposes of service. In addition, some tentative or long-range orientations must be set up as to the nature of the task and the possible goals. As a result, the social worker deliberately selects content that he deems significant and thus provides the focus for the participants concerning what they are to contribute and understand informationally and what they might work toward in the problem-solving endeavor. In sum, the practitioner encourages ordered thinking and selective cognition about events or conditions which formerly were incomprehensible.

REINFORCEMENT: In addition to the categorical means that are used to provide order, focus, and direction (e.g., questioning and guidance), there are other sources of control that are contained within the authority, influence, and importance ascribed to the social worker. These take the form of approval or disapproval, giving or withholding, and encouragement or dissuasion. Discussion of matters that are appropriate to the task at hand is likely to be met with verbal, tonal, and postural signs of interest and responsiveness. Conversely, discussion that strays from the purpose will likely stir such antithetical reactions as silence, apathy, or strained tolerance until the content is rechanneled.

Group pressures are still another potent force that urges conformity to expected norms for conduct, discourse, and content. The real or perceived threat of exclusion, ostracism, criticism, or ridicule sustains adherence to the rules of the group—whether it is a family, therapeutic, recreational, or task-oriented group.

The issue at stake, perhaps the most critical aspect of socialization, is that of the need for confirmation as opposed to the fear of disconfirmation. What any significant social encounter holds for us is its potentiality for confirming what we believe ourselves to be. Affirmative responses, interest, and concurrence reaffirm our being and reality—what we believe, know, and do. The polar experience of nonaffirmation in the form of silence, disagreement, or negation of any type threatens our self-perception and evokes anxiety and feelings of alienation.

DISSONANCE REDUCTION: The entry of persons into any type of change system is not without some measure of dissonance in the forms of conflict, ambivalence, or at least discomfort. Those persons who voluntarily seek professional services, whether for personal or concrete assistance, for social growth or social change, face the uncertainties, the accommodations, the requirements, and the unknowns that are unavoidable parts of the change process. Persons who are either unaware of available services or who resist them face additional kinds of dissonance that come with having to acknowledge the existence of some problem or their personal responsibilities (Goldstein, Heller, and Sechrest, 1966).

Socialization, then, is aimed at the reduction of these conditions and reactions which may impede continuance and engagement and/or block the desired processes leading to change. The practitioner may implement this aim in various ways. *Compensation* provides the client system with certain gratifications that offset or make up for feelings of apprehension or deprivation. Examples include sustained interest, attention and response, material rewards, recognition of needs, and flexibility in scheduling and programming in reaction to the requirements of the client system. *Cognition-producing measures* may also reduce dissonance. As the social worker brings to awareness the conflicting or ambivalent attitudes held by the others, they may be examined, consideration may be given to alternative means for dealing with the issues and problems, and of great importance, credence is lent to the feelings and attitudes of those involved. Finally, the attempt to achieve *mutuality* in reducing conflicting feelings may convey to the participants that they do not stand alone or in opposition, that concordance in movement toward the achievement of mutuality desired values and goals is possible.

## Indirect Influences

RESPONSIVENESS AND CONCERN: The social worker's ability to respond with positive and genuine regard for the other as a valued person in his own right creates a climate that eases the strain and tension inherent in change efforts. This response may also provide a new experience that can significantly alter the other's self-perception. These consequences may also be products of the group experience wherein members perceive the regard and concern of their peers.

However, responsiveness and regard may have other, somewhat oblique socializing effects. When a member of the client system brings to dyadic or group relationships his traditional maladaptive patterns for manipulating relationships to achieve some degree of predictability and security, the undisguised interest of the social worker, magnified by his ability to accept behavior without condemnation, places the client in a more ambiguous plight. Unable to call upon his typical patterns, he is thereby forced to deal with his ambivalence and learn more honest and functional ways of relating.

COMMUNICATION SYMBOLS: The major importance of communication as a relational phenomenon will be considered in its own right in another chapter. For the present, the socializing effects of verbal and gestural communication symbols will be considered.

The words, terms, and phraseology typically used in any social situation provide clues as to what the encounter is all about and the ways in which its members are supposed to relate to one another. Role, status, and expected behaviors are conveyed and perceived through the medium of communication patterns.

Where there is little disparity between the members of the system as far as the semantics and syntactics of language are concerned, mutuality and understanding may develop rapidly with few obstacles in the way of meaningful communication. In other instances, where differences in class, nationality, ethnicity, or culture prevail, members of the change system almost literally may not be speaking the same language. The consequence of this latter condition is the emergence of strain and confusion resulting from the human need to make sense of the experience and to achieve some degree of personal confirmation. Possible risks to the system are either its disruption or a tendency of persons in the subordinate role to accede too readily to the communicative style of the superordinate, thereby creating a charade. Thus the socialization process requires constant attention to the quality or lack of feedback.

On still another level, lexical forms of socialization occur as the social worker typically, and perhaps unwittingly, inculcates the other members of the system with his own vocabulary. In part, this is a natural outcome of the attempt to achieve convergence, for the "less knowing" to learn from the "more knowing." Examples are abundant. Persons first learn that they are "clients" or "group members" or that they are "indigenous." They become aware that they may be "resistant" or that they "project" or "intellectualize." A member may find that he wants his committee to speak to "relevant issues" about "policy reformulation" or to be aware of the "dynamics" of the group. While these are not necessarily negative outcomes and may, in fact, enhance smoothness and functioning, the extent to which these terms become the jargon of conformity and lose the genuineness of personal expression requires consideration.

THE SOCIAL WORKER AS A MODEL: The aforementioned behavioral influences, each with its own socializing properties, are reinforced and given substance when the social worker is perceived as an exemplar of one or many roles. As the embodiment of particular characteristics which are ascribed to him, he may serve as a model for desired behavior. The social worker's beliefs and ideals are selected and apprehended by those in relation with him. These attributes transcend what he says; they are demonstrated and conveyed with greater force and meaning in how he responds and acts as a whole person.

This aspect of his role results because the social worker's status of power and authority places him in a position of centrality that is subject to observation and critique by the other members of the system. This position is strengthened by the trappings of the professional role —his greater knowledge, his own achievements and success, and not infrequently the projected assumption that somewhere he has the answer, the key to the solution of the problem at hand.

He also carries and acts a gender role and in some ways represents what being a man, or in the case of a woman social worker, what being feminine is all about. Age, dress, and appearance also provide clues. Furthermore, the human aspects of the professional relationship make

it doubtful that the practitioner' _____ can
be concealed. His political lean _____ for
example, inadvertently or direct _____ he
eagerly curious and seeking ob _____
implicit orientations to life.

The change experience itself _____
organizational context, provide _____
client system to learn about th _____
ticularly as he uses himself to make the experience as free from debilitating behaviors and obstacles as possible. His attentiveness, concern,
and responsiveness indirectly provide a demonstration of what is optimal
and desirable in interpersonal relationships. This is notably true in the
group setting, a microcosm of human interaction where personal characteristics cannot be hidden and where standards and beliefs are manifestly open to view.

*Symbolic Influences*   Often overlooked are those symbols contained in
the physical and social environment of the change setting which, in
devious ways, convey to the client system some notions about where
it fits into it, to what it needs to accommodate, and the status that
it is expected to assume in order to benefit from professional services.
The following are just some of the more common phenomena encountered, particularly in those instances where services are provided in
the usual organizational structure. Other settings, including hospitals,
institutions, and centers each have their own symbolic influences.

THE RECEPTION AREA: Where the client waits to be seen and how he
is received tells the client something about how the organization sees
its clients and his value as a recipient of service. The comfort, decor,
degree of impersonality, individual attention, and the possibilities that
the area offers the client for retaining a sense of privacy and dignity
give that client some indication of the possible attitudes that will be
extended to him. How he experiences the setting affects his own mental
set about his role as a client. Persons for whom the need for assistance
connotes the admission of failure or substantiates the tendency for self-
depreciation are particularly vulnerable to the character of their reception, which may further strengthen the so-called resistance that the social worker encounters.

BUREAUCRATIC PROTOCOL: Most organizations tend to construct systems, forms, and procedures that must be followed as part of the con-

ditions for admission and partaking of services. Ostensibly, these requirements exist to facilitate the provision of the services typical of the organization. But as an organization becomes a kind of organism in its own right, these procedures may become a purposeless and mindless accumulation of rules and methods that are no longer congruent with the needs of the persons the organization was designed to serve. It is important for the socialization process to use these inceptive procedures; it is equally important that the procedures be timed to fit the readiness and ability of the client system to respond and understand their meaning. Critical factors are the clarity of information and direction that is provided, the way in which services are initially interpreted, the accessibility of appropriate persons, the specificity and relevance of the forms that are to be completed, the kind of information that the client has to give, and the use to which this information is put. The extent to which these procedures are personalized, the degree to which they bridge the gulf between applicant and client, and the way in which they are geared to the individuality and dignity of persons will affect how clients begin to understand and perceive what their roles are to be. When bureaucratic systems become a labyrinthian course that clients must negotiate, a form of bureaucratic socialization takes place. Becoming wise to the ways and learning the jargon, structure, and loopholes becomes a means of surviving within the monolithic bureaucracy. The social worker then becomes an arm of the mammoth. Professional responsibility requires an acute awareness of the extent to which the organization bureaucratizes its clients.

The examples of the symbolic influences chosen are obvious and are used to make a point. There are numerous others—the rapidity with which phone calls are returned and letters are written, the rigidity with which the setting maintains its hours (which frequently instructs clients to have problems only between nine and five, with an hour off for lunch), how relatives are treated, relations among staff and members of other disciplines, and promptness of interviews. The point is that socialization takes place in many realms, including those that precede or are apart from direct contact with the social worker.

*Recapitulation*

The discussion of the conditions which act as socializing influences and which define the social worker's role as a socializing agent may appear to point in one direction. One could assume that socialization is a unilateral process, that it only involves the client system. As will be demonstrated in a later examination of the systemic and relational aspects of change, this is not the case. To be effective and to achieve mutuality within the flow of interchange with the client system, the practitioner also becomes socialized to the customs, style of relating, and behaviors that he experiences in interaction. The singular and categorical approach was used here in order to organize and delineate the more typical socializing influences that the social worker conveys.

I have spoken of socialization as a natural phenomenon that takes place in any meaningful form of any social interaction and is markedly more profound in relationships that are unequal or imbalanced because of the dominant status of one of the members. Socialization is also a natural outcome of social processes which have a goal-seeking intent and which therefore require a certain order and system to attain their aims. As noted, the core of the socialization process is the transmission and exchange of values.

The issue, then, is not whether value expression—direct, indirect or symbolic—has any place in the change process; value exchange is its logical consequence. What is important is the meaning, effect, and potency of these values and their impact and implications. Not only can the social worker's values not be hidden, they are frequently sought out and evaluated by persons in relation.

At least two tasks emerge. Inasmuch as the practitioner's values are subject to observation, authenticity and verity need to be a part of his role and behavior. The attempt to effect a role or stance that is incongruent with one's essential value system or that evades or denies one's beliefs or preferences creates an atmosphere of, at best, confusion, or at worst, distrust. The observer is then forced to deny or denigrate what he thinks he perceives and has to attempt to identify with a model of behavior that is perhaps shallow, affected, inconsistent, deceptive, or manipulative.

Secondly, there needs to be concern about what the apparent values mean to and how they influence the client system. Of immense importance is the clarity of what is being valued and to what the client system is being socialized. Socialization not only attempts to establish order and sequence to the change process, but it also has some bearing on the beliefs and reactions which are carried over to other events and relationships and to aspects of society.

Consider, for example, the following instances not uncommon to social work practice which are linked to value considerations: the able student in trouble because he is fighting an ineffective educational program; a group of tenement dwellers who have been refused adequate housing ostensibly because of their race; the unwed mother who wants to keep her child but is being pressured to give it up; or a community of rural poor people who are cut off from access to services for political reasons.

Given these situations, how would a social worker's values guide the course and direction of his practice with these persons? To what ends would change be directed? Should clients be disposed toward adaptation to the existing inequities and deficits based on the belief that these conditions are irreversible? Should these conditions be, in fact, excluded from consideration and value placed primarily on the facility for internal adaptation? Should autonomy be valued, and should the client system be helped to sustain its own form of adaptation and encouraged to withstand the pressures and costs of nonconformity? Should the client system be approached as one that, in its own minute way, may be able to introduce change into the deficient social environment? Or should the value of convergence with similar clients be stressed in order to unify efforts aimed at changes in the larger system? Irrespective of the client's own choice, at critical points in the change experience he will have to deal with the values of the social worker as an authority figure.

It can be seen that whether the social worker is engaged in practice addressed to personal change or to more comprehensive forms of social action, he is not exempt from the consideration of his social values and his social vision as they are evident in his ideas about man and his relation to the social order and in the issues of adjustment and accommodation, conformity and nonconformity, and autonomy and subjugation.

*The Teaching Role*

The intent, at this point, is to treat this role in a somewhat discursive fashion as a precursor to a more definitive discussion in a later chapter. For now, it will be sufficient to spell out the role so as to round out the image of the social worker.

Ascribing a teaching role to the social worker at first seems irrelative; we tend to think of the teacher within the confines of a classroom engaging in formal and structured educational efforts. The educator, in the strictest sense, manages a learning process that has as its goal the acquisition of knowledge for growth and maturation or the development of special skills. The social worker manages a learning process that is primarily directed toward the acquisition of knowledge that will aid in the completion of certain tasks or in the resolution of problems related to social living. Although the specificity of the methods and techniques may differ, the process and sequence are essentially the same, the elements of which will be discussed in a later chapter.

If we look to John Dewey's conception of the typical ways in which man works out his problems in living, the linkage of the social work role to these efforts is evident. Dewey postulated that man is basically an acting being who engages in thinking mainly in the presence of problematic situations (in Prosch, 1964). At these points he falls back on principles he has learned in the past which are derived from his solutions to former problematic situations. When these principles do not work, he has to forge or invent new principles that will work in the new situation. And as he confronts the new situation for which he as yet cannot find effective solutions, new goals and purposes begin to form in his mind and force him to cast about for new means for their accomplishment. Thus each new problem situation requires both the construction of new principles and the reformulation of desired goals. How he accomplishes these endeavors takes into account their social meanings since man is a social being who inevitably lives and acts in the presence of others and whose actions impinge on them, as theirs do on him. Principles, goals and intentions, then, need to be thought of in terms of their social and interactional potential. If, for the moment, we bypass the specific methods and techniques of practice and reduce the social worker's activities to their elemental forms, the professional role can be seen in its correspondence to man's problem-solving strategies. The social worker provides and manages the opportunities and processes by which persons learn to resolve their problems. This can best be illustrated by some of the practitioner's representative role activities in typical practice situations.

PROVIDING INFORMATION: The extent to which one can maximize the positive outcomes of problem solving is in proportion to the adequacy of his knowledge about conditions related to the problem and to the steps that need to be taken to solve it. The required knowledge would vary in accordance with the task but could include information about aspects of the real world, about the client system itself, about aspects of the past that bear on present conditions, or about appropriate social behavior in given circumstances. One task of the social worker is to augment existing knowledge with what needs to be known so as to extend the range of alternatives for effective action.

PROVIDING OPPORTUNITIES FOR TRIAL-AND-ERROR LEARNING: Optimal social conditions within the interview or group setting offer the time, the support, and the feedback that permit its members to try out and evaluate new attempts to resolve their problems or complete a task. Within the change context, the social worker provides and guides the opportunity to consider, rehearse, and test out previously unconsidered, risky, or disordered problem-solving techniques.

PROVIDING INSTRUCTION AND GUIDANCE: In the course of the attempt to resolve certain problems, persons may be faced with a number of bewildering alternatives for action. The relative efficiency of these possible choices as they bear on the desired outcome may be an unknown. At this point, the more directive interventions of the social worker may serve to highlight and disclose the effectiveness of one alternative over another, unblock confusion, and make possible the most reasonable choice.

ENCOURAGING SELF-INITIATED BEHAVIOR: Although adequate information may be at hand and a surfeit of alternatives for action may be available, the learning processes leading to change may be hampered by the inability of persons to act on their own behalf or to assume responsibility for their own behaviors. It is assumed that in-depth learning, growth, and change take place only when they are consequences of personal commitment and conduct, when they are one's own responsible actions. It is, then, the social worker's task to assist in discriminating between behavior that is reactive and self-limiting and behavior that is active and self-initiated.

REDUCING DISSONANCE: Any movement toward change or the attempt to devise new principles for action stirs some measure of apprehension and anxiety that impedes or disables the problem-solving process. Although there may be little question about the salutary results of the contemplated change, modifications in existing states (which may, in themselves, be security operations), set into motion conflicting feelings and reactions. Clarification of the ambiguous elements by the social worker, bringing to light the ambivalences that are in operation, and providing realistic support, encouragement and time all serve to smooth the process of change and help those struggling with their dissonance to cope more effectively with the problem or task.

PROMOTING VALUE LEARNING: Any form of learning and change is consonant with a shifting of values, a rearrangement of priorities, or the assimilation of new values. In short, change requires some reconsideration of what is desired or preferred in persons' relations with their real worlds. The information that the social worker makes accessible may enlarge value choice and value sophistication. In addition, the experiential nature of the change experience—feedback, social observation, differentiation of individual needs, and the testing of beliefs, for example—provides the opportunity for persons to determine their essential preferences and to achieve correspondence between what they value and how they act.

PROMOTING TRANSFER OF LEARNING: The full meaning and impact of what is learned is not restricted to the consequences of the resolution of the problem at hand. How persons are able to apply newfound problem-solving skills to other problems or conditions in their lives is indicative of more pervasive growth and maturation, of deeper and broader learning about self, social relationships, and the real world in which one lives and acts. The social worker who can see potentialities beyond the immediate venture may thereby identify, encourage, reward, and reinforce the capabilities for transfer to other pertinent conditions or events.

These activities are merely a few of the indicators of the social worker's teaching role and serve, for now, as a prelude to a later examination of the teaching role as it is manifested in the transactional nature of the change process. It can be noted that, in contrast with what we think of as traditional teaching modes that are based on preconceived content and predetermined goals, the teaching role of the social worker needs to be somewhat more creative and ingenious. In the final analysis, the desired outcomes of the change experience are predicated on such imponderable factors as the needs, potentialities, and existential elements not only in the client system but in related systems. This requires attention to such issues as the readiness and opportunities for learning that sometimes arise unexpectedly or fortuitously; the implications of new learning, values, and behaviors for others; and the ongoing study of what needs to be learned in psychological and social terms.

## Summary

The intent of this chapter has been to enlarge upon the premise that the social worker, thought of in terms of his personal characteristics in combination with his technical expertise, acts to maximize the processes of social learning, social adjustment, and social change. Although his roles are differentiated by the specific social context of practice and the professional task, it is his influence which manages the transactional nature of the change process in interpersonal and group settings. An overview of pertinent literature and studies validated this premise and disclosed the significance of the personal style and attributes of the practitioner in relation to effective practice.

For purposes of analysis, three interrelated factors that contribute to the essential character of the social worker role were studied. The first concerned the practitioner's "self" as an observer of his world determined by constitutional makeup, life experiences, education, and philosophy. The second category included the sentient characteristics which effect how the practitioner relates, perceives, and responds to the human and relational aspects of the experience. These two, the observing self and sentience, merge with and vitalize the third, professional role performance, in rounding out the image of the social worker. It was noted that the whole image of the social worker is governed by and is responsive to personal and professional norms as well as the feedback received from the system with which he is engaged.

Further explication of the professional role disclosed three main properties: status—the position of the practitioner within the change system, values—the personal and professional beliefs and preferences that he brings to the event, and intention—his purpose and aim. By transposing these properties into operational terms, it was seen, first, that the worker's status within the unequal and imbalanced relationship produced a role of power and authority. The presence of values—personal, professional, and organizational—placed the social worker in a socializing role which ordered and directed the content and sequences of change. Finally, the intentional nature of his practice was seen to correspond with a teaching role that enhanced learning and problem solving.

# 4

## THE CLIENT:
## IN AND AS A SYSTEM

A common understanding emerging from widely divergent fields is that there is no substantial separation between things, objects, or events in the world. Philosophers and communication theorists, as well as scientists, have shown that linkages, time factors, organization, and patterns relate objects and events to one another. No longer are phenomena understood as artificial entities or coincidences; instead, there is an orderly movement toward the comprehension of the interconnectedness and the coherence of phenomena as they affect and are affected by each other.

Recent years have witnessed the increasing utilization of systems theories and models to explain the holistic meaning of various phenomena as well as the processes and properties which comprise the whole. The sciences—physical, biological, and social—have supplanted a molecular and mechanistic view of the phenomena within their purviews with a systems orientation that offers a conception of wholeness, organization, and dynamic interaction. This approach also cuts across the boundaries of each science's specialized domain and discloses the essential similarity of the objects of study.

Systems theory is no less applicable to the phenomena that are encountered in all aspects of social work practice. Here, too, we are concerned with matters of relatedness and coherence as we attempt to understand and treat the conditions attendant to a man's relationships with other men, with his various groups, and with society as well as their reciprocal effects. It is no longer useful to retain a view of man as an intrapsychic entity or of a group or a community as a closed, independent unit.

Von Bertalanffy, whose extensive work on the elaboration of general systems theory will be cited in the following discussion, states that the theory has its roots in organismic conceptions in biology (1968). Systems theory has also become an integral aspect of the conceptions of psychology and the social sciences. Where classical association psychology attempted to resolve mental phenomena into such units as sensation, intelligence, and motivation, gestalt psychology showed the existence and primacy of psychological wholes which are not the total of their elementary units. Similarly, the social sciences replaced the concept of society as a sum of individuals who are social atoms with the holistic concept of society, the economy, and the nation as a complex that is superordinated to its parts.

The purpose of this chapter is to demonstrate the relevance of the systems concept to the nature of professional practice we have considered thus far—namely, one that views man in molar terms as he is in interaction with his social environment. In order to animate this theoretical framework, let us examine a typical but hypothetical scenario for practice before proceeding with a more explicit analysis of the meaning and implications of the systems concept.

### A Practice Illustration

Mrs. Wright was referred by the County Probation Department to the Community Social Service Center. The referral was a consequence of a planned juvenile court hearing for her fifteen-year-old son, Bill, who had been arrested and charged with the possession of marijuana. Since this was Bill's first offense, the probation officer thought it might be helpful to use the center's services to aid this family. In addition, the probation officer was aware of the growing drug problem in the community. Knowing that the center was thinking of building a program that would attempt to cope with the community-wide conditions relative to the problem, he hoped that this referral might fit into the center's plans.

The center is a relatively new multiservice organization that was developed in response to the needs of a community in transition. Formerly a middle class suburban town that was dependent on small industry, the area's stable character had been altered by the recent growth of large industry, and an overtaxing of existing services has resulted.

Mrs. Wright's first appointment was with Mr. Able, one of the center's social workers. As a result of this interview and a follow-up home visit, Mr. Able recorded the following observations:

1. The family, comprised of Mr. and Mrs. Wright, Bill and two younger children, a son and a daughter, has had an uneventful but stable history until a year ago when Mr. Wright suffered a serious heart attack. Although he is partially recovered, his adjustment continues

to be difficult, and the family is experiencing a sense of dislocation and anxiety.

2. Bill, formerly a curious and active youngster and an above average student, has become somewhat withdrawn and hostile. His motivation and performance in high school has declined rapidly. The school is overcrowded and faces critical problems; therefore, it has not been able to provide any individualized help or attention.

3. Bill is a member of a loosely knit group of boys of his own age that has, reportedly, drifted into experimentation with drugs and random vandalism.

4. Mrs. Wright shares her concern with a number of other parents of adolescents in her neighborhood. They have talked about getting together to confer with some of the school personnel, but for one reason or another, these meetings have never taken place.

These preliminary observations also tended to substantiate Mr. Able's prior impressions about the drug problem. They are:

1. The Wright situation is indicative of a common set of problems in the community. The Wrights are only one of an increasing number of families that have recently come to the attention of the center either by voluntary application or by the referral of other authoritative or social welfare organizations.

2. The center has not been eminently successful in grappling with the problem. Despite the deliberations of the administration and the board of directors, they have not been able to devise a set of policies or a program to meet the growing problem.

3. Other social welfare organizations as well as representatives of the new industries have voiced concern and the desire to meet to discuss ways of dealing with the community's problems. However, these plans are still in a very formative stage of development.

Given this set of observations and conditions, what are Mr. Able's options concerning the most effective forms of intervention and approaches to the problem? There are two major interventive concepts that could guide his decision.

The first is based on and limited to the social worker's competency to work with, or to use his agency's definition of services to particular social units—individuals, families, groups, or the community. This interventive approach, with due regard for other conditions, would tend to treat the problem as it is manifested within the unit that falls within the purview of skill or policy. Because this concept of practice would delimit attack of other possible causal forces, it is not necessarily the most flexible, economic, or effective. The chances are that the social worker would be forced to deal with residual and symptomatic aspects of the problem in lieu of getting to its more critical sources.

The second means of access to the problem is based on an assessment of the total structure in which the problem is lodged. It is essentially a problem-solving orientation which, to be effective, would first locate the major forces accessible to change that are embedded in specific interactive environments (in a sense, the social context of the problem). This analysis would then generate the appropriate strategies and interventions for problem resolution. The following will illustrate this concept.

At first glance, it might appear that young Bill should be the target of service aimed at some form of therapeutic change in his self-perception and behavior. While he may well need this help, he also must be viewed as a symptom bearer, a prodrome of a still greater problem. Although he is a casualty of this problem, his destructive behavior contributes to its continuance.

Bill is also an active and reactive member of his family, a group of interdependent persons who may be in conflict about their respective roles, expectations, and values. He is, in addition, a member of a group of peers whose values and behaviors are in conflict with their society. These two groups are interrelated in that there is a collision of opposing values that excites reactive and defensive behaviors on the part of each group's members.

Both groups, in turn, affect and are responsive to at least one major social institution, the educational system as represented by Bill's high school. Because the school is overcrowded and lacks guidance personnel and recreational facilities, it not only offers little constructive help to these boys or their families, but it may tend to perpetuate or, in the group's perceptions, even justify hostile attitudes and behaviors. Conversely, the group's actions would have the effect of threatening the already precarious state of the school's program and resources, thereby limiting what little time and energy might be available to arrange meetings with interested groups of parents.

The Wright family is an interacting segment of a larger neighborhood, community, and economic system. It not only shares the ecological conditions and problems, it also converges with other families in terms of their mutual problems and their concerns about the welfare of their children, familial well-being, and the stability of the community. These families as citizens, in turn, are involved in a constant process of exchange with the institutions of the community—social, regulatory, educative, and economic. The new industries, for example, may feel the acute effects of the community's conditions in the form of absenteeism, lowered productivity, or personnel problems.

Another system comes into being as Mrs. Wright initiates contact with the center, and this system involves Mr. Able and his agency. Of greater importance is the fact that her entry creates the potential for interaction and negotiation between this system and the others just described—the Wright family, the group of boys, the neighborhood group of parents, the school, and so forth. Not the least of the consequences of her contact is its effect on Mr. Able's relations with his organizational system—its staff, policy-making bodies, and administration. For visual purposes, the following diagram illustrates the interrelatedness of the major systems involved.

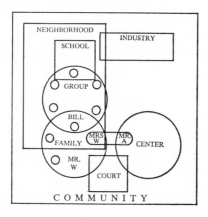

In order to simplify and clarify the systems structure, the description of these units in interaction progresses from the smallest to increasingly larger units. The same structure could be constructed from any vantage point in the total system. For example, members of the school board and representatives of industry could initiate a movement to study the problem and could involve the center at a later point in an attempt to secure professional assistance with the broader aspects of the problem.

What has been described is a major system comprised of a hierarchy of subsystems, each subject to the inputs of the smaller and larger systems contiguous to it. A systems orientation reveals the complex nature of the larger social problem as well as its impact on the specific persons or groups of persons in relation. Conversely, it elucidates the systems, persons, and behaviors which tend to perpetuate the problem and thereby identifies the points in the complex of systems where the most effective intervention is possible.

*General Systems Theory: A Definition*

Buckley defines a system as "a complex of elements or components directly or indirectly related in a causal network, such that each component is related to some other in a more or less stable way within any particular period of time" (1967, p. 41). The components may be relatively simple and stable or complex and changing. The relations between them may be mutual or unidirectional and may vary in degree of causal efficacy or priority. The particular configuration at any time constitutes the structure of the system at that time, thus achieving a "whole" with some degree of continuity and boundary. Concomitantly, some process of interchange is going on with other systems. In that this definition is applied to the study of human groups and formal and informal organizations, we may aptly refer to a "social systems theory" rather than to the more inclusive "general systems," which would take into account the analysis of biological entities and chemical and etiological systems, as well as computerized simulations.

In sum, social systems theory provides a framework for gaining an appreciation of the entire range of elements that bear on a social problem including the social units involved, their expansive and dynamic characteristics, their interrelations, and the implications of change in one as it affects all others. This approach stands in contrast with a reductionistic and static perception of individuals or collectivities of individuals.

The risks and possible misuses of this theory must be stated before proceeding to a more precise analysis of its components. As with all theories designed to order and explain the vagaries of human interaction, systems theory is, in essence, a reification, an abstraction of the real world. Hence, it only provides explanations in principle rather than in scientific or quantitative terms. It provides a framework within which concepts of human interaction may be organized and understood. In that it enlarges the perception and meaning of how persons, groups of persons, organizations, and communities affect one another and manage their existences, it is useful; to use the theory analogously would only succeed in returning to a mechanistic view of human behavior.

## Characteristics of a Social System

In the following discussion, the content will be drawn mainly from the works of von Bertalanffy, Buckley, Lennard and Bernstein, and Carson. Von Bertalanffy and Buckley deal primarily with theory formulation, analysis, and comparison. Carson's interest is in the use of systems theory for explaining patterns of human interaction. Lennard and Bernstein are interested in developing more effective models of treatment and consider the implications of a systems approach for what they term "clinical sociology."

*The Permeable Boundaries of Systems*   In contrast with the closed systems in mathematics and sciences, a social system is open: that is, it is in a constant process of change subject to the inflow and outflow of communicational stimuli. The property of permeable boundaries defines what is inside and what is outside the system (Lennard and Bernstein, 1969). These boundaries may be thin and vulnerable to external demands, or they may be too rigid and impermeable and therefore relatively isolated from other systems. The Wright family, for example, suffers from the input and impact of outside forces that too rapidly penetrate the family's boundaries—the behavior and values of Bill's group and the attitudes and actions of systems of social control, to name but two. This penetration leaves the family vulnerable and unable to initiate or call upon its own resources. In contrast, the educational system, as a consequence of its own internal malaise, sets up boundaries which repel external demands and attempts to isolate itself from surrounding systems. In the first instance, the lack of boundaries results in some loss of structure, cohesion, and function. In the second, increasing rigidification of boundaries is the consequence.

The boundaries of any system are defined by the observer and are related to the particular criteria that are applied. The boundaries of, say, an organization may be more objectively definable because of its policies, limitations, and objectives. A recreational group with very limited objectives beyond social activity would tend to have loosely defined boundaries sufficient only for self-identification. In any case, this concept points to the relative openness or impermeability of a particular system and serves as a general measure of accessibility to that system.

*Extrasystem Inputs and Adaptation*   How social systems work represents their solutions to larger problems presented by society. The way a system deals with external demands is indicative of the continuous adjustment and interactional patterning within the system that are required to accommodate the diversity of the external forces that impinge upon it. These inputs are the norms, the values and rules, and the instructions from the larger society about expected behavior and performance. When these instructions are congruent with the values and expectations of the system, adaptation is relatively easy and free of conflict or ambivalence. When the instructions are too diverse, incongruent, or inadequately articulated, conflict and deviance result.

The Wright family finds itself somewhat disabled by the discontinuity between its values, norms, and behaviors and those present in or expected by other contiguous systems. Part of Mr. Wright's difficulty may be the self-depreciation he feels because, as a result of his illness, he cannot fulfill the role that he believes society expects of him. Parent and child roles are in conflict because of the inability to achieve correspondence between two dominant sets of values, the family's and Bill's group's. Because the family came to the attention of the juvenile court, the message input is that, as parents, they no longer adequately meet the requirements as set forth by society. Therefore, a larger authoritative system threatens to assume part of the parental role. How the parents manage these inputs is indicative of their adaptive capabilities. Thus as the social worker enters the system he may be perceived either as another external influence who will further elaborate the rules and instructions of society or as one who will enhance the family's ability to articulate and strengthen its own values and rules in a more productive fashion. Whichever way they respond to him will then determine the social worker's input.

*Longitudinal Processes*   A single system can be compared to itself at different points in time as well as to its criteria for stability. Stability itself is a time function. Understanding a system therefore requires recognition of the temporal fluctuations in the nature of the system's stability, which gives evidence of its overall character. Here the importance of a social history comes to the fore—not for the mere collection of sequential episodes or individual milestones in the development of the system, but as indices of the continuity, permanence, and strength of the system's maintenance capabilities (Lennard and Bernstein, 1969). For example, it would be specious, if not harmful, to assume that the Wright family is pathological in its present state without reference to its heritage, to how it has managed its past problems and inputs. Similarly, any efforts to work with the subgroups in the community relative to the present fractures in its structure would require some study of what held the community together in a stable fashion for many years.

*Convergence*  Convergence is a system property resulting from interaction between individuals that tends to decrease dissimilarities in their expectations, goals, and behavior. Various studies of groups give evidence that the process of interaction results not only in movement toward symmetrical orientations, but also toward more similar patterns of communication (Lennard and Bernstein, 1969). Communication through interaction reduces imbalance and equalizes the distribution of information about specific role relationships and about the behavior and attitudes that are appropriate and necessary for the establishment, maintenance, and development of the system. Convergence, then, may be viewed both as a descriptive characteristic of the system and as an index of the degree to which the system does or does not provide opportunities for the kind of interaction and communication which would foster mutuality. The Wright family provides an example of the antithesis of convergence—what happens when convergence breaks down. As Bill breaks away from the expectations and values of the family and aligns himself with the values of his group, conflict arises within which the essential beliefs of the family are challenged and threatened. This threat in turn endangers the family's stability. It may be assumed that the condition which impedes the Community Social Service Center's ability to grapple with the community's problems is also the lack of convergence among staff, board, and administration relative to a common perception of the problem and the most effective means for dealing with it.

*Differentiation*  As any group proceeds toward the accomplishment of its purposes, varied patterns of performance are required in each sequential phase of its development. The groups become differentiated in character in each of the successive phases. Any family is a prime example of this process. Parental roles become differentiated as the child grows, shifting from, say, protective actions in the child's infancy to the intent to foster independence in the later teens.

We see that Mr. Able's role as a social worker would become differentiated over periods of time, as would the client system's with which he chose to work. The change process would necessarily begin on very general terms; but as data became available and the purposes and objectives became clarified, differentiated roles, responsibilities, and tasks would emerge on the part of the participants. Consequently, the characteristics of the change unit vary.

*System Regulating Processes*   We come now to those conditions which ensure the continuity, character, and stability of the system. Various systems theorists have used such terms as *equilibrium, homeostasis,* or *steady state* to refer to the stability of a system, its regulation, maintenance of its variables, and the direction of the organism to its goal. To frequently, one can find these terms used interchangeably as if they were, in fact, synonymous.

Von Bertalanffy presents a cogent argument for clarity about what these terms specifically connote (1968). To understand their respective implications for the means by which a system regulates itself, as well as for practice with the systems encountered in social change endeavors, it is first necessary to review the shift away from a mechanistic conception of man within the behavioral sciences.

In the first half of the twentieth century, American psychology was dominated by the concept of the reactive organism. Classical and neoclassical behaviorism, learning and motivation theories, psychoanalysis, and cybernetics all perpetuated this view. Destiny, according to these ideas, is determined by genes, instincts, accidents, early conditioning, reinforcement, or cultural and social forces. Thus social phenomena were thought of in purely causal terms in which a set of conditions of particular force and strength inevitably effected the emergence of another set of conditions.

This simplistic yet comfortable orientation has gradually been supplanted by a more complex principle, namely, that man is an *active* personality system. Hence, he is capable of self-initiated behavior. He has some measure of autonomy in his actions and is not necessarily subject or reactive to his environment in a probabilistic sense. This principle is evident in newer orientations to behavior: ego psychology, Piaget's child psychology, the self-realization concepts of Goldstein and Maslow, Rogers' client-centered approach, and the existential and phenomenological positions. Broader societal implications are evident in the extent to which the desirability of accommodation and conformity to established social norms and of maintaining the status of prevailing institutions are being questioned and tested. The ability of man to contribute to and alter his environment or even to create new environments is as much a property of human behavior as is his tendency to be affected by and to react to his environment.

Basic to a social systems orientation is this principle of an active personality. Seeing the organism simply in terms of its molecular units —reflexes, sensations, drives, traits, and the like—permits us to understand only its discrete functions, a view which not only mechanizes and dehumanizes that organism but also obviates the richness of the human experience. In contrast, a molar concept illuminates the bio-psycho-social properties of the organism in mutual and reciprocal interaction with all of its parts and processes. Any breakdown, whether individual or collective, is always a systems disturbance rather than the loss of a single function. Mr. Wright's heart attack, for instance, involves more than a flaw in a single organ; his illness not only disturbed the balance of his physiological system, but it also affected his psychology, his relationships with his family, the stability of that system, and the family's relations with contiguous systems.

The organism is intrinsically an active system with or without stimuli. A stimulus does not *cause* a process in an inert system; it *modifies* existing processes in an autonomically active system which is constantly directed toward the realization of certain goals and values. The human state is characterized by conceptions of time, awareness of the meaning of the heritage of the past and the anticipation of the future, the capacity to intend and plan, the presence of.ideals, morals, and values, and a striving for some interpretation of truth.

This expansive, mutable, and active conception of the organism militates against the notion of homeostasis or equilibration as the means by which small or large systems attempt to regulate themselves. Homeostasis is essentially a biologic reference and applies to those utilitarian activities which promote self-preservation. The term connotes the tendency for an organism to return to a state of rest that is relatively free of tension, a state which denies the pervasive strains of growth and creativity. The concept of equilibration refers to the attempt of the organism to achieve not a state of rest but a state of balance between forces that bear on the system. This also implies an absence of motion and pulse and is not in accord with the inevitable tension, ambivalence, and ambiguity that are hallmarks of human goal seeking, learning, growth, and spontaneous activity.

The concept of a *steady state* more aptly captures the way systems cope with and manage disruptive stimuli coming from external or internal sources. Buckley refers to this concept as an expression not only of the *structure-maintaining* capabilities of an inherently unstable system but of its *structure-elaborating* and *change* features as well (1967). This is, then, a concept of morphogenesis that alludes to how a system maintains stability and continuity while undergoing growth and change. Thus it is not the structure of the system that remains steady, for in order to maintain wholeness and continuity, some alteration of that structure may be a consequence of the system's endeavor to deal effectively with the inflow of stimuli. The superordination of roles, the reordering of performances, and the inclusion or exclusion of its members are structural changes that may be attendant to the system's attempts to sustain healthy stability, to mature and unfold.

The Wright family again provides us with a good example of a system in a steady state as it experiences disjunctions and attempts to do more than merely persevere. The family cannot return to its previous state of balance; the effects of Mr. Wright's illness and Bill's breaking away from the structure of the family preclude the resumption of previous relationships and patterns. They no longer work to maintain the structure of the family. While the family would have continuity, depending on how its members come to define the term "family," the roles, interrelationships, patterns, norms, and values would need to undergo change. For example, the parental roles could achieve greater strength and viability in dealing with Bill; Mr. Wright could emerge as the person in the decision-making role; Bill might be helped to find a set of values with his parents that would promote more affinity; confidence in behavior could accrue from participation with other families; or conceivably, Bill might need to leave the family. In any event, a new family structure would emerge and hopefully would be more able to manage and resolve other stresses as a consequence of the specific event.

This version of adaptation to stress permits a way of understanding the regulatory forces of a system as a *process* which deals with disruption by the reorganization of its parts rather than by returning to or maintaining a static state of balance. This view assigns to the system the potential to achieve a higher order of problem solving and a capacity to grow, learn, and change. It is also valuable in that it offers a way of perceiving or measuring the attributes and potentialities of the system as well as the nature and quality of its internal dynamics, strengths, and shortcomings.

I do not wish to dispense totally with the homeostatic concept of adaptation because it is useful when applied to systems that maintain a given, relatively high level of organization against tendencies toward reduction (Allport, 1960). It is useful for models of larger organizations, particularly those bureaucracies which tend to persist with little structural change despite, or even because of the tensions and pressures directed toward them. When continuity and survival rather than flexibility and change are the core forces, the organization will regulate itself by the restoration of its structure with few, if any, modifications of its parts.

## Summary

The concept of the client as defined in this chapter departs from the more traditional monadic view of the recipient of social work services. It bears repeating at this point that the term "client" is used in its most extensive meaning to include any individual or collectivity of individuals who benefit from the use of the profession's services either directly or indirectly through the participation of others acting on their behalf.

Social systems theory was used as a means of broadening the perception of the client to include the many forces that impinge on the practice experience and are, in turn, affected by that experience. It is also useful as a framework within which other concepts about human interaction can be organized—for example, interactional, group dynamics, organizational, bureaucratic, and community theories. In itself, social systems theory is not a form of practice; its use for the analysis of the problem-client configuration may prescribe interventions or modalities of service, however.

It can be argued that a loss of individuality may result from the attempt to study the individual not as an entity in his own right, but as he is in relation within a hierarchy of increasingly larger systems. I would disagree. A systems orientation enhances the many facets of personality as they become recognizable in the person's many social relationships, roles, and statuses. A holistic view impels us to understand the entirety of the social, psychological, and physiological organism and enlarges our appreciation of the creative and adaptive potentialities not only within the person but also within the systems in which he functions. We can come to know the real world of the client in the form of relations rather than as differentiated entities.

The organic nature of the systems concept also offers a framework within which the functions of social work practice may be arranged as variant perceptions of and approaches to the same problem. Therapeutic and social action strategies need not be viewed in polar terms but merely as differential remedies, the selection of which would be responsive to the study of the systems in question in their entirety. As the practitioner determines *where* within the systemic configuration intervention would achieve the most economic and effective ends, the matter of *how* would logically follow.

We can now return to Mr. Able and his client to illustrate these ideas. As he extends his study of the initially presented persons and problems to take into account all of the relevant systems in relation which affect and are affected by the conditions described, many avenues of attack are open to him. Which he selects depends upon the assumptions he makes about the nature and dynamics of the problem, his purposes and objectives, and the most effective point of entry. He could work with Mrs. Wright to strengthen her coping abilities and thereby enhance the family's. He could treat Bill to help him become more expressive and less destructive. He could engage the entire family in treatment to strengthen its adaptive potential. He might conclude that he could reach a larger number of boys with the same problem by working with Bill's group. Or with the intention of attacking the more pervasive conditions which bear on the presenting problem, he could offer professional leadership to the incipient neighborhood group of parents, offer consultation and his agency's services to the school, or attempt to arrange and lead meetings between representatives of industry and pertinent community groups and organizations. Finally, his knowledge about the intense implications of the drug problem might well be directed into his own system, his agency, as data that would be useful in deliberations about policy and program. It needs to be acknowledged that we have considered a hypothetical instance as well as a hypothetical social worker who would have to be the complete generalist in order to be effective in all of the functions noted. Nonetheless, a systems orientation, even within the exigencies and limitations of the practicalities of practice, would enable the social worker to determine and predict which sequence or combination of these functions would be most efficacious and where, within either his or other systems, they can best be implemented.

# 5

## THE CHANGE SYSTEM

The two preceding chapters attempted to explain the complex nature of the individual systems of the social worker and the client. Now, as we place the two into an interactional change context, we will see that the complexities are enlarged out of proportion to the numbers involved, for the conjunction of persons generates many variables requiring attention—confirmatory needs, concerns with what is at stake, and the determination of purpose, to name a few.

This chapter, then, will endeavor to examine the elements of the consociation that develops out of the purposeful, problem-solving link between the social worker and the client. Two major concepts are useful in accomplishing this end. The *social systems* concept will help us organize the structural and functional properties of the social worker-client configuration. The second, the concept of *relationship,* will be addressed to the dynamics of interaction contained within that configuration. The two, in conjunction, will be used to provide some grasp of the balance, form, and locus of significant factors within the system as well as the process and flow of interaction that occurs between its constituents. Or, in other terms, the social systems concept serves as a map by which the principal boundaries, properties, roles, and characteristics can be located, whereas the relationship concept offers a flow chart which depicts factors of affiliation, interdependence, and interaction.

### THE SOCIAL WORKER-CLIENT ASSOCIATION AS A SOCIAL SYSTEM

By way of introduction, I wish to refer to an earlier study by Lennard and Bernstein which demonstrates how concepts drawn from the social sciences can deepen the understanding of the complex processes of psychotherapy (1960). Their conclusions are valuable and illuminating.

1. Despite the major differences in the outlooks and behaviors of the participants in the change experience, there are major similarities in

the way interaction unfolds longitudinally. The experience itself, with its total and recurrent patterns of interaction, is the most important contribution to change.

2. The helping process is not a one-way street. That is, the practitioner is not merely a witness or an observer. Participants interact in the true sense of the term, and feedback plays an essential role. Value communications and influence are exceedingly important.

3. The requirements of the system take precedence over the expectations and conceptions of specific roles. Much of this occurs outside the practitioner's awarness. For this reason, system responsiveness could very well become a more self-conscious part of training. A systems-sensitive practitioner adjusts his pattern of activities to the other and to the demands of the system itself. Ultimately, he establishes an equilibrium with respect to the system's variables, and this balance maintains the system within the limits of variation which the system itself necessitates. Through the identification of system processes, an increased measure of responsiveness and control is made possible.

4. The change experience is a prototypic role-learning situation. "Role-learning goals" are achieved to the extent that the client is able to transfer what he has learned about role patterns to other significant role relationships. As a result, interest should be directed to the level of abstractness or concreteness with which role patterns are learned and generalized.

These conclusions are relevant to many aspects of this treatise. The first and second points bear on the discussion of relationship later in this chapter. The fourth point refers to the significance of learning in the change process, which will be discussed in the next chapter. Our concern at this time is with the importance of the system sensitivity noted in the third point. To begin, let us first examine the system's field, the environment in which practice takes place. As will be seen, the setting itself is a potent force which tends to shape, color, and direct the emerging association in its form and content.

## The Change Environment

This generic term for the setting which hosts, sanctions, or establishes the purposes and parameters of social work practice is used in place of the more traditional term "agency." Contemporary social work is no longer restricted to traditional types of social welfare organizations. Practice may be implemented in such non–social welfare settings as industry and agricultural unions. The private practice of social work is a reality wherein the practitioner creates his own setting for the change experience. Social action and social change endeavors may be transacted in settings where structure is minimal and temporal existence is limited. In still other instances, the social worker may practice in indirect or adjunctive change roles as a consultant, as an advocate, or in legislative functions quite apart from the more common social welfare realms.

The characteristics of the change setting may therefore range from the formal, indurate properties of a large bureaucracy on one extreme to a relatively pliant, problem-responsive, crisis-oriented type on the other. In any case, the specific change environment comprises certain systemic features which impinge on the way service is delivered. Knowledge about these features serves at least two major purposes. First and most obvious, the social worker should be acutely aware of his setting as a system and of what comprises that system. Practice without this awareness would be ambiguous, especially as it is experienced by the recipient of services who would not be certain about what the social worker represents. Second, this knowledge reveals the vital and dynamic rather than the static qualities of the change environment. Consequently, it would come into view not as a monolithic or inevitably persistent structure but as a composite of persons in interaction—a structure that is man-made, man-operated, and man-controlled. It is therefore viable, responsive to forces from within and without, and as with any system, subject to change. The study of the systemic properties of the change setting will be organized under two categories: the inter-system or more external and the intra-system or internal factors which influence the administration and implementation of practice.

*Inter-system Factors*   RELATIONSHIPS WITH THE SOURCE OF SUPPORT: Here we would think mainly of the linkages that are related to financial support of the setting's operation and program. Certainly, continuity and the breadth and quality of services are dependent on monetary factors. However, there are other contingencies in the relationship with the supporting body. How moneys are disbursed affects the type of planning that is possible—whether the setting must operate on a year-to-year basis or whether it can make longer-range plans, for example. The restrictions that are placed on the use of funds may affect the extent to which the setting can make its own decisions relative to the determined needs of its constituents, which may change from time to time. Finally, and in relation to the preceding, how the setting is accountable to the supporting body bears on autonomy and decision making.

SANCTIONS AND EXPECTATIONS:    In that the change environment and its program exist in response to some social problem as defined by society, its authority to provide its services is ascribed or delegated to it, usually with some set of accompanying conditions. The stringency or latitude with which sanction to practice is given will affect the intensity, quality, and limits of the setting's penetration into the workings of the social problem. For example, the sanctions may establish who can be served, how, and under what terms. The attendant expectations for performance and outcome similarly bear on how the setting defines and carries out its purpose. Autonomy, policy formulation, program formation and development, and the level of competence expected are responsive to sanctions. Thus a public welfare department may be sanctioned to treat the ills resulting from poverty, but it may find its endeavors hampered by the additional expectation that it will reduce a sizable portion of its rolls despite the unreality of financial independence on the part of the majority of its clientele.

RELATIONSHIPS WITH OTHER SOCIAL WELFARE SYSTEMS:    How the setting's program is carried out needs to be considered in relation to where the specific setting fits into the network of other relevant organizations within the social welfare structure. What types of associations exist with contiguous systems? Are the relations formal or informal? Do the systems operate on cooperative or competitive terms? Are the organizations accessible or relatively isolated from one another? Are there established modes and channels for communication, the opportunity for the exchange of information and ideas? Is the social welfare system structured along horizontal lines in which relative equality exists among the respective settings? Or does it comprise a vertical structure, a hierarchy of settings within a particular power structure? These questions affect whether practice is accomplished in accord with the broad sweep of the social welfare system's interests and intentions or whether it is a rather isolated or idiosyncratic endeavor.

INTERPRETATIONS OF SOCIAL PROBLEMS:    Lodged within the aforementioned systems variables are the critical issues of problem definition, analysis and planning, and the resultant division or delegation of responsibility concerning how and by whom the problem will be treated. Whether the various organizations and services coincide or conflict in how they define the problem and how priorities are assigned governs the degree to which the individual setting finds itself struggling in an isolated realm of practice apart from other resources and programs or in consonance with other endeavors. Consider the plight of the crisis-and-treatment-oriented center for delinquent youths in a law-and-order community.

*Intra-system Factors*   The change setting, like any organism, is comprised of parts that are reciprocally resonant. For purposes of analysis, categorization is necessary. In this instance the internal properties of the setting will be ordered into three major domains—the structural, the functional, and the output.

STRUCTURAL PROPERTIES:   These are the conditions within the change environment which directly or indirectly determine, guide, and organize the change process. Structure not only denotes the parameters of service but also governs the intentions and mode of delivery.

The *physical setting* itself provides a substantial backdrop for the change experience. As a theatrical stage setting unobtrusively enlivens the drama that unfolds before it, the physical setting also affects the real world within which both the practitioner and the consumers of services act out their respective roles. Privacy, accessibility, appropriate facilities, decor—these are but a few of the environmental conditions which, at least, set the tone and climate for practice.

*Policies, regulations,* and *protocol* set the boundaries and norms for assistance. What can be done, through what means, for whom, and under what conditions are some salient parametric factors governing practice. Their significance lies in the way in which they are concordant with the definition of the problem, the needs of the setting's constituents, and the extent to which these norms and rules are flexibly responsive to the ultimate human situation.

On a less definitive level than the regulatory norms, but no less influential, are the *guiding theories and beliefs* of the change environment. These include the implicit and explicit philosophies to which the setting addresses itself, its notions about what is optimally valuable or "good" for people. The precepts and values upon which the setting was founded and which have persisted through time set a guiding culture in which its practices are embedded. The setting's valued theories used to explain behavior, personality, interaction, or society would inevitably govern how it defines the social problems falling within its purview and, hence, the proper means for treating them. Overriding these issues is the extent to which these beliefs and theories are accessible to expression and review and to the testing of their usefulness and function.

The *assigned roles and related norms* of the setting's members are bound into its structural properties. Conceptions of responsibility and behavior (how one is to be a helping person, how one helps) directly bear on service delivery. How these individual roles are interrelated tells something about the quality of communication among the members and the measure of congruence about the function of the setting. Tied to the role system are the norms for performance which, in addition to providing common guidelines for performance, indicate the freedom to innovate, the amount of autonomy that is permitted, and the means by which conflict about purpose, policy or services is resolved.

The aforementioned conditions not only comprise the structure of the change environment but create a *culture* as well. Over a period of time these entities tend to fuse into a set of beliefs and behaviors generally shared by the members of the change environment. While they may or may not eventuate into a conscious level of expression, a culture does form—a kind of climate or ambience that tends to characterize the particular setting. The outsider, client, or colleague senses the resultant aura of, say, freedom or restriction, formality or informality that identifies the setting and accommodates to it if the contact is sustained. These cultural norms become tacitly understood and shared regulatory mechanisms evident in attitudes as well as procedures and routines, in the way people communicate and the jargon that is used, and in other styles of performance.

These structural factors are, in systemic terms, major self-regulating mechanisms which in turn set the boundaries and conditions for service and consequently influence the nature of practice. In optimal terms, these mechanisms would have dual functions: to enable the system to maintain a steady state of adaptation to strains that promote growth and to provide a structure within which the needs of its clientele can be met most effectively.

FUNCTIONAL PROPERTIES:    Function denotes purpose, direction, and intent—in short, the utility of the change environment. In anatomical terms, structure comprises and skeletal and neurological properties of the change system, whereas function is its raison d'être.

The *stated purpose* of the change setting relative to some social problem or set of social problems is the overriding factor that determines its function. Within any social welfare complex, it is how any one setting delineates its particular mission that gives it identity in relation to other relevant systems. Purpose may be extensive, elaborate and multifaceted, as in the case of large bureaucratic structures designed to meet an array of needs. Or it might be specific, short-lived, and designed to solve some single issue or problem—for example, a citizens' group organized to carry out a demonstration project or special service. In any event, all action and strategy derive from the setting's purpose.

Clarity about the function and purpose of any change environment is tied to the extent to which the setting defines its particular *responsibility* for the piece of the social problem for which it is accountable. The current problem of drug addiction illustrates this point. Although many organizations in a given community may have as their purpose the treatment of the drug problem, their respective functions are more precisely related to the specificity of their intentions relative to the problem. One setting may aim at legislative reform, another at rehabilitation, and still others at resocialization or reeducation. We can refer to this dimension of the setting's purpose as its primary function. Contained within this frame are other orders of function which are indicative of the specific ways and means by which the setting's purposes are activated and are responsive to the requirements of particular practice situations.

The *range of variants* that the change environment is prepared to encompass under its umbrella of purposes affects and defines its function. Although a particular setting aims at the resolution or amelioration of certain aspects of a social problem, it has little control over how the problem is manifested by individuals or groups. Hence, the availability of other subfunctions may be required. Let us say that an organization intends to increase and enhance citizen participation in the community's decision-making processes. To implement this function, three groups of mothers on welfare are organized. Two groups readily decide to direct their efforts toward the support of certain pieces of legislation. The third finds itself bogged down with urgent family problems. How, then, does the organization define its function in this instance? Does it prudently hold to its specific intent and find services elsewhere for these mothers, or does it broaden its function to offer services in accord with the evident needs?

Another facet of the same issue is the factor of *desired outcomes*.

Although a setting may spell out what it intends or is designed to do in attacking a social problem, the kind of results it plans to achieve also contributes to the definition of its function. Returning to the drug problem as an illustration, if rehabilitation of addicts is the stated purpose, then what is the desired outcome? Is it reliance on methodone, elimination of the addiction, or temporary abstention? In another instance, if the intent of a setting is to involve neighborhood residents in the attempt to create better housing conditions, the desired outcome may be the formation of an active organization of concerned persons, a change in building codes, or the stimulation of latent indignation for effective action. Function needs to be thought of in terms of palpable ends not only to offer the consumer some clarity about what might possibly be achieved, but also to provide the potential for qualitative or quantitative measurement of the setting's purposes.

The *practitioner's interpretation* of his own function mediates and finally expresses the aforementioned vectors. How he identifies himself as part of the change environment and how he relates to the social problem and its victims will affect how he makes purpose, plan, and program operational. The defined function of any change environment cannot be fully comprehended without reference to this human component.

Function, then, is a system property that cannot be viewed as an abstract statement of purpose or a grandiose and all-inclusive scheme ("to reduce the incidence of poverty") on one hand or as a constricted, single-motive plan ("parent-child counseling") on the other. In order to achieve identity, clarity, and viability, function must first be defined in its broadest scope in relation to its connection with a specific social problem. Then, with increasing refinement, the boundaries, the contingencies, the modes, the outcome, and ultimately, its human translation in practice can be spelled out. Thus the change environment as a system takes on motive, vitality, and direction.

OUTPUT: Performance, in the final analysis, can be a valid measure and expression of an organism's intentions and capabilities for action. We tend to identify and learn about phenomena by searching for their utility and operation. In this instance, output is the final product generated by what the change environment determines is its function and purpose.

Rather than referring to a type of service that is offered (for example, community planning or family counseling), the term "output" is used here to delineate the composite of factors that characterize the nature of service. Hartman stresses the ambiguity and confusion that results from reference to practice in purely categorical terms and that definition is needed to forestall indiscriminate application (1971). Therefore, to speak of casework or group work services as output provides one with only a general idea about the size of the social units that are served. Reference to counseling for the aging or youth offers some notions about the broad problems of particular population groups. What we are concerned with here, then, are the typical performances of the cange system, the way it goes about its business of fulfilling its purpose.

COMMUNICATIONAL SYSTEM: Exchange of information is fundamental to professional performance. Social work is primarily a lexical profession that relies on communication exchange to carry out its varied functions.

The performance of a setting generally relies on two dimensions of communication. The first has to do with the communicational modes employed to acquire and transmit information. Formal modes might include applications or other forms used to collect data required to complete a social history or to determine the feasibility of or eligibility for services. Questionnaires and interviewing schedules gather information about attitudes, beliefs, and the like. Interviews or group meetings may be the modalities of practice within which communication exchange is effected.

The second dimension of communicational exchange is the type of information and content with which the change system usually deals. For example, settings which aim at personal or interpersonal change are concerned with verbal and affective productions. These settings rely primarily on subjective appraisals of affective and narrative expression with less interest in the reliability of the content under consideration. In instances where the aim of the setting's services is change in larger systems, greater emphasis would be given to objective data that are verifiable—statistics, minutes of meetings, documents and corroborated facts, for example. Although many settings use some combination of communicational modes, their predisposition for certain types of systems, modalities, information, and language is an index of the performance of the change settings.

INTERPRETATION OF DYNAMICS: In line with its structure and function, each change environment has its own way of explaining both the overt and the covert forces that bear on the problem or task or that are operative in interpersonal and group exchanges. How these forces are interpreted affects how they are treated and thus, how the setting typically performs.

The fictional Mrs. X., in this instance a recovering tubercular patient, will illustrate this point. We will consider the interpretation of her lengthy narrative of how she felt as an adolescent about having had to care for her dying mother, as told to the other members of her patient group. In one setting, the group leader might record the event as one in which "Mrs. X., as a result of her dominant position within the group, succeeded in splitting the group into two factions. One sympathized with her account; the other faction was repelled by her tendency to monopolize the time." In another setting, the group leader might interpret the same event as "Mrs. X.'s need to exacerbate earlier hostility about having to deny her own dependency needs in favor of her mother's." Both interpretations may well be correct. But the point is that each interpretation tells something about the valued output of the settings in which the groups operate. The first, mainly concerned with the dynamics of the group, would aim at strengthening role adaptations in interpersonal relations. The second emphasizing intrapsychic factors, would aim at insight and self-understanding. Thus both settings may claim the same purpose, but their interpretations of salient dynamics would influence performance style.

SELECTIVITY:   In that the change experience is not a random set of events, the management of the experience through forms of selectivity is typically related to each setting's output. On both explicit and covert levels, determinations are made about which persons will be accepted as consumers of services and what factors will constitute the parameters and content of the change process.

Series of selective actions are exercised even before there is contact with the client system, and they continue through the course of association. By means of policy or informal protocol, the change environment sets the criteria for the client role. Frequently, some screening procedures channel clients who meet these criteria into the setting's program. The socialization experience itself is a process of selectivity by which behavioral and attitudinal standards are imposed on those who carry the client title. The succeeding change experience comprises a series of choices and selections regarding what is significant for the process in achieving immediate or long-range goals.

The rationale for selectivity and focus transcends procedural and performance issues. Effective practice requires some partialization of the problems coming to the attention of the change system into units that are manageable and that lend themselves to probable resolution. This statement does not suggest a diminution of intent or the reduction of practice to circumscribed and rigid areas. Instead, a dual vision should be operative in selectivity. The selection of a vector of the problem for attention is based on (1) parsimonious actions for (2) the greatest possible affect. Or in other terms, the following predictive questions need to be asked: "Which significant person or groups of persons should be engaged to work on which significant aspect of the problem in order to produce the most salutary outcome?"

The selectivity of the change environment provides a highly visible index of the setting's performance and output. In some measure, it incorporates the structural and functional factors previously described in order to refine the "what" and "how" of practice by pinpointing the components of the social problem to be treated, the populations to be involved, and the related conditions for service, as well as the means to be used to achieve the desired ends.

### System Characteristics of the Social Worker-Client Configuration

Upon undertaking the task of explicating the properties of any helping system, it is necessary to acknowledge the risk that is inevitable when one attempts to reduce the complexities of a human situation into its categorical parts. Yet it is essential to map the parameters of the experience to forestall needless and random wandering in what could become a maze of interpersonal experiences. It is through the use of pertinent generalizations that the unique elements of specific encounters may be revealed. Therefore, the reader is properly advised to consider what follows as a blueprint in much the same way that he would examine the plans of an about-to-be-built home, in predictive and probabilistic terms.

The following discussion will be restricted to those factors that contribute to the beginning stage of system development. This is obviously the crucial stage which sets some guiding patterns for the emerging and continuing character of the system.

A primary assumption governing this organization of concepts is that as members of the prospective system converge, they bear disparate orientations to or expectations about what their roles are to be. Irrespective of their functions, practitioners share some common beliefs about their roles as helping persons and as effectors of the learning-change processes. Members of the client system, in contrast, have divergent or diffuse expectations about their roles, if they hold any at all. Therefore, the first tasks of the social worker, perhaps transcending attention to the presenting problem, are to provide the means and opportunity for the client system to learn how to become a member of the change system and to learn how to use the experience. Then he must seek to attain at least a beginning consensus about objectives; and to determine how and through what means these objectives are to be reached. This activity is what Lennard and Bernstein refer to as *role induction,* a form of socialization that includes the teaching and learning of behavioral roles and norms (1969). If role complementarity is not clarified and achieved in the initial stage, if behavioral allocations are not resolved early, then the continuing uncertainty and need to determine one's status will interfere with orderly efforts at problem resolution. Conversely, a successful solution at the outset leads to a decrease in the frequency of role discussion and thereby frees time and energy to attend to the problem or task. We might speculate that in some instances role resolution may, in itself, be the core experience for certain clients. Persons who chronically have been unable to achieve success in interpersonal relations because of their confusion or conflict about expected or effective roles could well profit from working out the role strains accruing from their participation in, for example, citizen or peer groups or the intimacy of the one-to-one relationship.

Lennard and Bernstein define this knowledge as *role system information,* the knowledge that the participants require in order to achieve complementarity of behavior and expectations. At times the practitioner may overlook the need for this knowledge because of the certainty he has about his own role. But the client needs to become aware of who is to do what, when, and how often; the behaviors that follow one another; and the required views and attitudes. These are learned by direct and indirect information giving on one level. But the essential learning about one's role derives from the experiential level of the interactional experience itself. The following, in whatever way they are transmitted, are categories of initial role system information as devised by Lennard and Bernstein.

*Activeness*  Who will take the initiative and to what extent? Will the practitioner assume major responsibility for action, or will he take a more passive stance to encourage all or certain members of the client system or group to take the lead?

*Authority*   Who exercises control, about what issues, and through what means? Although authority is consonant with the social work role, the client system is expected to be the final arbiter about certain conditions and objectives in his own life situation.

*Selectivity of Topics*   What content and issues are relevant for discussion? How are they related to the definition of the problem and the desired goals?

*Reciprocity*   To what extent can response and interchange be expected? How much feedback can the client system expect?

*Concordance*   To what extent will disagreement be tolerated? Will the members need agreement, or will the system survive differences?

*Formality*   To what degree will the association be casual or formal? How is intimacy defined by the members, and what are its boundaries? Are the rituals of social amenities to be observed and for what period of time? Formality is a systems characteristic that has to be observed longitudinally with regard to the rate at which it develops and then declines and gives way to a mode of relating that is spontaneous and typical of the system.

*Attitudes*   TRUST-MISTRUST: To what extent can the interactors rely on each other? While we would tend to think of this question in terms of the client's attitudes, the importance of the social worker's trust in his clients cannot be minimized in its effect on his role performance.

HOPE-DESPAIR:   To what extent is there reason for hope? This question applies equally to all members of the system. The practitioner's attitudes about the potential for change would ineluctably govern how he approaches and treats the problem. How the members of the client system will invest themselves in work on the problem or task will depend, in part, on how they can envision the probabilities for change and relief.

FREEDOM-RESTRAINT:   What do the members believe about the freedom to discuss certain issues or express feelings? Are there attitudes of caution or expectations of openness?

*System Expectations*  This factor refers to expectations about the integrity of the system itself in terms of the following issues.

GOALS:   What will be accomplished by the experience? The question of goals is not limited to specific objectives but takes into account all areas in which change may occur—interpersonal relations, policy changes, financial stability, and so forth.

CONFIDENTIALITY:   To what degree will communications be confidential and privileged? If they do not remain within the confines of the immediate system, who else will have access to information, on what terms, and with what implications?

CONSTANCY:   How highly structured are the circumstances of system operation? Can it be expected to continue and on what terms? To what extent are its conditions open to discussion, change, or restructuring—for example, in terms of time, frequency, cost, and setting.

## Role Strain

Movement into a new role is not without some amount of strain and conflict, particularly as the role entrant begins to envision the responsibilities that accompany that role. At the outset, the role taker is beset by uncertainties about what he has to let go of in his old role and what he has to take on in the new. The assumption of the client role, whether by a father seeking help for his family or by a business man joining a community action group, involves certain risks and doubts. Some established patterns of daily living need to be modified. Expected rewards for the amount of conformity and energy required are not immediately forthcoming. Anticipated quick solutions are not readily apparent. And what might have appeared to be a simple, straightforward task may, for the time being, seem to turn out to be rather ambiguous and convoluted. Hence, the social worker's recognition and appreciation of role strain and his readiness to deal with the phenomenon bears on the successful completion of the role induction process.

The ways in which persons deal with role strain are as numerous as the range of behaviors permits. A most obvious means is departure from the role itself, wherein persons actively divest themselves of the client label. This is not an unfrequent occurrence and is at times abetted by the change setting's readiness to work only with "willing" clients rather than pursuing the resolution of conflicts that block role assumption. Labels such as "unready" or "resistant" simplistically place the onus onto the prospective client and thereby relieve the setting and the practitioner from responsibility.

Persons may also dissemble as they attempt to simulate the ascribed role as a means of coping with role strain. The projection of responsibility, the placing of the major burden for change on another member of the system, is a familiar technique. Overemphasizing the importance of other's roles and obligations is a similar strategy. There is also the common tactic of game playing to divert or dissipate the role induction process. The formative processes in groups offer their own unique opportunities for reduction of role strain through such devious means as hiding among the numbers, outward compliance, or alignment with resistant subgroups.

The concept of role strain is significant for two reasons. First, it is a natural and expected phenomenon; therefore, its emergence should not be viewed as necessarily negative or deviant. A person's struggles in taking on a new role may well be an indicator of a strong and intact personality, one that does not fluidly shift from one role to another merely for the sake of compliance. In fact, it would be well to question the substance of those persons who readily conform and are willing to change their role colorations. What consistency might be expected of them over a period of time?

Second, awareness of role strain extends the practitioner's sensitivity about factors that interfere with role assumption. In addition to the dissonant conditions within the client system, he would look to factors within the change setting itself that may be contributing to role strain. He may need to question the clarity or ambiguity of his communications and the reality of his expectations. The change setting may intrude into the process of role induction by the imposition of rituals, restrictive policies, and questionable procedures.

### Power and Balance

The consequence of successful role induction is the building of a cohesive system that comprises a set of hierarchical roles. Whether in two person, family, small or large group systems, an imparity exists between the emerging roles of teacher and learner, guide and follower, group leader and group member, facilitator and actor, provider and receiver, or influencer and receptor. Members of the system also maintain ascendant or descendant roles with other members of the immediate system as well as with others in peripheral systems. For example, a group member may simultaneously act out a secondary role in relation to the group leader, emerge as a primary force within a subgroup, and have relatively little status in his own family.

The inequality in role relations leads to the evolvement of power, a phenomenon we have already discussed. Yet in interpersonal systems that are goal directed and require some amount of congruence and reciprocity, effective movement toward the goal cannot take place when a power imbalance prevails. Therefore, a smoothly working system of this sort typically strives toward a reduction of the differentials between its members. This reduction is accomplished by the establishment of a set of norms which, in turn, effect a workable balance. The emergence of these norms, some pragmatic and having to do with procedural aspects, and others abstract and concerned with interactional factors, serves to place the presence of power within workable bounds and provides the subject of power with a measure of predictability. That is, as members of an imbalanced system agree to a set of rules concerning how each is to behave, the need to apply power and confrontations about the facts of interdependence are avoided, thereby reducing anxiety and uncertainty.

Certain social work principles are, in reality, norms which serve to reduce the inequality and imbalance of the change system and to afford an appearance, if not the actuality of equality. "Self-determination" probably heads the list. This principle states in effect that "you [the client] are equal to me [the social worker] because you are free to determine for yourself, to make your own decisions, even though I possess the power in this relationship." It is the partial truth contained within this prinicple that gives credibility to the idea of equality. Aside from the freedom to leave the change setting (and only in certain instances), the client is only theoretically free to make his own decisions regardless of the extent to which the practitioner wills this idea. When there is interdependence combined with influence, particularly in those situations where the client system sorely needs what the practitioner can provide, freedom to act and decide is contingent on the role activities of the practitioner. Any self-determined action would need to be qualified by the real or imagined perception of the implications of the intended act for one's status and relations with the superordinate other.

"Acceptance" in another principle/norm which states that "we are equals because I [the social worker] can accept what you [the client] feel, say, or do." Such a statement is itself a paradox inasmuch as the assumption of the right to accept or to view another as an equal can only be made from a position of power. In any event and under whatever guise, each system moves toward an internalization of a set of norms that prescribe behavior and reduce the frictions, strains, and inequities of power imbalance. The significance of these norms also lies in the remarkable extent to which they uniquely tend to characterize the particular system.

My concurrent experience with two groups of social work students a few years ago reveals quite strikingly how norms of this nature that are idiosyncratic to the particular system develop. The two groups were identically matched in size as well as in composition. The age, sex, and level of education of the members of both groups were the same. Therefore, it was expected that both groups would probably develop along the same lines, particularly because the groups were formed at the same time and for the same purposes: to learn about group processes experientially and to deepen self-awareness as emerging professionals. To enhance their experience and hasten learning, I deliberately avoided the imposition of structure with regard to procedures, order, or the definition of my role as the leader. What was significant was how the groups used a large part of the experience to develop their own norms. Each group, despite its similarity with the other, arrived at a very disparate set of rules and behaviors aimed at reducing the power differential between the members and their perception of me as the leader. One group addressed me on a first name basis and reduced the distance further by the use of informality and an aura of camaraderie. While no restraints were placed on this behavior in either group, the second rarely attempted to breach the difference and adopted a more formal and deferential approach to me as the leader. Interestingly, the first group depreciated leadership development within its own ranks, whereas the second ascribed authority to various members at certain times. As the leader, I found myself acting two distinct roles in response to the two groups. In the final analysis, both groups achieved approximately the same ends and gains with regard to what they learned about groups and about themselves as participators in the interpersonal experience. But the means, governed by the respective norms, differed markedly.

*Contracts*

As norms evolve out of the professional encounter and fall into some configuration, they can be understood and referred to as contacts—the organized set of explicitly or tacitly understood ways in which the inter-actors in a system agree to carry on their business (Carson, 1969). On a more sophisticated level, contracts continue to serve the purpose of reducing the anxiety resulting from power imbalance by giving the system's members definitive guidelines for behavior without repeatedly having to employ authority or direction.

At the outset, ad hoc contracts govern the initial, tentative behaviors enacted by the members of a newly formed system. This form of interim contract may be exemplified by the following: the agreement to continue for a certain number of interviews or group meetings; the testing out of certain feelings and attitudes by the client system and the response they evoke from the social worker, leading to agreement about how they will communicate; and the agreement about the information that is required and how it will be secured or provided. With time and as the many facets of the association become exposed, the terms of the ad hoc contracts become revised accordingly.

These interim contracts eventuate into a master contract which determines how the members of a system will interact over a sustained period of time. "I [the social worker] will be responsive and helpful as long as you [the member of the client system] continue to cooperate and participate freely" is an oversimplified contractual statement about a number of specific types of expected behaviors that can be stated from both vantage points in both direct and indirect ways. Violation of a contract would lead either to termination or to the negotiation of a new contract that would alter the nature of the system. A master contract is not dissimilar from the idea of the *commitment* of the system's members. What is involved is not only an assumption of responsibility for the roles and tasks required to achieve a desired end but also a warrant to maintain and sustain the change system.

*Recapitulation*

The preceding discussion provides an organismic view of the change system that elucidates its specific structural, functional, and output characteristics at any point in time and that reveals the properties which permit the ongoing processes of growth, change, maintenance, and continuity.

These latter properties refer, in fact, to the conditions that make for the steady state of the system. Roles, norms and contracts, in their active forms, are the mutable forces within the system that ensure the cohesiveness and continuity of the system. They are the means by which the system manages and adapts to strains and forces within and external to the system. Just as the systems concept has been useful in achieving a clearer understanding of the client system, it also offers an expanded perception of the phenomenon of persons in interaction within a particular structure, which in turn enables the observer to construct some asumptions and predictions about the system and its constituents.

THE SOCIAL WORKER-CLIENT RELATIONSHIP

Relationship is a concept that has long been indispensable to the characterization of social work practice. The reader will recall Mary Richmond's early efforts to stress its importance and meaning as well as the subsequent contributions of the Functional school, which proposed that the relationship was the major impetus for change. Traditionally, however, the concept has been more typically applied to two-person systems. This is not an invalid idea for relationships literally refer to the bond, affinity, and interactions betwen two persons.

While we may speak of relating to larger units—a marital pair, a family, a group, or even such units as organizations or community sub-. groups—such a statement is a reification of what is, in reality, a complex set of mutual relationships and interrelationships among numbers of persons. The terms "family," "group," or "community" are labels and abstractions that refer to a configuration of individuals in relation who bind themselves or are bound together for such salient reasons as interdependence, survival, economics, kinship, or goal seeking. Consequently, when the social worker confronts a more than two-person social unit, he places himself in a position that holds the possibility of a relationship of some sort with each of the members of that unit. At the same time, he enters into existing relationships among the members of that unit. A kind of triple vision ensues that includes the discernment of what is taking place (1) between the practitioner and specific individuals, (2) between other individual members of the unit, and (3) within the latter relationships as they are influenced by the presence of the practitioner. Relationship, then, is a concept that is immensely useful for attaining an understanding of the interactions within any of the forms of human association encountered in practice.

Having stressed this point, I now have to state the paradox that exists about a concept of such significance. Within the allied helping professions as well as within social work, there is great unanimity about the importance of the relationship. This association has been assigned the potentialities for growth, learning, change, unfoldment, corrective experiences, and the like. However, there is considerably less agreement about the definition of the concept and little common understanding about how the relationship does, in fact, promote change, growth, and so forth. For example, a study of the self-reported practices of thirty experienced social workers revealed total accord about the significance of the relationship for practice (Goldstein, 1970). But one-half of this population averred that the experience of relating was the primary basis for change while the other half thought of the relationship as a climate for or a prerequisite to the effective use of specific methods and techniques.

If we view any relationship in the light of its experiential character, it is understandable that the concept would elude a universal or precise definition. It is, in fact, a moment-to-moment experience between persons which is marked by the unique and long-practiced patterns of association of its members and colored by many internal variables and motivations not fully accessible to perception. What we term a relationship has no ultimate meaning. It is a phenomenon that is observable only at a point in time; therefore, at that point in time it is different than what it has been, and it can be expected to change in how it will be.

If this is the case, are we then engaged in a most significant aspect of the change process that, in the end, denies explication? In part, the answer would have to be yes: one cannot fully capture the essence of what occurs in meaningful interactions between persons. R. D. Laing notes that each of us experiences the same world differently, and in a sense, we therefore live in different worlds (1969). Thus one cannot really experience the world of the other as the other does. Only inferences can be made based on observed behavior and communicational cues. But even these inferences are colored by the observer's own narrow range of experiences which delimit what he can really "know" about the other.

Yet we cannot dismiss the relational event as a purely existential phenomenon: to do so would be to eschew the fact that a certain rationality and purposeful intent is part of human conduct. Thus it is within the constraints of the transiency and the affective and personal meanings of a relationship that we shall attempt to construct some hypotheses about the factors that contribute to relationship development and what takes place between the persons who comprise it. To accomplish this end, it is first important to examine the prerequisites for relationship formation, the *preconditions* which make the event possible. It will then be feasible to study the transactional nature of the relationship or its *experiential quality* in order to gain some understanding of its uniqueness. Finally, an appreciation of its movement and change potential can be gained from the consideration of its inclination or *directional motility*.

### Preconditions Affecting Relationship Formation

Affinity between persons does not just happen because of physical proximity. At least a minimal state of readiness and some measure of accessibility, either latent or overt, precede the first movement toward relationship evolvement. In addition, before persons can begin to relate there is certain information that each has to have about the other. First meetings comprise a subtle testing and search for knowledge and conditions that are assumed will provide a sound basis for continued association. These efforts provide answers to such questions as "How are we alike?" "What do we have in common?" "What do you expect from me?" and "How will we deal with differences?" To achieve a more precise view of these preformative conditions, the following factors will describe selected variables that prepare the ground for the beginnings of a relationship.

*The Ability to Relate*   When the social worker practices within an interpersonal context, it is his task to make some assumptions about the other's capability for entering into some forms or sets of relationships. This judgment by one of another's ability to relate can be based only on subjective criteria, on what the social worker has learned and believes about the affiliative potential of persons. It is obviously a critical judgment in that it can affect whether and how a particular relationship develops. This determination has to be tempered by the following qualifications: how he perceives the other with whom he is to relate, under what conditions, and in what kind of social situation.

The ability to become personally involved in interpersonal associations varies greatly from person to person. A myriad of predisposing and interlocking variables influences the extent to which one can let himself into relationships and the style with which he carries it out. These variables might include one's personal security and self-identity, whether one has experienced past opportunities for learning how people interact, the ability to know and understand the meaning of another's behavior, the appreciation of symbols and cues, and some positive success and rewards derived from experiences in other relationships. Within the spectrum of relationship potential, persons on one extreme may evidence inordinate trust, freedom and willingness to enter into relations with others, while persons on the other extreme may be so inhibited, fearful or confused that they inevitably alienate themselves from significant human contact. Most persons fall somewhere between the extremes and manifest many ambivalent feelings—those that impel entry into relationships out of the fear of alienation and the need for human affiliation countered by the fears of rejection, failure, or loss that may result in the creation of self-protective and possibly well-rationalized barriers.

The manifest properties of the social context may greatly effect how persons use their potential for entering into relationships. For instance, the matter of similarities or differences in the interactors' age, sex, class, and culture may either speed some measure of mutuality or create obstacles that will need to be clarified or worked out before the relationship can evolve. Of equal importance is the specific problem-solving situation and the amount of involvement that is required to achieve the desired resolution and change. One must question how deeply the participants must involve themselves in relation, for what purposes, and over what period of time. Here I do not speak of imposing particular controls; instead, the question refers to the reality of the expectations that are placed on the prospective members of the relationship.

Time itself is not necessarily an index of relationship intensity. The relationship factors in a brief contact that achieves its purposes are of no less importance than those in long-term services aimed at, say, restoration of strengths or major reorganization of community disjunctions. It may very well be that a short-term association may call upon the participants to invest themselves quickly and with some risk, whereas a long-term association may offer the time and latitude for its members to involve themselves at a more natural pace.

If it is assumed that adequate potential to relate is evident, then it is possible to consider the other factors which affect relationship development and which involve the social worker as well as the other members of the system.

*Physical and Emotional States of the Participants*   We know that we are not the most congenial or expressive when we are burdened by a malaise of physical or emotional origin. In addition to the ways in which these conditions affect the tenor of the relationship, they are also significant for the beginning stages of the relationship when the members have not yet come to know one another well enough to be sure if these transient reactions are or are not typical of one's behavior.

*Presence of Self-conscious Anxiety*    Anticipatory feelings, either pro or con, establish readiness for entry into significant human association. Whether one is to join a group of peers, become a member of a task group, or meet with a counselor, uncertainties about norms and expectations, fear of rebuke or ostracism, and the possibility of reward and gratification of some sort generate a more acute awareness of self and the attempt to project one's self into possible future conditions. The self becomes prepared to act and to respond, atunes itself to the critical immediacies of the encounter, and thereby sharpens perceptual acuity. Needless to say, where risk or insecurity is overwhelming, extremes in self-absorption preclude adequate recognition and appreciation of the essential presence of others and inhibit involvement. But in general, this preparation for attention to relationship requirements opens the possibility for involvement.

*Expectations*    Persons frequently tend to anticipate, well before they first come into affiliation, what possible gains, losses, or experiences will accrue to them out of the event. How the event is perceived in advance has much to do with persons' readiness to relate and how they will behave once the relationship becomes a reality. Goldstein has given much attention to the issue of expectations (1962). Based on a review of pertinent studies, he finds that expectations are, in fact, major determinants of behavior; how persons' expectancies are confirmed or disconfirmed will affect how they will come to understand the relationship and feel and act within it. A person's expectancies are communicated in various ways and, within interpersonal experiences, do influence the other's behavior. They also have prognostic implications, for the degree of improvement that accrues is related to the extent to which the expectations are realistic. In short, if persons are expected to improve, do better or complete a task, or if these persons assume that the relationship will make these ends possible, then it is likely that these outcomes will occur (assuming that they are within the range of achievement).

These findings point to the need to strive for clarity about the hopes, doubts—the expectations that persons bring to the change relationship (including what the social worker expects) so as to reduce the intrusion of unwarranted misconceptions and misinterpretations about intent.

*Minimal Sharing of Values*  Before a cluster of individuals can become persons in relation, it is necessary that, on some level of consciousness, they perceive the fact that they hold some basic values in common. There needs to be a common ground concerning certain beliefs and experiences. This does not necessarily refer to values that are transmitted and assimilated; I speak, instead, of the need to seek out some value domains which serve to establish sufficient commonalities of experience. Without them, a persistent sense of distance or alienation will prevail.

It is inevitable that certain differences between persons will color the change relationship. Since the context itself is one that has to do with social change or adaptation, the participants will, no doubt, hold divergent views about the value of the experience, whether it is even needed, or what outcomes are desirable. In addition, the interactors may experience conflicting cultural values or see their respective worlds quite differently. Despite these discrepant values, the participants will, if the relationship is to flourish, search for aspects of their respective value realms that are congruent. These spontaneous pursuits are most evident and typical in the first stages of group formation when the members actively search out that which they hold in common—political, religious, or social attitudes; child-rearing practices; life experiences; geography; and so forth.

*Perception of the Other*  Persons in propinquity do not necessarily recognize each other's real presence, "real" referring to something more than physical or stereotypical being. Appreciation of the other beyond objective, categorical, or labeling techniques affords the awareness of the affective, attitudinal, and behavioral attributes which uniquely characterize the person. Thus the elements of a relationship make it essential to permit one's self to be known as well as to strive to know the other. The consequences of settling for a simplistic understanding or relying on labels or stereotyping, whether they be clinical or social, are at best pseudorelationships, a charade between persons who play ascribed roles, or at worst the state of disconfirmation of self.

*Influence of Other Social Forces*  The preceding factors and potentialities for convergence are also affected by how others, either within or contiguous to the immediate system, may exert or may be perceived as exerting influence on the formative relationship.

When the development of a particular relationship is taking place within a set of other relationships, what takes place between the social worker and specific individuals is highly visible to others immediately present. The practitioner's singular relationships with members of a family, a small group, or a committee exemplify this point. Many messages are contained within the relational transactions which convey to the others something about the potentials for relating with one another and with the practitioner. The possible ramifications are numerous. One emerging relationship may serve as a model for how persons can interact without the use of devious forms of control or manipulation. This learning by observation or identification may reduce barriers of fear and doubt and may thereby hasten the development of other affiliations. In less positive terms, the evidence of a growing relationship between certain members of the system may stir reactions of threat, competitiveness, or ambivalence on the part of the others. Such reactions can be expected when the social worker enters a system that is firmly structured, for his alliance with certain members of that system would pose a threat to its equilibrium. Many families, bureaucratic subgroups, and street corner gangs are good examples. Consider the effect of a positive relationship between a black social worker and a white member of a group that has strong racial biases, or the consequences of a warm relationship between the practitioner and a youngster whose parents have brought him for treatment because they see him as the cause of their disharmony. These reactions are by no means irreconcilable obstacles. Assessment of how they impede relationship development may quickly reveal latent problems that contribute to, if not actually determine, the condition requiring assistance in the first place.

Similarly, input from persons who are outside the context of change but are affected by the event will influence the rate and nature of relationship evolvement. These could include other family members, cohorts within an organization, and relatives and friends. Conditions within the change environment may also obtrude, particularly when the system's expectations are antithetical to the client system's requirements. How the social worker extricates himself from external demands that are opposed to the client's needs affects the prospects for a sound relationship and his role within it.

*Recapitulation*

The foregoing points represent the attempt to delineate the factors which antecede and impinge on relationship development. In many respects, they are all facets of the same stone. Each refers to and bears on all others. For example, one's expectations reveal one's value system; one's physical and emotional states affect how he will perceive the other; and some level of anxiety is attendant to all functions of relating. Yet each element must be given attention as significant entity in order to forestall constriction in a relationship that is deficient in depth, openness, or the potential for social growth.

*The Experiential Characteristic of Relationships*

Relationships can best be understood in the ways that they are enacted and experienced by their members. Such descriptions as "warm," "positive," or "transference" are merely reifications and convey little about their essential properties. Despite the elusive nature of human association, an approximate but workable comprehension can be attained through cognizance of the behaviors and communications that take place between persons in relation.

This does not depreciate the immense significance of the sentient characteristics noted earlier for inferring where persons are in relation. There is no doubt that some practitioners are so endowed with these attributes that they are able to sense the inner worlds of others with a marked degree of verisimilitude. But even these precipient inferences are drawn from observed words, gestures, and expressions. Those of us who are more ordinary mortals must rely more on our cognitive faculties as we process what we see, hear, and sense into assumptions that provide something other than a random response. The intent, then, is to sort out the generic characteristics of the relationship experience that tend to reveal where the interactors are within it at any point in time.

*Role Security*    A primary measure of the conditions of the relational experience is the comfort and assurance that the interactors evidence in their role status and performance. As has been previously noted, the extent to which members are free to pursue their desired goals depends on the degree to which they know where they stand, what their obligations are, and what they may expect of self and others in relation.

*Reward and Satisfaction*   Persons will remain in relation insofar as the experience provides them an amount of gratification that is sufficient to compensate for whatever tensions, frustrations, or disappointments are present. In addition, the kind of gratification which one evidences may be indicative of the meaning that the particular relationship holds for him.

Whether persons voluntarily seek professional help or are sought out, they discover that no immediate rewards or changes are forthcoming, that in reality they may have to endure an assortment of frustrations before the desired end is achieved. Hope, the possibility of something better, may provide enough recompense to forestall dissolution. Or some temporary gains affecting the immediate situation may enable persons to envision what lies ahead. But the major source of fulfillment, I believe, is the relationship itself, whether it is with the practitioner or with one's peers. The experience of constancy, interest, attention, concern, and caring; the absence of retribution, dishonesty, or other social penalties—these qualities of a professional relationship sustain, support, and encourge involvement despite the presence of discomfort and uncertainty.

*Commitment and Obligation*   We come now to the resonant characteristics of a relationship. The extent to which the interactors' behavior imparts to the relationship the quality of importance or primacy is indicative of *personal investment;* the extent to which there is freedom to interact and to divest one's self of usual disguises and controls is a measure of *personal involvement.*

As the interactors move toward a level of mutuality in the ways with which they confirm their commitment to their association, a climate of *interdependence* evolves—a state in which reliance on the predictability of the other's constancy, behavior, and attitudes is evident. The emergence of interdependence is consonant with a reduction in testing and trial-and-error searching. Involvement, investment, and interdependence are, in combination, expressions of the commitment of the members to the maintenance and significance of the relationship.

The corollary of commitment is obligation. Persons cannot interpose themselves in human associations without assuming the responsibilities that are linked to that action. Most formal associations spell out the obligations that are inherent to membership; the civil laws relating to marriage and the rules and bylaws of organizations and clubs are typical examples.

Change relationships are not bound by such explicit rules, although they are characterized by the norms that are built into their operation. These norms do imply certain obligations: the initial commitment to participate in the service plan and to accommodate to necessary procedural conditions, for example. Subsequent obligations may also be assumed by the client system with regard to the behaviors and attitudes required to achieve the desired outcomes. These may include the need to present one's self as authentically as possible, dealing with content that produces tension or discomfort, and concern with or about others in the case of group participation.

As a consequence of his commitments, the practitioner has an obligation to the agreed-upon norms that sustain process and balance. In addition, his obligations include an unrelenting concern for the needs, feelings, and state of the members; an open and honest presentation of self; and a readiness to deal with any intrusions emanating from self, others in the system, or persons outside the system which would threaten the continued growth of the relationship.

*Affective Character of the Relationship*   Relationships that produce growth and change are distinctive in that sufficient freedom is present within them to permit the expression of feelings that are appropriate to the particular configuration of persons in that relationship. Freedom of affective expression does not connote a license for uninhibited outpourings of feelings without regard for their impact on others. Consequently, how persons open their emotions to view may indicate their security and comfort within the relationship; how they are atuned to and take into account the feelings of others may show their values about the relationship.

Beyond the mere expression of affect is the potential for a *communion of feeling*. Expression of feeling by itself may offer some benefits as burdensome emotions are lifted by the act; but communion of feelings is indicative of the extent to which the interactors are able to spontaneously share affective reactions and thereby gain a deeper understanding of each other.

*Cognition*   In usual social relationships, the aforementioned habitudes and patterns may evolve and exist on a purely subjective level without much question or examination. For the most part, the nature of one's association with another is rarely articulated except at poignant moments of discovery or real or expected loss. A mark of the change relationship is its potential for bringing to conscious awareness that which is taking place between the actors as well as its meaning and implications. The cognition of one's own behavior, responsibilities, role, reactions, and so forth offers the possibility of a critical learning experience. Feedback and interchange teach persons about themselves and about others as social beings—particularly the specific ways in which persons affect one another, which in turn crystallizes the awareness of self. Personal change relationships in dyads or groups may emphasize this awareness purposefully and deliberately. But this cognition may also accrue indirectly from the integrity and candor in relationships and systems that have other purposes—a well functioning recreation or task-oriented group, for example.

### Recapitulation

We have considered the various dimensions of the relationship experience as they are manifested in behavioral and interactional terms. The necessity of role security was stressed as a foundation for a productive experience. The input required to sustain the relationship was discussed, as were the gratifications that are derived out of the experience. Finally, the products of the relational experience were adverted to in the form of consequences of affective expression and opportunities for social learning.

### Directional Motility

A third characteristic of a relationship is its tendency to take on motion and direction. Even as it begins to assume the attributes of continuity and stability, these conditions permit the relationship to evolve and change. In short, a relationship begins to take on its own life and direction as it reflects the growth, change, and purposes of the persons who comprise it.

A relationship would remain relatively static and inert if its members continued, over a period of time, to ritualize behavior or to refrain from introducing new issues or adding new information. Stagnant marriages and cautious and inhibited associations with fellow workers or neighbors are typical examples. In contrast, motility, particularly in change relationships, develops as problems or issues are introduced or redefined, new knowledge is examined, alternatives are considered, and goals are determined. And as these events occur, the relationship begins to move with direction and purpose toward the determined goals. Increasingly, the participants in the experience are able to at least broadly define from whence they have come, where they are, and where they are heading at particular times. To expand on this point, the following factors are noted as giving the relationship its particular bearing.

*Time*   The time structure in which the relationship is embedded directly affects the nature and rate of the experience's movement. The length of time available for the completion of the problem-solving task, for instance, would determine the breadth of the problem that could be dealt with, the rapidity with which necessary events would have to take place, and the opportunities for testing and evaluating new roles and alternatives. Similarly, the frequency with which the members meet might be a variable which would affect the intensity of the relations between persons and the content to be considered.

Of equal importance are the interactors' attitudes about temporal conditions. Whether time limits are imposed on the change process as a result of conditions beyond the control of the participants or as an element of the practitioner's strategy, there are some indications that the common awareness of these limitations speeds up the flow of purposeful interaction. Using the analogy of the animal that increases its speed as it comes closer to its goal, Goldstein hypothesizes that the imposition of individualized time limits will increase the effectiveness of the change endeavor (1966). Taking into account the need to carefully assess persons' responses to temporal events, he suggests that keeping the end point in awareness has affective and motivational value.

*Operational Purpose*   The character and inclination of each change relationship will be shaped by its purpose and intent. A number of factors influence the relationship's operational design.

How persons in association will tend to relate to one another is affected by the broad purposes that bring them together. We would expect that persons who convene in order to revise certain policies within an organization will tend to interact on more formal and deliberate levels than, say, members of a recreational group. Thus the nature of shared intent sets certain norms for how persons will behave with one another and how the relationship will evolve.

Within the relationship's operational purpose, the potentialities for change and the number of possible alternatives are also factors which affect how its members interact. Where there are a number of choices for action or the route to problem resolution is relatively smooth, persons would tend to relate differently than when the possibilities for change are constricted or blocked. Consider the contrast in practice with school drop-outs in a culture of poverty and with those in a affluent area. The variables of hope and despair, apathy and hostility, obstructions and opportunities would ineluctably influence the bonds and contracts between the members.

Finally, we again need to consider the intent and purposes of significant persons outside the immediate relationship. How they will endure or accept certain outcomes is a variable that may bias the direction that the relationship takes.

*Behaviors Governing Direction*   It is the behaviors that are enacted between members of a relationship that direct its flow, pace, and inclination. Three types of behavioral activity occur simultaneously and may be identified as giving the relationship its particular movement and direction. The three are *interventive behaviors,* representing the practitioner's activity, and the *patterned* and *educed* behaviors that are peculiar to all members of the relational system.

INTERVENTIVE BEHAVIORS: The assertive actions of the social worker, deliberately employed to influence or mediate social learning and change within or on the part of the client system and in accord with certain objectives, intentionally dispose the relationship toward a particular orientation and end. The social worker who advances insight, for example, will aim the relationship over a different course than one who attempts to bind destructive behavior. In addition to these manifest activities, other factors intrude to shape the nature and consequences of intervention.

How the practitioner interprets the situation he is facing tends to predispose the relationship's current. His own orientation and his strategy and tactics, as well as those of the change environment, will determine the range of his interventions and how he affects the thrust of the experience. Where the change experience is taking place is another variable that bears on directionality. The interventions of the practitioner in the one-to-one context take on a qualitatively different meaning and affect than those executed in a group. Factors of intimacy, contagion, and interdependence are but a few of the conditions which influence not only the nature of interventions but their interpretation, weight, and effect. Similarly, whether the social worker is acting within the confines of his home grounds or in the residence of the client or other settings will govern the course of the relationship's progress. Whether the client is a subject within the social worker's domain or whether the reverse is true will necessarily tinge the nature of his interventions with the degree of comfort and security he feels about his status and role.

PATTERNED BEHAVIORS: The patterned way with which the social worker puts his professional intent into action can be referred to as his style of practice. The pattern of his interventive behaviors, employed to achieve a particular effect, is one aspect of all of the personal and professional variables that, in their synthesis, form the whole of professional style. The social worker's empathy, gregariousness, curiosity, values, and the like combine with his technical skill to give what he does a personal flavor, and if present, élan. These characteristics are contained within the authoritative role of the social worker and invest the relationship with its particular thrust.

Similarly, the relationship is affected by the typical modes of behavior that the client system brings to it. As has been noted, persons tend to invoke prior forms of problem-solving behavior when confronted with new situations; hence, the challenges and stress that the relationship stirs cause persons to act out these behavioral patterns. The security or reponse that these actions are used to achieve then directs the way its member interact and tend to give the relationship its character—for example, cooperative, competitive, verbal, restrained, resistant, or conforming.

When the two patterned forms are combined, the consequences are more than the sum of the two, for what emerges out of the interactions is a new patterned way of relating and responding, a reverberation between the interactors. Understanding how A and B relate demands more than just an awareness of how A behaves toward B and of how B, in turn, behaves toward A. It is also necessary to know how B experiences and perceives A's behavior, how B behaves toward A on the basis of his perception, how A experiences and perceives B's behavior, ad infinitum. In sum, the behavioral styles that evolve out of ongoing interaction between persons make sense only when they are viewed within that interactional context. This kind of observation can tell us much about the direction in which a particular relationship is moving—easily flowing toward the accomplishment of a certain task, or obstructive, conflicted, ambivalent, and so forth.

EDUCED BEHAVIORS: A fine but important difference exists between this category of relational behaviors and those preceding. What is referred to here are the latent and potential feelings, attitudes, and capabilities which the special qualities of the relationship bring into the open and thus into action.

While emerging behaviors may be the adventitious product of human interchange, they are also sought for and encouraged by the social worker in his endeavor to enable persons to discover more productive behaviors within themselves. As persons in groups, dyads, committees, or families become aware of and trust the expression of their own solutions, they find these potentialities encouraged and reinforced by the practitioner or their peers. They are then able to begin to test the usefulness of these behaviors, and as this happens, the relationship begins to "turn a corner," to quicken its pace toward the desired goal.

Educed behavior is not restricted to the client system's experience. Sparked by the unique qualities of the relational experience, the practitioner may discover that he is capable of acting in new and more helpful ways, that he can wander from his well-worn technical paths to test out behaviors that are peculiarly responsive to what is taking place between himself and his client. Social work literature speaks of "the use of self" or of how the personal characteristics of the practitioner may be used as a force that modulates and enhances the change experience. I would refine the concept of educed behavior as "The use of *that part of self* that is evoked by an encounter between persons." Within relationships of substance it is not the entire personality that is brought forth but rather those salient characteristics that are selectively responsive to the personality and the ethos of the other. The special empathy that touches a hurting child, the response to the loneliness of a certain member in the midst of an active group, the newfound and helpful aggressiveness that the social worker discovers within himself after a period of ardous work with a hard-to-move board—these are meager examples of this concept.

*Summary*

It has been shown in this chapter that it is possible to gain some useful perceptions of the client system-social worker configuration through the application of social systems and relationship concepts in combination. The former provides a structural view which helps locate the constituent parts in interaction, including the input from internal and external sources. Understanding the structure, function, and output of the system in question as well as the roles and statuses occupied by its members directs the observer to a holistic comprehension of the professional system that is more productive than a person-by-person analysis.

The concept of relationship enables one to capture the flow and process in what is taking place between persons in affiliative interaction. It was also seen that relationships are not merely dyadic experiences but also pertain to the networks of human association that are integral to larger social units. Relationships take on meaning when they are studied in terms of the preconditions which make relating possible and underlie their formation and continuation; their attributes of form and content as these are experienced, perceived, and enacted by the members; and their direction and movement as they are influenced by the purposes, behaviors, and internal changes of their members.

# 6

## SOCIAL LEARNING
## AND SOCIAL CHANGE:
## THE OBJECTIVES OF SOCIAL WORK PRACTICE

The concept of social learning seems, at first glance, to be alien to the vocabulary and knowledge base of the profession. The term learning itself tends to evoke a number of semantic impressions that have to do with pursuits and exercises that are exclusive of the profession's purposes. The formal classroom with its structured teacher and learner roles, the techniques of reconditioning and desensitization, or a period of individual study are some of the images that are called to mind by the term. Even these diverse examples show that learning can be interpreted in many ways.

The reader is asked to put aside these or other presuppositions about the concept and to think of learning in its fundamental sense—namely, as the acquisition of knowledge or skill—and then to consider how learning is germane to the profession's purposes. This chapter proposes to show that social adjustment and change are products of a logical series of learning experiences irrespective of the modes, techniques, or schools of practice employed to achieve these changes. It bears stating that social learning is not a method of practice or a technique in itself; instead it is a means for constructing a conceptual framework within which specific methods or orientations can be ordered, studied, and explained.

However, this concept cannot be fully appreciated without some reference to the aims and goals to which it is directed and the processes of exchange which comprise its content. Before we can sort out the elements of learning that are typical of social work practice, we will first need to consider what is meant by goal seeking, the activity that gives social learning its purpose and thrust. This will be followed by a brief examination of the communication processes by which learning is negotiated—the exchange of information and knowledge as expressed in actions, ideas, facts, attitudes, and feelings. With these dimensions of learning established, it will then be possible to develop an operational view of the social learning experience in practice.

## Goal Seeking and Change: Some Philosophic Questions

The search for some desired end, immediate or future, is a constant motive that is typical of the human condition. Whether intent is directed toward finding means for survival (e.g., food and shelter), or toward a more abstract need (e.g., happiness or contentment), the human organism is persistently involved in the search for and accomplishment of some goal.

On considering the ramifications of goal seeking, we are immediately plunged into long-enduring dilemmas having both practical and philosophical facets. In the former case, a plethora of possible solutions to social problems rush toward us from varied sources. The fragmentation of the social and behavioral sciences into brittle-boundaries disciplines has produced a conflicting array of possible solutions to any one problem. Consider, for example, the evident problem of poverty and the varied economical, political, psychological, and sociological estimations and prescriptions that are set forth. Basic income plans, compensatory education, the readjustment or revision of institutions, and individualized services are proffered as valid remedies. Even as we reduce goal seeking in its relation to the specific individual in search for a solution to his problem, the implications of the possible directions, choices, and alternatives that bear on his existence are great.

But the philosophical quandary is more pervasive. Hopefully, some of the more pragmatic questions will find at least partial resolution when both cause and method become more objectified through study, testing, and experience. Can we answer with any certainty, however, whether goals should indeed be set? Does the social worker or a member of any of the other helping professions have the moral right to participate in, if not to actually influence the decision to strive for one outcome or another that will affect another person's life situation? Again we find the principle of self-determination used as a ready answer to this disturbing question. If we believe in the dignity of the individual, we cannot doubt that persons have the ultimate right and responsibility to make their own choices in accord with their capacity to do so. But how much of this principle is really an illusion of autonomy, a simple aphorism that avoids a plaguing question? Because of the range of predicaments encompassed by the profession's broad purposes, persons seen in practice are more often than not victims of some profound social problem. Or they themselves may perpetuate these aberrant conditions or bear the symptoms of the inequities in our society. In many instances, these are persons who feel that they have no control over the larger systems that bear on and direct the course of their existence. What determinations, then, are available to them? How many choices and alternatives are within their reach? And among those, are learned or inherent capabilities accessible that will permit effective action? Is not self-determination really an ideal rather than a principle, or as has been stated previously, a norm, a kind of optimal condition that we strive toward as we work within the constraints and defects of the conditions encountered?

For now, let us bridge the philosophic question of the right to intervene and set goals by relying on society's sanctions to practice and the guidelines and norms inherent in the profession's Code of Ethics. The continuity of public and private social welfare organizations which employ social workers is, at least, an implicit expression of agreement by a sizable part of society that social workers have the right to intervene and, since interventions are purposeful, to set reasonable goals. When these goals are set forth in broad terms—rehabilitation, strengthening of family life, increased democratic participation, and the like—their worth cannot reasonably be disputed. Who cannot favor such ends? However, when these goals are made more explicit in response to a particular set of conditions, we are faced with another variation of the philosophical question. Given a particular configuration of persons, systems, and problems, what should be the optimal outcomes and on whose terms?

I will cite merely a few illustrative examples. If we speak of the rehabilitation of a mental patient or a delinquent, are we referring to a push toward conformity to the social pressures which contributed to the pathology in the first place? Who bears the onus of change? Who sets the rules for the behaviors that are labeled "normal," "abnormal," "pathological," or "deviant"? Once the label has been appended, how do we disburden its carrier of that label and those within his system of its ramifications? Or what do we mean by strengthening family life when we are engaged in the attempt to reduce disability and damage caused by marital strife? Is the marriage an end in itself? Do we indirectly encourage divorce by helping partners face their essential incompatibilities? Or do we strive toward the maintenance of the marriage irrespective of the cost? And how do we help minority groups to become participants in a democratic process? Do we underwrite aggressive action, encourage working within the system, or press for conformity to disabling controls for the present?

It can be argued that goals and the means of change obtain from objective study, evaluation, and planning. These procedures are, in fact, essential to the plan of practice in the model presented in these pages. I suggest that these more scientific and less random approaches to goal setting have validity only when it is assumed that what each practitioner studies and evaluates is limited and governed by his own range of perceptions. These are guided by personal predilections, beliefs, identifications, and his own experiential history. It is a natural an inevitable tendency to filter out of one's possible range of observations those factors which do not make sense or are not explainable in some way. Thus each of us sees only what the boundaries of our minds allow us to see.

The social worker who has never experienced the condition of severe poverty may either tend to deny what he sees when it is out of touch with his personal experience or, on the other extreme, may become overawed by the severity of what he sees and tend to emphasize the degradation and hopelessness of the condition to the exclusion of its latent strengths. The sociologically oriented practitioner may select elements of societal or bureaucratic malaise as his target of action, whereas the psychoanalytically oriented practitioner may focus mainly on the internal costs of the same problem. Goal setting, then, implies the influence of distinctly personal factors which, in turn, will affect what will be sought and done.

Finally, we are faced with the variety of ways in which goal seeking and goal setting can be explained and understood. It is typical in our culture and our profession within it to assume a teleological stance. We look for causes that contribute to certain ends. The pervasive influence of Western philosophical thought automatically, and at times mindlessly, points us toward questions about how things came to be and what is needed to change what needs changing in order to achieve other ends. Thus we tend not to look at what is and perhaps lose its meaning in our historical and scientific search for what was and its relation to what can yet be.

Do we not also need to be aware of other pathways and possibilities for gaining a more profound awareness of the human and social phenomena that we encounter? An epistemological way of seeing, for example, would forewarn us about the limitations of what we can really know about another. All too often the social worker uses cause, truth, and knowledge as absolutes; manipulates these data into firm conclusions; or transposes a series of human events into a psychosocial explanation that sets him off on a course of action toward explicit goals. A more humble appreciation of truth and knowledge, in contrast, would impel the practitioner not to seek particular ends. Instead, he would jointly engage with the client system in seeking to unearth the ongoing knowledge that establishes some tentative meanings of central issues in persons' lives and experiences as a basis for what can be. Or in phenomenological terms, can the social worker be content to appreciate man as he is now? Is the proper goal for social work or the allied professions the enlargement and expansion of man's present existence without great regard for anticipated results? And finally, do we pay sufficient heed to the ethical questions that enter into practice with other humans? To what extent are the goals that are set reflections of a systematized, a priori set of ideas, pragmatic necessities, or symbols of organizational or cultural protocols? How often is the dignity and the need of the individual shunted aside under the guise of procedural requirements, methods that have worked with others, or some positivistic theorizing?

My purpose in raising these ideological considerations at this point is to stir some thought about the crucial issues that are inseparable from the human event in which one person influences another's goals and strivings. I have not, by any means, given these questions the profound and extensive examination they require. Rather, my intent is mainly to interject the more pertinent questions; to underscore the fact that goal seeking is not a mechanistic, cause-and-effect endeavor; and to suggest that a consensus of both means and ends will always be a question in a society that offers even minimal freedom to make choices about what constitutes the "good life."

In so doing, I leave these questions unanswered, hoping that others will take up the fascinating search for meaning. Returning to the little that we do know, I now pick up the teleological thread that approximates the approach of this work and proceed to identify the nature of goals within the purview of social work practice.

## Goal Seeking and Change: Some Concepts

The use of these two terms in combination is purposeful. Specific goals cannot be envisioned without some reference to the changes entailed; conversely, allusions to change generally carry some consideration of the ends to which they are directed. Whether I am planning a weekend vacation, a speech, or some improvement in my son's study habits, an immediate consequence is attention to the modification in action, attitude, or cognition required to attain the specific goal. Or if we speak of some alteration in behavior or thinking, these changes refer, if only implicitly, to their value for some desired outcome.

I would define change as that which takes place in *persons,* as the major or minor adaptations made to life situations that are ultimately manifested in behavioral forms. Change involves the entire organism and is not restricted to particular functions of the brain, mind, or body. Change also impinges on and has implications for others in one's social milieu, for it calls upon these others to make certain accommodations to new actions.

The assertion that change is ultimately lodged in persons is not incongruent with more sweeping or expansive emendations of larger systems—for instance, social legislation, economic innovations, racial integration, or modifications in a community's structures and institutions. We tend to abstract these phenomena, to see them in nonhuman, institutional, or societal terms as if they were occurring in a self-enclosed sphere. They are, in reality, human endeavors brought about *by* persons who are committed to the need for change, reform, or modification. They are, in the final analysis, change events only as they have some significant meanings *for* the life patterns of certain persons, individually or in concert.

Whether change is of massive or minute proportions, how each individual reacts to and incorporates it is determined by his own unique characteristics. This concept militates against the simplistic cause-and-effect notion that specified stimuli will produce fairly predictable results. The neophyte practitioner is frequently disappointed when his well-considered plans miss their mark—for example, his belief that financial aid would encourage a family to improve their ways of functioning or that undeniable facts would move a committee into action. As has been noted, the cumulative experiences in persons' lives that affect their perception of the world will influence how they perceive the stimulus to change. They will then call upon their previous repertoire of learning and action, anticipate certain outcomes, and ultimately act on the basis of propensities. In sum, our convictions about the values of certain social reforms or enrichments in interpersonal relations need to be tempered by an appreciation of the peculiar nature of the systems to which these intentions are directed.

### Types and Dimensions of Goals

Let us imagine a conversation among three social workers during their lunch break. The first states that he will soon be able to reduce or even eliminate his participation with a group of teen-agers, for they are coming to a point where they are able to work out their own plans for programming their activities and, therefore, have less need for his help. The second social worker expresses some relief that his hospitalized patient has come to see the impulsiveness of wanting to leave the hospital prematurely and now wishes to remain and continue therapy. The third also claims success in his morning's work as he describes how he has succeeded in helping a community advisory board to stop haggling and begin to attend to some needed revisions of policy.

All three are speaking about specific goals and related changes. Each, however, refers to a different level of change as part of the same overall process. Each description alludes to a particular task based on the evaluation of role, behavioral, interactional, and inclinational factors.

The first social worker is talking about the *optimal goals* about which there is concurrence and commitment on the part of all of the participants. The measure of change that is sought in this instance is the group's autonomous pursuit of its own aims, a change that is at or is on its way to a state of completion. Optimal goals, then, comprise the ultimate desired outcome to which the change experience is directed.

The second social worker talks about *interim goals,* those objectives that are significant mileposts on the route toward the optimal goals. That is, before the final objective can be realized, a series of intermediate objectives need to be met. In this instance, the practitioner had to help the patient accept the need to remain in the hospital before they could proceed toward other potential goals.

In the third example, the social worker is pursuing a variation of the preceding goal that, in its own right, can be termed a *facilitative goal.* Here he is attempting to make the change process more useful and progressive by modulating those behaviors that impede goal seeking in order to expand the options for change. A facilitative goal, then, is one that has more to do with the process itself. Other types of facilitative goals might include meeting basic needs for food, housing, or employment as precursors to the amelioration of more profound causal conditions; strengthening coping abilities during periods of great stress; and enhancing decision-making abilities.

It is not infrequent that the three goals are pursued simultaneously, although one may receive primary attention. The change process is, first of all, guided by the vision of certain desired outcomes. To achieve these, certain interim goals must be realized (in a sense, as a series of step functions). And to achieve these ends, process conditions within the system must be enhanced by reducing or modulating impeding factors or strengthening potential capabilities.

*Categories of Goals*   It is important to delineate the particular nature of the goals that are sought so as to refine the understanding of the problem or task and the means for its resolution. The following are major categories of goal seeking typical in social work practice. They are, of course, determined by the participants in the process and take into account the factors of parsimony, potentiality, and the realities within the change system. The sequence of presentation does not necessarily indicate either hierarchical or discrete characteristics.

CONCRETE GOALS: Included is the attainment of material ends—for example, housing, income, health care, and food. While these goals may be ends in themselves, they may also be sought to make other goals attainable (foresight goals, for example).

CURRENT REALITY GOALS: These have to do with immediate conditions requiring change or amelioration. Aside from what these goals accomplish in their own right—say, crisis interventions or a short-term resolution of a chronic problem—a number of pro and con beliefs are held as to the value of this category of goal setting. A "first-aid" point of view acknowledges that it may have some temporary value but avers that the more profound aspects of the problem have to be resolved for any permanent good. An existential position points to the fact that immediate problems are microcosmic representations of the total system's operation; therefore, immediate changes have greater implications for the organism in that they enhance and expand the potential for growth in broader areas of living. A third view considers the resolution of immediate conditions as a step function within an ongoing, more extensive scheme of problem solving.

STRUCTURAL GOALS: In still another order, the aim of practice may be the modification of the composition or balance of a particular system—a family, small group, or organization. While the final value of this goal may be in or for the members of the system, the primary target is the system itself. Attention here is directed to factors such as membership as well as to role relations, equilibrating processes, regulating mechanisms and communication networks, the interactions which link persons in relation.

FORESIGHT GOALS: This goal is based on the assumption that the human mind can be characterized by its future-oriented approach to the world. Once desired ends are identified, they can be achieved through rational planning. This goal emphasizes the strivings and aspirations of persons, individually or in combination.

VITALISTIC GOALS: These are predicated on the belief that the human organism is always in the process of general forward movement and growth. That is, persons cannot remain static without the consequences of stagnation or death. Growth and the unfoldment of potentials thus are necessary for survival. Whether vitalistic goals are pursued under the rubric of concrete or specifically purposive aims, the basic value of change lies in how it nurtures the capacity of persons to be all that they can be and more than they were.

Another way of perceiving goals is presented by K. W. Deutsch (1951), who reduces the concept of goal seeking to four orders, each in a successively higher order of purpose: (1) seeking immediate satisfaction; (2) self-preservation, which may require overruling the first; (3) preservation of the group; and (4) preservation of a process of goal seeking beyond any one group.

The first order refers to actions aimed at achieving gratification without regard for the consequences to self or others. The second does take into account possible dangers or threats to one's self; yet these strivings are still self-centered. In contrast, the third order takes the group's goals into account and thereby requires the subordination of individual goals when the integrity of the group is at stake. The highest order adverts to the wholeness of self-determination and self-actualization, the maintenance of the right and competence to strive for one's goals. While this endeavor would not exclude the needs of the group or others, at the same time it does not permit group forces to denigrate honest personal intent.

Hence, clarity about the level and nature of the goals pursued in practice complements and discloses much about the purposes of the enterprise, the level of strivings and needs of the client system, and the character of social learning necessary for goal achievement.

## Communication: Some Concepts

The social work process as a goal-seeking enterprise comprises the exchange of ideas and alternatives, a pursuit of knowledge and understanding, an ordering of the disarray of perceptions, and an increase of information. These ends are accomplished through the various levels and styles of human communication. Once we acknowledge that the practitioner does not unilaterally effect change through the application of techniques and methods and that the client cannot be studied apart from the immediate social context, we find that the social worker and his client are interactors in an elliptical process of information exchange.

Again, how A affects B cannot be understood without reference to how B affects A within some communicational context. Even as I attempt to make these ideas decipherable for unknown readers, how I arrange them is based on some anticipation of how they might be understood and what reaction they might receive. But this task is simple when compared to the complexities of actual person-to-person transactions, particularly when these persons attempt to have impact upon each other, for their communications take place on more than just the literal level. The social context of interchange, the conditions that preceded the message and those that follow, the accompanying gestural and tonal characteristics—these nuances tell more about the message itself than the words that are conveyed.

For our present purposes it is possible to extract only a few of the salient concepts and principles from the growing field of communication theory. The intent here is to sensitize the reader to the immense significance of communicational processes for the social learning event rather than to fully inform.

Watzlawick, Beavin, and Jackson have developed an idea about human communication which serves as a foundation for the discussion of social learning that follows (1967). This they call the "Black Box" concept. The authors argue that it is impossible to see the mind "at work." Subject and object are identical, for as the mind studies itself, any resultant assumptions have an inevitable tendency toward self-validation. This recognition led to the adoption of the Black Box concept from the field of telecommunications. Applied originally to certain types of captured electronic equipment which could not be opened and studied because of the possibility of destruction, this concept suggests that it is more expedient to disregard the internal structure of a device and concentrate on the study of specific input-output relations. While inferences can be made about what goes on inside, this knowledge is not essential for the study of the function of the device in the greater system of which it is a part.

If we apply this concept to social learning and change, we need not rely on unverifiable hypotheses about intrapsychic processes and can limit ourselves to observable input-output relations in the form of communication and feedback. So-called deviant and pathological behavior, social dysfunction, social conflict, institutional disabilities, and so forth can be better understood as functions of adaptation when the communicational field is subject to observation. For example, it is possible to obtain a more accurate and useful understanding of schizophrenia, beyond its clinical label, by studying the typical communication patterns. Similarly, the inner workings of a larger bureaucratic structure becomes manifest when we examine the messages that are fed into the structure by other systems (the community, client population groups, other organizations), and compare this with its typical output. In both instances, malfunction may be revealed in how each processes the input of information and whether what is produced is relevant to that input. The extent to which there is lack of complementarity determines the social worker's role. He may need to correct or clarify the message input, deal with the way the messages are processed, or enhance more functional kinds of expression. Hence, the schizophrenic may be helped to comprehend the messages that are transmitted to him from what he perceives as an alien world and to learn how he may make contact with that world. The dysfunctional organization may be helped to identify the blocks that separate it from other systems so as to achieve greater concordance with the populations it serves. These are admittedly oversimplified propositions; they do, however, point to a means of perceiving dysfunction in less speculative and hypothetical terms.

Ruesch presents principles of communication that are fundamental to the processes of social learning (1959). In addition to the preceding theoretical structure, the following points explain the operational aspects of communication processes.

1. People relate to each other through communication, a process that is both observed and experienced.

2. The unit of study is not one person but includes all with whom there is habitual exchange.

3. The artificial division of individual, group, and society therefore need not be maintained. All messages originate in human beings, traverse human beings, and find distinction in human beings.

4. To communicate, one must be able to perceive, evaluate, scan, and compare new impressions to the old and make decisions.

5. Messages must be phrased in terms that are understandable to others. This refers not only to the semantics of communication but also to the ability to observe the other's readiness, motivation, and capacity to understand.

6. The accumulation and arrangement of signs can be referred to as knowledge if it is inside persons and information if it is accessible to others.

7. Language itself is meaningless unless it is accompanied by instructions in the form of timing, tone, and gestures. One arrangement of words may evoke information or may persuade, depending on expression. If I ask my son, "What did you do at school today?" my demeanor might convey that I am interested in knowing how his day went (evoking), or that I am reinforcing my wish that he did not get into trouble as he did yesterday (persuading).

8. Feedback, perceived by the other, has impact. It is relayed to clarify, extend, or alter the original idea. Thus if my son reacts to my evocative question as if it were persuasive, his reaction helps me either change my style of questioning or clarify his misperception.

9. In the learning and change process, interest is not only in the content of communication but also in the form. The communication and feedback processed reveal how persons cope with their immediate relational situation by the forms of their communication.

It is apparent, then, that the communication process as well as the evolving communication network is a primary vehicle by which problems are ascertained, goals are determined, and change is implemented.

## Social Learning: A Theoretical Model of Practice

It bears stating, at the outset, that the discussion of social learning as a model for social work practice is not precisely related to psychotherapeutic techniques that employ learning theory. Examples of some of these learning positions include Wolpe's reciprocal inhibition therapy, Salter's conditioned reflex therapy, and others' use of Skinnerian operant techniques (Eron and Callahan, 1969). These are specific techniques in their own right and stress the need for the manipulation of only one independent variable. While these techniques and the model presented here may share some common theoretical foundations, the former is a prescription for therapeutic activity, whereas the latter provides a means for organizing and elucidating the stages and components of practice in its broadest meaning.

Learning theories are, in fact, diverse and diffuse; the very process of learning eludes precise definition. For our purposes, it would be helpful to introduce the concept of learning through the use of D. T. Campbell's hierarchy of "knowledge processes" which explains certain processes of learning (1959). These processes are found at different evolutionary levels of what Campbell terms "complex adaptive systems" and are useful in demonstrating movement from simple one-person attempts to socio-cultural levels of problem solving. They are: (1) *blind trial-and-error problem solving;* (2) *learning*—the retention of prior adaptive response patterns for subsequent use, thus cutting short the trial-and-error processes for familiar problem situations; (3) *perception*—visual exploration is substituted for the overt exploration of possible behavioral alternatives; (4) *observational learning*—observing the outcomes of another social being, with the result that the observer profits from the other's experiences; (5) *imitation*—the acquisition of a model for behavior by perceptions of another's behavior; (6) *linguistic instruction*—learning about the nature of the world and the correct responses to it through the use of words; (7) *thought*—the symbolic rehearsal of potential behavior against a learned model of the environment; and (8) *social decision making*—pooling the observations of many persons into a single, more adequate model of the environment.

The first three knowledge processes may or may not involve interaction with other social beings. In any case, an interpersonal component is not essential for the achievement of adaptation at those levels. My attempts to assemble my child's bicycle without instructions, my learning that I can handle two martinis but that three will cause some drastic results, or my attempts to visualize the relationships of the parts of a puzzle before I attempt to solve it may, by chance, involve others; but their participation is not required in my learning.

The last five knowledge processes and problem-solving techniques are consonant with the concept of social learning inasmuch as direct or indirect interaction with other persons is a requisite for successful learning and task achievement. Observation or imitation clearly call upon and refer to specific persons or composites of behaviors of many persons in one's social environment. While thought may be a solitary event, it is likely to include a reconsideration or interpretation of episodes of social relations. Verbal direction obviously requires communication between persons, as does social decision making.

It is apparent, then, that social learning is not a process that is restricted to purposive change endeavors. It refers to all of the adaptive means used by persons in their day-to-day experiences, to the way in which persons or formally or informally structured groups of persons learn to become efficient and effective members of their social environment.

While learning goes on unevenly, depending on what needs to be solved or known, there are significant times, relations, and events in persons' lives which more acutely stimulate these knowledge processes. The various stages of maturation and growth are critical periods wherein prior conceptions of role behavior are no longer functional. Adolescence, parenthood, the middle years, and retirement are episodes that require new knowledge, a reassessment of one's self-expectations, the opportunity to observe others, and some verification from other sources in order to facilitate the transition from one stage to the next. It is only when one has certainty about how and what one is to be that conflict and tension are reduced and smoothness of movement into the new role is made possible.

As persons enter into and intensify their relationships with others, numerous forms of direct and subtle learning are encountered. The ascription of importance to the role and status of others within these relationships may create role models whose life styles can be emulated and authority figures from whom one can learn. Relationships that are affectional and intimate offer the opportunity to experience and therefore to learn about the meaning of trust, caring, and commitment. On the other hand, conflict-laden relationships place persons in positions where they discover what their beliefs are and what they stand for as they attempt to clarify or defend their stance. In those relationships that are complementary, where the linkage of differences between persons forms the foundation of the relationship, members can learn their special value and significance, their characteristics that meet the other's needs. Similarly, equalitarian relationships may serve to identify and verify shared characteristics.

Situational conditions also contain certain important elements of interpersonal learning. Such crisis events as death, accident, illness, or unemployment inevitably pose a certain number of alternatives among which choices have to be made and acted on in a social context. These choices may result in regression, growth, or maintaining the status quo. The basis for choice may be a return to what was previously learned, or a search for new information may be required. Further, the experience of being subjected to a critical turning point in one's life may reveal potentialities for creative action that, to that point, were not known or available to perception.

Similarly, persons discover, to their dismay, that their control over their world is more tenuous than they thought. Families lose their stable characteristics over a period of time, neighborhoods change, peer groups lose or gain members, and organizations no longer fulfill the purpose for which they were designed or may become constrained by policies and programs that are no longer functional. In addition, the state of the world changes from day to day. On any morning, our newspapers may inform us of the vagaries of the political structure or the fluctuations in the economy. Thus despite the tendency of humans to structure their future with as much predictability as possible, unforeseen events call upon  them to make significant changes in perceptions, life styles, and patterns from time to time. Only as there is access to new knowledge and feedback can new learning and readjustment take place.

The concept of social learning, then, encompasses a broad array of behaviors and orientations. Social adaptation, psychotherapy, reward and punishment, stimulus and response, advice and guidance, reinforcement, consultation, group dynamics, social interaction, formal instruction, socialization, identification, community action—these comprise only a partial list of either specialized techniques or abstract principles which may be subsumed under the concept. This being the case, how do we distinguish between the types of social learning that are characteristic of ordinary daily living and those which are contained within the boundaries of professional practice?

First of all, usual social learning is an ongoing social enterprise that does not proceed at an even rate or with a constancy of force. Most learning, except for the transitional or acute periods noted above, is relatively casual. Usually there is not a great deal at stake in the process, some latitude for error exists, or rectification is possible. In more critical situations, the upsurge of learning is temporary and generally task related, and the organism later tends to return to its usual state.

In contrast, the key factor that differentiates social learning within the professional change experience from usual social learning is intensity —the intensity of the need to be fulfilled or the goal to be achieved, the intensity of the commitment to the endeavor that is required, and the intensity of the exercise itself. The special needs faced in practice are generally indicative of critical social conditions that may, in some ways, be related to the maintenance, stability, or even survival of persons, groups of persons, or larger systems. Here something significant *is* at stake. This is not to say that the awareness of these needs or the recognition of the necessity for help or change is always manifest on the part of the target of service. It may take the anxiety of others affected by or responsive to the conditions to set the change process in motion—for example, friends or relatives of families that are foundering, members or the clientele of organizations that rock along out of touch with those they are supposed to serve, or relatives of individuals who destructively repeat patterns of behavior without regard to the consequences.

Social learning, in this instance, is further differentiated by its design and structure. That is, it is predicated on a series of steps, each to be purposefully accomplished before it is possible to proceed on to the next. As already noted, persons with or representing a difficulty or problem need to be induced into the client role, important events and knowledge have to be ordered into a comprehensible form, and so forth. Thus social learning in professional practice can be considered a special form of a typical human process. The intentionality and management aspects of the professional role give the event its special qualities.

It is important to add that a social learning orientation tends to supplant the more traditional and monadic approaches to problem resolution. These focus primary attention on the bearer of the problem and either exclude or minimize the social field in which the problem is embedded. As a result, symptoms within persons or structures become the major issue rather than processes between persons or systems. Social learning denotes the interpersonal component in how individuals, families, groups, organizations, or community substructures go about the business of problem-solving. Social learning describes the resolution of problems of human interaction through the processes of human interaction.

### Some Theoretical Considerations

Despite the vast amount of research and energy that has been invested in the field of learning, only recently have the implications of knowledge about learning been considered for their relevance to endeavors aimed at achieving psychological or social change. Goldstein takes issue with the tendency of the helping professions to ignore the ideas stemming from concept attainment, reinforcement, discrimination learning, and the host of other research topics in the field of learning. He refers to the very limited number of treatises on the subject that refer to psychotherapy as a study of ways for changing behavior in specified directions (1966). He contends that "whatever else it is, psychotherapy [which he defines in the broadest of terms] must be considered a learning enterprise . . . it may be specific behaviors or a whole new outlook on life, but it cannot be denied that the intended outcome is a change in the individual that can only be termed as manifestation of learning" (p. 213).

Strupp and Bergin, in their study of patients' reactions to and the outcome of psychotherapy experiences, validate this opinion in their conclusions (1969). They state that psychotherapy (in their definition, "a multi-faceted conglomeration of fuzzy meanings") should be viewed as a form of education or as what Freud called "after-education." It is most evident that what the patient acquires are new perceptions of self and others; he learns new patterns of interpersonal behavior and unlearns maladaptive ones. Strupp's conclusions are similar to those of Berenson and Carkhuff. In their terms, change occurs on a broad front and is independent of the therapist's theoretical position and professional affiliation (1967). What is learned are new techniques for effective living. This learning is facilitated by three conditions: (1) the experiential, (2) the didactic, and (3) the role model that the therapist presents.

If knowledge about learning has been applied so meagerly to the field of individual and interpersonal therapies, its deliberate use, up to this point, in group, organizational or community practice, or in attempts to achieve social change have been virtually negligible. This is indeed a paradox, for these aspects of social work practice are closely related to the knowledge and procedures in the learning field. Despite the fact that practice with groups has long been allied with educational objectives and methods and that practice with communities does comprise many elements of didactic and cognition producing learning theories, the link between learning knowledge and social work practice has rarely been acknowledged. Jehu has recently made a pioneering effort in this direction in his book on learning theory and its significance for the profession (1967). Among the few who have studied the issue is Picardie, who cites the values of learning theory for social work practice (1967)

As a result of a study of thirty-five psychiatric patients in which a classification of learning processes was used, he found that learning theory models of behavior provided a more comprehensive way of looking at client-social worker interactions. These models provided a simple and more satisfactory perspective than that contained within the vast and unwieldy body of knowledge derived from analytic and eclectic approaches.

J. P. Guilford defines learning as a change in behavior, a transition form one behavioral state to some other (1967). Change in behavior, in turn, causes some change in perception preceding or following the change event. Perception is a decision process, a response to the real world in which inferences are made about phenomena on the basis of prior experience—that which is known or understood in one's own terms. The correctness of perception, then, depends on the frequency with which the phenomena have been encountered and prior successes in dealing with them, as well as distortions that may result from attitudinal predispositions or biological impediments. The distinction between perception and behavior is arbritary; whatever actions persons employ in response to their environment is predicated on how they perceive that environment. Or in other terms, we can say that persons exhibit such an extraordinarily strong need to maintain consistent relationships between their actions and perceptions that, in the course of any given action sequence, either may be modified to bring it into accord with the other (Carson, 1969). Hence, as we add the social component to the learning event, we can see that social learning becomes the way in which persons call upon or modify perceptions and behaviors in order to adapt, adjust to, or alter their social environment in individual or collective ways.

The significance of this concept for social work practice and the related teaching role of the social worker is more pronounced when it is narrowed to its problem-solving function. Here John Dewey's elaboration of problem solving as a model for behavior is useful (Guilford, 1967). As early as 1910, Dewey proposed the classic steps or stages, the discrete and episodic nature of problem solving: (1) a difficulty is felt, (2) the difficulty is located and defined, (3) possible solutions are suggested, (4) consequences are considered, and (5) a solution is accepted. With minor modifications, these steps have been rather persistent over the years. Guilford asserts that problem solving is linked to creative activity, that they are one and the same phenomenon. The relationship, then, of this model of learning and change to the fundamental growth–generating processes of social work practice is evident. Social work practice does comprise a series of steps, each predicated on the accomplishment of the previous step, to achieve not only the resolution of some problem, task, or condition but to also bring about the opportunity for the expansion and growth of human potential.

This premise deserves some elaboration. Whether the intent and content of practice is directed toward an increase in insight or self-awareness, the achievement of a corrective emotional experience, task or role attainment, or efforts for social change or program formation, client systems are exposed to and are encouraged and enabled to assimilate new knowledge in order to reassess previously held knowledge about pertinent substantive, psychological, and social factors. The specifics of the process that takes place will be discussed shortly; for the present, it is safe to say that this process of learning is episodic. It takes place in logical and sequential stages which are characteristic of the human ways of problem solving as set forth by Dewey. That is, it is impossible to attack a problem until it is definable in terms that make sense and which render the problem available to manipulation through various intellectual, affective, and behavioral means. We must have certain information at our disposal before other alternatives can be considered, and as they emerge, we must attend to the range of possible consequences of these alternatives. And finally, the selected alternative is implemented through some form of behavior. Each of these stages places creative demands on the learning organism, for each depends on the capacity to evaluate and make judgments, to expand knowledge beyond current boundaries, to project one's self into future events, to imagine and intuit, and to deal with relationships, abstractions, concepts and symbols. These and other requirements draw on the potentials of the entire thinking and feeling organism.

As has been noted, these processes are also typical of the efforts of persons to deal with the complexities of their social existence in everyday living. When the social worker enters this process, either to identify a need or difficulty or in response to a request, it is because these usual problem-solving techniques break down, new techniques are needed, or external resources required for task achievement are not available. His responsibilities may be relatively simple (such as providing the data that the system requires to enrich its existing problem-solving capabilities), or complex (for example, persuading others to acknowledge that there is a problem in the first place or helping to revive or rework the ability to deal with difficulties). His actions in the first instance might involve referral to appropriate resources, giving information about child rearing and the like, or providing demographic data that would permit an action group to complete its task. Examples of the second might include intensive work with groups of delinquents, persons who are victims of the inequities of society, shattered families, or deficient organizations. Although the content may differ, the essential courses of practice is the same. With this introduction it is now possible to go on to examine the problem-solving function of social work practice in more precise detail.

AN OPERATIONAL MODEL OF LEARNING AND PROBLEM SOLVING IN SOCIAL WORK PRACTICE

The proposed model (see page 174) is designed to demonstrate (1) the stages of problem solving, (2) the accompanying learning processes, and (3) the input of the teaching role of the social worker at each stage. This model represents a two-dimensional communication system. The vertical arrows indicate the direction of information flow within the system (the client), and the feedback loop arrows depict the flow from outside the system (the social worker). It should be noted that the model or flow chart is of a generic nature and is designed to elucidate the elemental steps, processes, and inputs. The model cannot fully represent the diversities of human experience nor can it fit every episode of problem solving. Therefore, it would need to be modified in accordance with the particular types of problems dealt with as well as variables of motivation, capability, and the patterns of the persons or groups involved. For example, the learning processes might well terminate at an early stage when motivation is not sufficient to promote movement to the next stage. Or the model may need to be elliptical in instances when attempts at formulating the initial problem were incomplete or erroneous or when unforeseen condition forced a return to previous stages of problem solving. In still other instances, a regression to earlier stages might be necessitated by an insufficiency or distortion of information.

The generic character of this model permits its application to the various types as well as to the particular schools or systems of social work practice. The steps of learning and the accompanying input of the practitioner's role activities are pertinent to practice with two-person as well as group or larger systems. They are present in practice with

AN OPERATIONAL MODEL OF PROBLEM SOLVING AND RELATED
INPUT OF THE SOCIAL WORKER'S ROLE

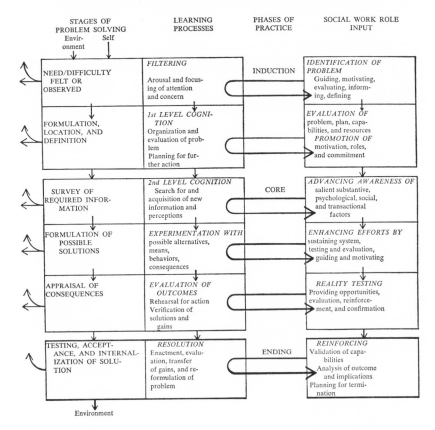

social, situational, environmental, organizational, and community problem entities and in the various psychological, psychiatric, and psychosocial orientations to practice.

It should be emphasized that this structure can only be used as a
model within which practice can be organized and explicated and not as
a technique in itself. It explains rather than prescribes the elements of
technique and therefore intends to make the professional enterprise
more comprehensible. To repeat, its intrinsic value is in the extent to
which it presents a symbolic representation and therefore a replication
of the sages, processes, phases, and inputs typical of that which is so-

cial work practice. Before proceeding to an elaboration of the process, some clarification of the categorical terms is in order.

STAGES OF PROBLEM SOLVING: Problem-solving activity is a sequence of steps, each requiring some degree of completion before movement to the succeeding step can be effected. No reference to the complexities or the temporal factors connected with each stage is intended. For example, when persons seek out services voluntarily, the problem-solving tasks of the initial stage may be disposed of very quickly, whereas the primary stage might well constitute the largest measure of the total experience when movement into services is initiated by another. It should be noted that the arrows at each stage indicate, in addition to forward movement, the possibility of exit from the process at that point or a return to some previous stage.

PHASES OF PRACTICE: A consideration of practice as comprising three distinct phases provides a time-divided framework within which the tasks, objectives, content, and interaction pertinent to each phase can be ordered and comprehended. The *induction phase* includes the period and activities which establish and clarify the respective roles of the participants (or more precisely, enable persons to become clients), identify the problems needing attention, demonstrate the course of action to be taken, and resolve the problems and issues that would ordinarily impede the ongoing learning and problem-solving process. The *core phase* is that period in which the practice system is stabilized; a mutuality of patterns, roles, norms, and objectives is achieved; and intensification and refinement of problem-solving activity takes place. The *ending phase* is the period in which problem resolution is achieved, termination is in sight, and preparations for dissolving the practice system are the primary tasks. While the phase concept defines the entirety of practice, whether it is of long or short duration, it may also refer to any segment of practice (one or more interviews or group meetings). Each practice encounter or cluster of encounters contains characteristics of each of the three phases.

SOCIAL WORK ROLE INPUT: This column defines the functions and activities of the social worker—those role behaviors which facilitate the learning process. As noted, the arrow is indicative of a feedback loop. That is, the social worker's investment in the problem-solving event is not unilateral. The technical, cognitive, and affective abilities that he employs are regulated, changed, or modified by the nature and quality of the system's response.

PROBLEM-SOLVING STIMULUS: The terms Environment and Self refer
to the primary sources of the problem receiving attention. Environmental stimuli might include conditions in the physical environment (lack of
housing, poverty, inoperative policies), the reactions of significant others
to the problem (family members, citizen groups, persons in authority),
or the social worker who identifies the problem in the first place. Self
adverts to one's own cognitive or affective awareness of the existence of
a condition requiring professional help.

*Operation of the Model*

*The Induction Phase of Practice*   Two stages constitute this phase. The
objective of the first is the attainment of a level of conscious awareness
of the particular nature of the problem, task, or need that effected entry into the change system. Awareness may be on cognitive and/or
affective levels. In either or both cases, what is entailed is the process of
sorting out the pertinent factors so as to refine the nature of the problem in terms that will give it substance and permit some consideration of
subsequent planning. The related role input of the social worker is
multifaceted. His participation in the identification of the problem involves guiding and ordering the other's perceptual abilities, validation
of significant findings, and attention to motivational, affective and extrasystem factors bearing on the task.

The second stage comprises movement toward a more precise formulation of the problem, where it is located within or outside the immediate
system, its dynamic meaning, the factors that contribute to its existence,
and the conditions attendant to achieving resolution. The last considers the major issues relative to how persons can or will assume the client
role and factors of dissonance, capabilities for engaging in the problem-
solving endeavor, probable goals (immediate and long-term), and the
planning that is required for implementation. The role input of the social
worker, relative to bringing these factors into awareness, is aimed at the
eduction of relevant facts about the problem. He assists with the ordering and formulation of knowledge and is simultaneously attentive to
the meaning, dynamics, and implications of engaging the others in the
client role for subsequent planning and action.

In summary, the induction phase is primarily geared to the process
of enlarging and enhancing the client system's capability to identify the
problem, to remove it from the realm of confusion, uncertainty or resistance, and to assume responsibility for the efforts that are required

to resolve the difficulty. Although attention is given to the problem and its import, severity, and adaptive meanings, the basic task is the engagement of the client system. With adequate information, clarity of purpose, and hope, the client system then can move into the next stages of social learning. Without the achievement of these interim ends, the ongoing learning and change experience would continually need to return to the initial phase in order to reconsider and relearn purpose, role, and problem.

*The Core Phase*   This phase is characterized by a shift away from major attention to role questions, expectations, and dissonance to concern with the ways and means of problem resolution. Although these issues continue to be an essential ingredient of subsequent transactions, a substantial degree of comfort and assurance about role, status, norms, and expectations permits the transfer of learning energies to the problem or task itself. The three stages of learning encompassed by the core phase have to do with the development of knowledge and awareness which, in turn, lead to the development of possible solutions and alternatives and then to their implications and possible outcomes.

The first of the three stages aims at the generation of information and its analysis. Data that are already known and learned, that are known but not assimilated or tested, or that yet need to be known are brought into the open and subjected to examination. Knowledge might come from information sources within the system (social history, perception of significant events, past patterns of behavior with similar problems, special competencies), within a group (shared experiences, common strivings, interactional patterns), from data sources outside the system (statistics, bibliographical sources, other relevant systems), or from the social worker's own expertise. In this stage, the role input of the social worker is directed toward ways of expanding knowledge. He may engage the client system directly or exploratorily in the search for the required information. He may provide the information that is needed in accord with his judgment of the system's readiness to utilize it, or he may use other resources for information input. In this strategy he uses evaluative techniques to sort out, achieve order about, and make comprehensible the knowledge required in response to variables of readiness, motivation, and the feasibility of possible alternatives.

As an array of possible solutions and alternatives for action emerges out of the welter of information, the options are considered in relation to their potential for achieving certain desired outcomes, their economy and efficiency, and the means by which they can be implemented. Their possible consequences and implications as well as questions about how the change system or others are to be involved in their implementation are also factors requiring attention in this, the second stage. The social worker's correlative efforts are aimed at enriching and reinforcing these attempts at problem solving through the use of various strategies. He supports motivation to work on the problem and deals with the obstacles that block consideration of possible pathways. He helps reduce and refine the number of choices or potential courses of action by assisting in the consideration of their efficiencies relative to the desired outcomes. In this regard, he encourages thought about their respective values and how they correspond with the value systems of those related to the outcome. Concomitantly, the social worker attends to the exigencies produced by the ferment of change. These may include the ascendant anxiety and emotional levels as persons begin to think about change in the abstract terms that can arouse the fear and uncertainty and that can only be dispelled by the realities of effective action. Disruptions in relational patterns as well as in the cohesiveness of the system may also require his intervention. Doubts about progress and questions about the meaning of the relationship or the value of the group or committee are not atypical examples. Thus this and the succeeding stage are periods which place demands for creative thinking and perceiving on the participants, not only in regard to envisioning possible new avenues for change but also in how persons can best interact with one another to achieve a rich social learning experience.

The third stage of the core phase is a logical consequence of the preceding stage. Here the more visionary and abstract ideas are translated into palpable forms that lend themselves to testing and evaluation. In sum, this is a period of rehearsal for action in the real world of the client system. As selected courses of action are determined, they may be tried out within the arena of the change setting itself and/or experimented with in other social settings. The results and impressions then become subject to evaluation as to their validity and usefulness as well as to the meaning of their impact on significant others. The social worker's major role at this stage corresponds to these activities. In providing the occasion to test the reality of the selected actions, he offers the support of the relationship or encourages support within the existing network of relationships. He provides his concern and his skill to undergird this rehearsal in thought and action. He helps bring to conscious awareness the emerging new patterns, their value and efficiency, and how they are indicative of strength and creativity. He is prepared to deal with the consequences of failure and disappointment as well, and mitigates their effects by his broader vision and his commitment to his evaluation of what is possible. Through the entire core phase, a period of expected disruption, the social worker acts as a lender of strength, hope, and vision and as an interactor in the learning experience who enhances the purpose and value of the change system and the potentials of its members.

*The Ending Phase*   This stage of problem solving is achieved and completed when the alternatives and solutions find assertive expression in the social environment, the consequences are evaluated and dealt with, and the problem-solving techniques become significant parts of the patterned repertoire of the particular client system. That is, what were once objectified alternatives now become integral functions within and of the system. Further evidence of change lies in the extent to which successful problem-solving abilities are transferable to related tasks or problems. The consequence of change, therefore, is not solely the development of specific skills but includes the growth of the entire organism, whether an individual or a group of individuals, in how it can deal more creatively with many aspects of living. The discovery of one's own potential to resolve what was formerly seen as unalterable and to engage in the social processes of learning and change should increase feelings of mastery—the ability to take charge of other aspects of the real social world.

Validation and reinforcement of problem-solving capability and creativity constitutes the role input of the social worker in this stage and phase. As persons begin to claim these capabilities as their own, as they become internalized and patterned ways of dealing with plans and problems, they become de-objectified and not readily available to appraisal. Those who leave a successful change experience are frequently unaware of their own transformation or what they have contributed to the event or to others when the experience involved others in interaction. Thus it is the social worker's task to bring to awareness what has been accomplished, to vivify these changes, and to demonstrate the capability for transferring these problem-solving skills to other areas of social living and action. Throughout this process, he also engages in

planning and preparation for termination by anticipating possible reactions and evaluating the need for other services or contingencies.

*Outcome*   The results of the problem-solving process inevitably find
expression within the environment. Although movement through the
sequential stages is indicative of change within the system itself, learning, as noted, is changing behavior within the social environment of
the system.

*Recapitulation*

Some general observations about the implications of the model of
social learning are indicated. To repeat, it is of a generic character and
cannot be used analogously. The model is designed to explicate the
fundamental but pervasive factors which are essential to the stages and
processes of problem solving within the phases of practice. The specific
properties and features of each stage depend on many variables, singu-
larly or in combination—the size of the particular social unit, the nature
and intensity of the problem, whether it is located inside or outside the
system, the resources available, personality, role and age factors, and
the amount of information that is available, to name a few. For example, the sequence, timing, control, and content of the problem-solving
experience in practice with a couple seeking to resolve a marital conflict
would differ markedly from, say, the efforts of a citizens' group to
reverse certain proscriptive welfare procedures. Yet the basic principles
of the problem-solving scheme and the related role expectations of the
social worker are fundamentally the same.

Because the flow within the model refers to a human interactional
experience, it is subject to many variations. It is not the property of
complex human systems to move forward with rationality or with
machine-like precision. Allowance, therefore, needs to be made, when
this model is applied, for backtracking at any stage to previous stages
and phases. For example, initial stimuli may need to be reevaluated
if the premises they created prove to be invalid when the formulation
of solutions is attempted. It might be discovered that the range of
alternatives devised is too meager and that reconsideration of available
knowledge is required.

In addition, exit from the problem-solving process might occur at
any stage. The problem, once clarified, might not appear worthy of
further study; or conversely, the participants may find it to be too

monumental to be undertaken at that particular time. The attempt to work out a solution might have to be held in abeyance due to the lack of required information. Or the anticipated expression of newly learned methods might well evoke responses from the environment that would negate what could be attempted.

Finally, the social work role has to be attuned to the emergence of creative abilities associated with each of the stages of learning. Learning is not restricted to narrow corridors leading to singular solutions; instead, it is indicative of growth, imagination, risk taking, intuition—of the expansiveness of latent potentialities within the particular system, whether it be a solitary individual, a family in interaction, persons working together in a group, or segments of an organization or community. Thus it is incumbent on the social worker to look beyond the immediate problem or task and to seize the emerging opportunities to reinforce evidence of mastery and self-actualization.

# PART TWO
## THE STRATEGIES AND NEGOTIATIONS OF SOCIAL WORK PRACTICE

# MODELS OF PRACTICE

With a conceptual framework for social work practice firmly established, we now have the base from which we can begin to look at practice in operational terms. This implies movement down the scale of abstraction to the principles, procedures, and guidelines for professional activity—to a level at which professional practice takes on structure and sequence. These factors are subsumed under the terms *strategy* and *negotiation*—the former denoting a schema that guides specific actions and the latter referring to the fact that practice activity is not unilateral but is modulated by the variables that are peculiar to the particular interpersonal situation. In short, while the practitioner's activity is governed by certain propositions and norms, how these are translated into actional terms is contingent on his perception of and input from the system with which he is working.

The present endeavor is to integrate the disparate elements of practice into a comprehensive model that relates to the practice experience. This is, indeed, a complex task, one that cannot be fully achieved due to the many facets, levels, and motives that are integral to this human event. Any model can fit only certain aspects of the practice situation as a multilevel, interactional phenomenon. In the previous section we have examined two useful models. The first, a social systems model, offered a structural view of the systems encountered in practice as well as the change system itself. The second, an operational, problem-solving model, organized the logical stages of learning and change and the role requirements of the social worker at each stage. Thus where one depicts structure, the other reveals sequence, content, and action (each quite valid for the aspect of practice it fits).

It is worthwhile to note that other variables were considered, each pointing to a critical area of practice, in the attempt to construct the model that will follow. There is, first, the *problem/goal* variable which refers to practice in terms of the broad social problem it intends to treat and the goals it attempts to achieve. In some measure, this vari-

**185**

able is represented in the "fields of practice" concept which relates the problem area (medical, psychiatric, family welfare, etc.) to the actual nature of practice. Bartlett makes a cogent argument against the use of "fields" as a way of perceiving practice (1971). She states that fragmentation of practice can be avoided only if the notion of "fields" is interpreted with the idea of a common base and differences are understood as variations in the application of the common elements.

A second variable is the size of the client unit using professional services. It is this variable that defines the casework, group work, and community organization conception of practice, the notion that the size of the unit prescribes a fairly consistent and definitive form of professional activity. Even if this is so, caseworkers frequently find themselves working with families and groups, group workers have to deal with individual members, and community workers encounter all forms of human association. Thus practice defined by this variable alone would produce a set of inconsistent, fragmented, and overlapping principles.

Finally, there is a *function/goal* variable. This also takes into account the purposes and outcomes of practice and, in addition, makes specific the means and the ends. Schneiderman offers a thoughtful analysis of a practice model based on this variable (1969). On one axis he lists three major objectives of social work practice: (1) system maintenance—the preservation of existing norms and arrangements; (2) system control—bringing nonconforming and threatening behavior under control; and (3) system change—promotion of change in the direction of increased effectiveness. On the other axis he lists the range of the profession's societal functions as they are related to the three objectives:

1. Treatment—including restoration, maintenance, and enhancement;
2. Direct provision—the administration of material aid;
3. Mediation—bringing persons with unmet needs and existing resources together;
4. Change enabling—the mobilization and motivation of the client system for the purpose of achieving specific changes in social reality;
5. Documentation—the translation of programs into services or accounting;
6. Analyzing and planning—the analysis of social problems, policies, and goals; and
7. Advocacy—problem analysis and policy and program development beyond the goals of any particular client.

As can be seen, Schneiderman's model accurately depicts another aspect of practice—the function of the social worker in broad terms as it is related to major objectives.

Depending, then, on the facet or segment of practice one wishes to explicate, a number of models are available for one's purposes. Since we are concerned with the strategies, transactions, and role obligations of the social worker in his practice with the range of client systems that are typical of practice, it is necessary to consider certain variables in synergetic terms. If we wish to comprehend the strategies of the social worker, we must take into account the variable of time. What he plans to do becomes differentiated over the span of time he is working with a particular system. Strategy and time, in turn, are modulated by the nature of the system that is the target of practice. The three human and interactive variables in combination—strategy, time, and target—are useful in capturing the flow of interchange in sequence and contribute to the construction of what shall be called a *process model* of social work practice.

It is worthwhile to note again that the proposed model as well as the others that have been considered neither have hierarchial significance nor compete with one another as being most representative of social work practice. A model is useful only in its "goodness of fit" to the reality it is intended to represent. While one model may adequately portray the functions of practice, it may be less depictive of the stages through which change takes place. Therefore, each model can be regarded in terms of its utility for gaining greater organization and comprehension of the elements or processes it intends to describe rather than as an all-encompassing prefiguration of practice. To reiterate, the selection of a process model serves the purpose of gaining a more precise awareness of the interactional, sequential, and human factors in the practice event. The model is constructed with the recognition of the dangers of oversimplification stressed by Bertalanffy:

To make it conceptually controllable, we have to reduce reality to a conceptual skeleton—the question remaining whether, in doing so, we have not cut out the vital parts of the anatomy. [1968, p. 200]

With this admonition in mind, the reader is referred to the content of the preceding section of this book to give this model substance. He is reminded that its vitality lies in the specific ways it is translated into action within the realities of practice.

**A PROCESS MODEL OF SOCIAL WORK PRACTICE**

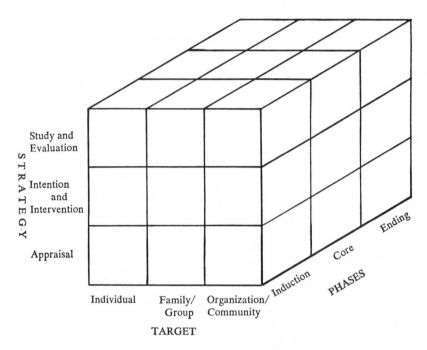

The process model comprises three variables of practice in interrelationship: strategy, target, and phases of practice. The following section briefly describes these terms as a prelude to a subsequent elaboration of their implications and meanings.

*Strategy* incorporates the three major role activities of the social worker. *Study and evaluation* are concurrent processes geared to collecting and processing data as a basis for establishing the assumptions that will guide interventive activity with particular client systems in each phase of practice. Study is the securing of facts, information, and data about the system that are relevant to the problem or issue and to the problem-solving process itself. Evaluation is the transformation of pertinent information into rational constructions that give meaning to the client system/problem/process configuration in action. *Intention and intervention* refer to the complementarity between aim and action. The former takes into account the purpose and planning for action that are bilaterally related to the evaluative process. Intervention is the manifest expression of intentionality—that act of coming between the client system and the problem or of influencing task resolution so as to enhance, modify, or augment learning and change. *Appraisal* adverts to the practitioner's withdrawal from interaction in order to evaluate the outcomes and implications of the preceding processes. Consideration of congruence, meaning, correspondence with reality, accuracy, and parsimony, as they are related to plan and goal, provides direction for subsequent alternatives and procedures. In summary, strategy includes the processes of refinement of perception, decision making, action, judgment, and review, which are differentiated in the various phases of practice in relation to specific targets of service.

*Target* refers to the type of social unit receiving professional services and this instance is defined as one of the usual social configurations found in society—individual, family, group, organization, or community. This distinction does not imply that these are discrete units; practice with any one unit requires awareness of how that unit is part of, includes, or is in relation to all others. However, the structure that is common to each poses certain implications for strategic and temporal variables. Although the target is most frequently the actual consumer of service, in its broadest sense the term may allude to practice with certain systems on behalf of some client system outside the arena of service. For example, a social worker may work with a family on behalf of a hospitalized mental patient or with a concerned community group on behalf of certain deprived citizens.

*Phases of practice* has to do with the stages through which the change experience progresses. In each, some types of role differentiation are required on the part of the social worker and the target system. The *induction* phase is that period within which the focus of practice is directed toward the clarification, development, and assumption of the client role concurrent with the identification and evaluation of the problem or task. The *core* phase is that juncture within which the change system is stabilized, emphasis is placed on problem-solving capabilities, and efforts are directed toward resolution and change. The *ending* phase is the terminal period of service wherein resolution of the problem or task is achieved and evaluated and consideration is given to subsequent planning.

As will be demonstrated, this process model organizes the content of each of the variables of practice in relation to all others. That is, each of the strategies with particular social units can be identified with any one phase of practice. What follows is an elaboration of this model using the phases of practice as the means of organizing its content into a sequential and logical order. This format will first elucidate the characteristics of each phase and then successively describe those strategies that are fundamental to social work practice in general and those that are specifically applicable to the requirements of the structure and composition of the particular social units.

# 1

## THE ROLE INDUCTION PHASE

*A. Characteristics*

As persons move into association with one another, their awareness of the immediate event and their expectations of what is to follow are derived from gained impressions and information. Impressions follow the exposure to and experience in the interchanges that include behavior, attitude, and affect. Information is the more literal expression of transmitted facts, ideas, knowledge, and direction. Hence, what is transacted at the outset of the formation of the change system to some degree influences the quality, character, and direction of all that follows.

In their first contacts, the social worker and the individual or group begin a process of system construction that will create a model of sorts, a set of guidelines, for their subsequent interactions and negotiations. This is not to say that a fixed, unyielding pattern emerges; corrections may be needed to give the system its own vitality and growth. But generally, relationships tend to assume a direction and quality that reflect the first observations and assumptions about role expectations and conceptions. Thus the immense importance of clarity, perceptiveness, and specificity on the part of the social worker cannot be overstated, for they affect how he sets about the task of helping the potential recipients of service take on the client role. This task is incorporated in the following explicit characteristics of this phase.

1. CLARIFICATION AND ASSIGNMENT OF ROLES AND RESPONSIBILITIES: In the initial phase, that which is transacted between persons directly and indirectly clarifies the participants' beginning ideas about what their roles are to be (as they are perceived by themselves and by others), as well as the obligations that are attendant to these roles.

2. THE BEGINNING OF A SYSTEMS REGULATING PROCESS: As the change system begins to take form, both explicit and implicit processes designed to ensure the stability and continuity of that system are set in motion. The emerging roles of authority and status, both assumed and ascribed, are accompanied by norms and measures that tend to keep

**191**

inequities in balance. By demonstration and direction, the participants indicate how they will interact and what kinds of responses they expect. At the outset, certain ad hoc rules and norms are set up to provide the basis for a subsequent contract that will guide and order the system's continuity and growth.

3. THE INITIATION AND DEVELOPMENT OF THE CHANGE RELATIONSHIP: While it is difficult to define how bonds of affinity and interdependence grow, the social worker is responsible for maximizing the worth of the beginning association between persons. Achieving clarity about what the participants expect from one another assures attitudes that are reality based. The establishment of functional communication patterns opens channels for the resolution of obstacles that would block relationship development. The social worker's presentation of himself with genuineness and integrity provides both a model for the client system and a means for diminishing maladaptive or game-playing behavior.

4. CLARIFICATION OF THE REALITIES AND BOUNDARIES OF SERVICE: By increasing the understanding of conditions and ground rules for service, ambiguity and confusion may be reduced, thereby releasing the energy needed for the problem-solving task. Fees or other obligations need to be stated and dealt with in terms of their implications. The frequency and timing of interviews, group meetings, or other means of contact not only establish order and continuity but also provide the client system with the security that time limits allow. In addition, there needs to be some clarity about what the change environment can and cannot offer. When there are specific limitations, alternatives need to be considered. Speculation about possible ends and goals has the effect of providing direction, offering realistic hope, and denoting that solution, on some level, is possible. Finally, the issue of confidentiality requires attention.

5. DISCLOSURE OF THE NATURE OF THE CHANGE PROCESS: In most instances, the assumption of the client role is accompanied by confusion as to how this new endeavor will work. The social worker can neither display a program nor visible technologies or artifacts that will give the client system some symbolic representation of what the process is all about. Thus the induction phase has much to do with both the demonstration and interpretation of the change experience. For example, the practitioner's direct and deliberate actions show how he can be helpful and how, through his genuine interest and commitment, the change relationship will differ from other attempts at problem solving. The client

begins to learn his responsibilities in the process (whether minimal or intense), particularly as he finds that there are no magical or ready-made solutions to the problem. The kinds of themes and information that are selectively considered begin to bring order and direction to the process and set in motion the problem-solving scheme.

6. THE EMERGENCE OF A COMMITMENT OR CONTRACT TO PROCEED: The culmination of the induction phase is the attainment of either a connotative or denotative expression of a personal investment in the change system as a short-term or long-range enterprise. This commitment not only assures at least the beginning involvement of the participants; it also serves to legitimize their respective roles. It confirms the rights, expectations, and autonomy of the members of the client system and grants the social worker the influence and right to intervene.

## B. The Strategies of Study and Evaluation
### Characteristics

Although these strategies are significant components of the induction phase of practice, they are also pervasive aspects of the succeeding phases and are present in all of the transactions with the change system. As will be seen, their characteristics differ in accord with the intent and purpose of each phase. At the outset of the social worker's encounter with the change system, he is engaged in a search for meaning and coherence in order to develop certain assumptions as a basis for planning and action. Increasingly, however, his intent is to involve the members of the client system in this endeavor as they evidence their readiness to do so. Study and evaluation are accomplished in three major ways which follow.

1. THROUGH PURPOSEFUL INQUIRY: This is the direct and planful acquisition of needed information that can be appropriately derived from the client system and/or the social environment. Examples include securing developmental data and social history, facts needed to determine eligibility for services, statistics, demographic data required for planning, and information from referral sources.

2. THROUGH OBSERVATION: The immediate transactions among the client system or between the client system and the social worker offer a rich source of knowledge. How persons interact and how they perceive their own roles or those of others offers some clues about their perception of self (individually and in relation), as well as their typical patterns of adaptation.

3. THROUGH VALIDATED INTUITION: Above and beyond rational cognitive processes, the practitioner may be able to sense and understand behaviors and conditions which have no apparent basis in fact. For example, he may perceive hostility cloaked in an aura of compliance, links between events that on the surface appear to have no relevance, or the impact of other conditions that would ordinarily seem to be out of relation with the problem at hand. However, to be useful, these intuitive reactions must be validated at some point as to how they correspond to reality.

## C. The Purposes of Study and Evaluation

These are multilevel strategies which are reflective of the complexities and breadth of the problems encountered in the practice situation. The search for meaning can never be complete; thus it must be conceived of as a joint quest that will build the substance of learning, action, testing and resolution, frequently in repetitious or cyclical terms.

1. TO DISCLOSE THE NATURE OF THE NEED OR DIFFICULTY: An obvious purpose of the collection and assessment of information is to crystallize and place in proper context the problem requiring the mutual attention of the participants. This endeavor refines and defines the problem and provides a basis for continued exploration, intervention, learning, and change. Meaning is thereby given to the encounter, a sense of direction is achieved, order succeeds ambiguity, and the function of the participants relative to desired changes is confirmed.

2. TO DETERMINE THE SIGNIFICANCE AND MEANING OF THE NEED OR DIFFICULTY FOR THE CLIENT SYSTEM OR RELEVANT OTHERS: The identification of the problem provides one of its dimensions; another dimension is how its seriousness or import is perceived by those persons affected by it. For example, severe social problems may be rampant within a particular neighborhood, or a family may be caught in a series of crises. How or whether these conditions are experienced by these persons tells something about how they perceive their world, if and how they will participate in the change process, and thus the approach that the practitioner will need to take to engage them in efforts aimed at amelioration.

3. TO UNDERSTAND THE CONDITIONS WHICH PRECIPITATED ENTRY INTO THE CHANGE SETTING: In most instances, the problem has existed for some time before it has come to the attention of the professional or his setting. The timing of entry may well tell something about the toler-

ance, motivation, and anxiety level of members of the client system. Similarly, whether contact was self-initiated or accomplished through the efforts of others provides some clues about the awareness, investment, and expectations of those involved.

4. TO ASSESS THE LOCUS OF THE PROBLEM: Here we go beyond the definition of the problem to determine where its sources are located within the relevant social systems. For example, a child's learning problem may be attributed to personal deficits, family tensions, peer relations, or discontinuities in the educational system. The use of a social systems framework assists in the determination of the potent personal, interpersonal, social, environmental, or societal factors that impinge on the problem and therefore helps determine the most effective point of entry and possible goals.

5. TO DETERMINE IF AND HOW THE IDENTIFIED PROBLEM IS RELATED TO THE ADAPTIVE NEEDS OF THE CLIENT SYSTEM: If behavior, individual or collective, is seen as purposeful, it is necessary to understand how it serves the system in how it adjusts to its particular social environment or in how it maintains itself. Thus the social worker's plan and interventions will be governed by this understanding. How he approaches the residents of slum housing who have nowhere else to go or the seemingly paranoid patient who fears attack will be affected by his knowledge of why these behaviors are so persistent.

6. TO DETERMINE THE SIGNIFICANT FACTORS THAT CONTRIBUTE TO THE CONTINUITY OF THE DIFFICULTY OR NEED: While this aspect of assessment is similar to the fourth point, it also serves to sort out those conditions which maintain the force of the problem in transactional terms. That is, while certain practices employed by a social institution may be oppressive to certain population groups, it is equally important to understand how those groups react to these practices. For instance, a group's actions may seem to provide justification for or conflict with these practices and thereby give credence to them. In addition, the duration and chronicity of factors that bear on any problem may reveal typical coping mechanisms and the extent to which these factors are accessible to change.

7. TO IDENTIFY AVAILABLE RESOURCES, STRENGTHS, AND MOTIVATIONS: Of no less importance than the more negative conditions cited thus far are the latent or obvious strengths within or outside the immediate system that can be called upon. It is much too easy to become overly concerned with the dysfunctional elements to the exclusion of

strengths. Consider, for instance, the substantial character of persons who can endure poverty, alienation, and social deprivations of all sorts. How does the person labeled "psychotic" cope with his fears, his isolation, or the dehumanizing nature of many mental hospitals? How do many families maintain themselves when there seems to be no end to a string of crises?

8. TO INVOLVE THE CLIENT SYSTEM IN AN ORDERLY PROCESS OF PROBLEM SOLVING: The very process of striving for a more structured and orderly way of gaining information and placing this information in a more rational frame has an educative quality. Judgment and decision making are enhanced, and the client system, is enabled to learn more productive means of perceiving, thinking, learning, and acting.

9. TO DETERMINE THE APPROPRIATE MODALITY OF SERVICE: The strategy of study and evaluation leads to some assumptions about the form of human association that will provide the most meaningful context for problem solving. The evaluation of whether the one-to-one relationship, a group experience, or collaborative contact with others will be most useful derives from what is learned about the problem/client system configuration.

## D. The Content of Study and Evaluation of Client Systems

Before we consider the specific elements of major client systems that are subject to evaluation it is important to note that the format that is used in no way suggests a departure from the social systems orientation described earlier. No schema currently exists within which it would be possible to order a simultaneous appraisal of various systems in interaction. In addition, each system or social unit can only be studied in accord with certain conceptual schemes—the individual in terms of personality factors and larger systems in relation to interaction, group dynamics, organizational theories, and constructs. Yet it is apparent that analysis of the individual cannot omit evaluation of the family, group, organization, or community with which he interacts. The study of any organization has to take into account the characteristics of the groups that comprise it as well as the persons who are moving forces within them.

Hence, as we begin to survey the strategies of assessment in a progression from the smallest to the largest systems, the reader is encouraged to keep in mind the linkages between these systems. In short, he is asked to establish these linkages in his own mind by perceiving the individual as an interactor within his group, the group as a force within larger systems, and the like.

1. FACTORS IN THE STUDY AND EVALUATION OF THE INDIVIDUAL IN ANY SYSTEM (DYAD, FAMILY, SMALL GROUP, ORGANIZATION, COMMUNITY)

a. PRECONTACT FACTORS: Certain initial assumptions (subject to later evaluation) can be gained from knowledge about events or conditions preceding actual entry into the change setting.

(1) Factual data drawn from application forms, letters, and phone conversations sensitizes the social worker to certain characteristics of the client system and problem. This awareness effects a state of readiness and preparation, and in addition, the use of this knowledge conveys to the members of the system some sense of worth and importance.

(2) Knowledge about how the individual became known to the change setting (i.e., voluntarily or as a consequence of the influential activity of others) alerts the social worker to the kinds of attitudes and motivations that the person brings into the interview.

(3) The conditions that brought about entry at this point in time relative to the severity or longevity of the problem can be informative. Does this timing indicate an immediate reaction to an acutely critical situation, an inability to continue to endure a chronic predicament, or an impulsive act?

b. CONSTITUTIONAL FACTORS: These are, briefly, the discernible physical and intellectual states that bear on the nature of the problem and may affect participation in the change experience.

(1) The presence of physical illness or disability affects not only how the individual can enter into the change experience relative to energy potential but also the focus of the endeavor. The extent to which the condition affects perception of the problem needs to be taken into account, as does the influence of significant others on the continuity or possible cure of the illness.

(2) Current and potential levels of intellectual functioning have a profound affect on the problem-solving process. The level of cognitive development will determine how the person deals with language and symbols and the style with which he engages in problem solving. His perceptual abilities reflect how he sees his world and

translates events around him. What requires appraisal is the capability for improved intellectual functioning and the environmental, social, and internal conditions that impede it.

c. SOCIO-ECONOMIC FACTORS: These refer to the situational, concrete, and cultural factors which may either be the source of the difficulty or bear directly on it.

(1) Economic factors have both substantive and psychological meanings. Adequacy of income and level of subsistence obviously affect one's style of life, aspirations, perception of self-worth, and value system. How the person characteristically uses money provides some clues as to patterns of adjustment.

(2) A person's type of employment and attitudes about it are indicators of his aspirations and identity. Patterns of employment may reveal, for example, strivings for security at any cost on one extreme (when one clings rigidly to his job), or instability or nomadic searching on the other extreme (when the employment history is discontinuous).

(3) Cultural, ethnic, or racial identifications are key factors, particularly as they are understood from the individual's point of view. To what extent do they offer a sense of identity and belonging? It is also important to sort out the meanings of behavior in cultural terms, especially when the client and the social worker represent different cultures. Deviant behavior may well reflect cultural differences rather than internal psychopatholgy.

(4) Similarly, religious identifications are linked with attitudinal and behavioral states, for they are indicators of significant value systems, norms, and practices.

d. PERSONAL VALUES AND GOALS: While this aspect of evaluation is selected for consideration in its own right, it is a factor that permeates, if not determines, all other factors. While it is important to achieve some understanding of the individual's preferences and aspirations—in short, what he wants and expects out of life—the following qualifications need to be considered.

(1) The presence or absence of congruence between the person's values and how they are expressed in action point to patterns of adaptation. Does he use compromise, denial, and the like in dealing with the dysjunction between belief and behavior, and what are the costs to the person? Or does he strive for consistency?

(2) Whether there is congruence between the individual's values

and those of his immediate system or society has to be assessed as a possible source of conflict. For example, a seemingly rebellious member of a bureaucracy desires to modify a rigid or prejudicial practice or a so-called "unfaithful husband" seeks meaningful fulfillment outside a deteriorating marriage. What patterns are apparent—conformity, compromise, deviance, or authenticity?

e. ADAPTIVE FUNCTIONS: On another level, these functions allude to the behavior patterns typically used by the individual to resolve conflicts in social and interpersonal relations so as achieve some degree of security and to diminish anxiety. In short, they refer to how the person copes with his social world.

(1) The manner with which one presents himself to others, particularly within the stressful change setting, offers some general clues. How one is attired may indicate something about his self-image. His posture, or what has been referred to as "body language" may show how he views himself in relation to others or how he perceives the other.

(2) Styles of communication, both verbal and nonverbal, may symbolize how the individual attempts to link himself (or to avoid linkage) with others. Thus both the literal and latent implications of his messages need to be understood. The affect and posture that accompany the words illuminate their real meanings, as does the timing and implications of what is said. In addition, how the person deals with conflict or differences may be revealed in communication patterns that tend to confirm, disqualify, or avoid his own or other's beliefs, ideas, or commitments. Finally, the level of ability to express appropriate emotions may be an indicator of constriction, inhibition, denial, spontaneity, or freedom.

(3) The presence of symptoms or symptomatic behavior, a most complex aspect of personality, may also be considered a form of communication. Briefly, what does the symptom do for the individual as an adaptive technique?

(4) Similarly, behavioral patterns that become visible can disclose the modes typically used to achieve certain ends. One may attempt to achieve control over his social environment by overly aggressive behavior that minimizes the potency of others, or one may engage in compulsive behavior that keeps the world orderly and in control. Behavior may have as its purpose the control of what are felt as undesirable or fearful impulses, drives, or needs.

The achievement of certain types of gratification may be another end, as exemplified by the overly dependent or exploitive individual. Or he may act in ways that attempt to compensate for assumed lacks (for example, the tyrannical father who questions his own competence). In the final analysis, these patterns may also signify the individual's perception of self—the balance between feelings of competency and adequacy and those of self-debasement and self-doubt.

(5) The social roles that one assumes and has ascribed to him open a significant source of understanding. The competency with which he acts out these roles (masculine, feminine, parental, marital, vocational, leadership, etc.) aids in determining how personal and social needs are fulfilled. Further, there needs to be sufficient clarity about how the individual views his role and his own expectations about that role. In turn, this needs to be matched with the expectations of significant others about that same role. Of importance, then, is the extent to which there is congruence between the diverse roles that each person carries and the expectations about them that are held (role adequacy). Thus the inconsistent behavior of a parent may be a consequence of different perceptions of his role by himself, his mate, and his child. At the same time he may perform quite adequately in his roles as businessman, community leader, and the like. The value of the social role concept enables the social worker to move from a global view of behavior to a more selective appraisal of aspects of strength and dysfunction in social performance.

(6) As previously noted, persons enter into relationships with others for the gratification of certain affiliative needs. Drawing from both the observed behavior in immediately visible relationships and the reported behavior it is possible to determine the kinds of gratification sought, whether this gratification is in reality available, and the means used to gain it. Hence, some persons may seek healthy forms of authentication in their relationships but may find that others merely want to play games. Or conversely, the individual may use relationships to repeatedly justify his certainty that he will inevitably be rejected. Again, how all of the pertinent actors participate in the relationship process must be viewed transactionally.

Relational behavior may disclose, first of all, the person's capacity for intimacy. How capable is he in involving himself with others, and depending on the level of intimacy expected for the particular dyadic or group change relationship, what can be anticipated in these terms? Second, these observations point to the existing balance between independence and dependence. In what aspects of living can the individual function independently yet permit himself to depend on others? Conversely, does he see himself as helpless and needy, refuting an ability to manage certain aspects of his life? Finally, and in more general terms, does he evidence a tendency to be accepting and open in his relationships with others, or on the other extreme, is he cynical and exploitative?

f. DEVELOPMENTAL FACTORS: Thus far we have dealt with indices of the here and now of personal adjustment. What these factors do not reveal are the historical and experiential events that shaped the evolvement of the individual's unique patterns of perception, learning, and behavior. That is, while two persons may perform their social roles quite similarly, the conditions that disposed these persons toward these behaviors might differ considerably and thereby pose quite different implications for planning and change.

(1) Complementing the earlier discussion of role adequacy, we are now concerned with chronological development, with role development and maturity. First, it is important to know the kinds of learning that one was exposed to that would enable him to or would block him from understanding the ingredients of a particular role. For example, a man raised in a totally female environment might conceivably find some difficulty in assuming certain masculine roles and may be confused by the expectations that are made of him. Second, role performance needs to be equated with particular life stages. The expected inconsistent behavior of the adolescent would appear irrational when seen in the patterns of the newly married young adult. Or we are struck by the incongruities of persons in their middle years who refuse to yield their identity with the younger set.

(2) The actual events in a person's life are not as important here as how they are perceived and used for present adaptive purposes. One cannot adequately report on his own history. Memories of early childhood experiences must in themselves be inaccurate because they were either perceived through the eyes of a child or later translated by an adult far removed from the actual event. In

addition, the reporter can only present his version of the event and therefore has to omit the transactional dimension. Finally, any report inevitably carries with it a self-justifying quality; we tend to describe that which conforms with some needed views of our world. Hence, the impressions, the selectivity that is used, what may be omitted, and the purpose and timing of the report may hold more value than the description of the event itself. So while facts about one's family or certain significant events will add to a growing appreciation of the individuality of that person, how these are interpreted and used in the service of adjustment and identification gives richness and meaning to the immediate circumstances in his life. It is well to add that the client's impressions of certain successes, failures, and losses are of some moment. Views of himself as a martyr, a victim, or a master may be rooted in these events.

(3) In more specific terms, we are interested here in the particular way in which the individual has dealt with tasks, conflicts, or problems in the past as a basis for determining the presence of certain abilities or the need for new tactics. With what level of efficiency did he cope with his circumstances, how did he engage others in the endeavor, what kind of results were achieved, and what is his appraisal of the episode? Is there, for example, a surfeit of confidence that would enable him to attack the current problem with some assurance, or has a series of perceived defeats placed him in a disabled state? This knowledge has still other values. First, the exploration of these past events may make conscious that which has become lost to awareness in relation to specific skills and competencies. That is, as the client becomes aware of how he has coped with past problems, long-forgotten techniques may become accessible to current use. Second, this knowledge may illuminate the possibility that the uniqueness of the current problem has no precedent in prior problem-solving experiences. The client may be totally befuddled because he has no previous point of reference that can be used to guide him in the present event. This, in turn, directs the social worker regarding the nature of his interventions.

g. EMERGING ATTITUDES ABOUT THE CHANGE EXPERIENCE: Equally significant and not separable from the assessment of the individual per se are his responses and reactions to his beginning involvement in the dyadic or group context for change. In fact, without this appraisal, the foregoing can become meaningless because it is useful and purposeful only in relation to its application to a change process that requires the investment of that individual. Hence, it is important to gain some understanding of the individual's level of motivation and interest and the conditions that sustain or diminish this motivation. These might include factors of dissonance, confusion, or uncertainty that need reduction or clarification. Finally, the consummate importance of this knowledge lies in the readiness and capacity for a personal commitment to the role and responsibility of a client participating in the change experience.

2. FACTORS IN THE STUDY AND EVALUATION OF THE FAMILY: The assessment of the family as well as that of the small group requires movement into other orders and concepts of study. Here we will utilize systemic, relational, and transactional concepts in order to gain some impressions of these social units as acting, purpose-oriented organisms. Inevitably, these units, and organizations and communities as well, need to be understood as composites of individuals and as structures that can be identified by their unique qualities and characteristics.

a. THE FAMILY AS A SOCIAL SYSTEM: As previously described, a systems orientation provides a valuable tool for the analysis of the structural and functional variables of the unit in its own right and of where it stands in relation to other significant systems.

(1) The family has a relationship to contiguous systems. In that any family is a responsive and contributing unit within a network of other social units, no assessment can be complete without some understanding of its position within these systems. The reader is referred to the earlier discussion of the fictional Wright family regarding boundaries and their permeability or rigidity. This knowledge can provide an appreciation of the extent to which the family is either isolated from the input of other systems or is disabled by it. Similarly, the nature of the input with which the family is attempting to cope may indicate the attitudes held toward the family by other groups or organizations, the visibility of the family, and the demands that are made upon the members. Hence, the family receiving public welfare or beset by chronic illness has to deal with the kind of label that is placed on it, the bureaucratization that accompanies the use of public services, and the input from the various authority figures who in some measure determine how that family is supposed to act. Still another factor is the extent to which

the family fits into the cultural mold and expectations of the larger system in which it is located or the degree to which it is considered deviant. This measure affects how the family can maintain relative autonomy. Consider as a case in point the black family that moves into white suburbia or the communal family group in a middle class neighborhood.

(2) Concerning the roles and status of respective family members, we are interested in two levels of role performance: the formal roles of husband, wife, parent, son, daughter, or sibling (this does not exclude the roles of other members in the case of the extended family); and such informal roles as scapegoat, decision maker, controller, follower, and the like. In the first instance, the roles are mainly assumed; in the latter, they tend to be ascribed. Thus the structure of the family comes into clearer view as these roles are delineated in terms of the specific individuals who carry these roles and their interactional implications in relation to the other members who complement them. For instance, an understanding of the decision-making role must include the conditions under which decisions are made, who supports or permits these decisions, and who is affected by them.

Once these roles are identified, assessment of the degree of concordance about them follows. The extent to which family members agree about the assignment of roles and how they are to be performed is an index of family unity and cohesiveness. And one must consider how the various roles are interrelated. Do they make for some kind of "fit" within the total configuration of the family and sustain or fragment family stability?

(3) The stability of any system is maintained by a set of rules that provide order and determine interaction. In most instances, these rules exist beyond the conscious awareness of the family members; they develop over time and become patterned ways of dealing with the vicissitudes of family living. As a consequence, the social worker can become aware of them through such means as observing the family in interaction, a visit to the home, or in lieu of these, by asking the family to describe the details of typical daily experiences. In this way he can determine those rules that tend to reinforce stability, those which nurture maladaptation, the extent to which they are subject to modification, and how their conformation defines the family's unique life style.

(4) Related to the preceding factors is the peculiar way the family being observed communicates and provides information to its members, conducts its business, uses symbols, imposes controls, and so forth. Again, how the system operates in these terms obtains from observation. An understanding of the communication network discloses who sends the major messages about what elements of family. The quality of these messages—their clarity, ambiguity, or latent content—is equally significant. Do members rely on threat, seduction, or reward in imposing controls or in the attempt to gain forms of gratification? Are the messages of the type that clearly indicate the kind of behavior that is expected in response, or is the listener left in a quandary as to what he is supposed to do and the sanctions that will be imposed if he does not do it?

b. DEVELOPMENTAL STAGE OF THE FAMILY: This factor places the problem within the context of the phases that families progress through beginning at the point of marriage and moving through the arrival of children, the middle years, the emancipation of children, retirement, and preparations for death. Thus conditions that may be problematical for one stage may be typical of transitional adaptive processes at another. As the development of the family is viewed retrospectively, it is important to determine the ways and means of problem solving at earlier stages as well as the shifts in role responsibilities that have occurred over time. To illustrate, the mother who was the homemaker at one point and then went to work would effect some change in certain areas of responsibility and the management of the children.

c. SUBSYSTEMS OPERATING WITHIN THE FAMILY: These would include the marital pair or certain parent-child and sibling relationships. At various points in time, around certain issues, or as a consequence of a particular affinity, alliances form within a family that are purposeful and have some sense of continuity. Assessment of these subgroups would aim at determining their function in regard to family stability and how they complement or conflict with other subsystems or the family as a whole.

d. PHYSICAL AND EMOTIONAL NEEDS: From the array of needs that family life is designed to meet, it is possible to sort out those that are most exigent for the family's stability and structure. These may well be indicative of the level on which the family is currently functioning, particularly if we see essential needs arranged in a hierarchical structure that requires fulfillment on one level before the next order of needs can be pursued. Hence, the family that is concerned with biological needs (the problems of health and well-being) would have difficulty amassing the energy necessary to seek out fulfillment of its social needs. Similarly, families on the latter level of functioning would not yet be ready to focus on the gratification of more creative needs that involve the pursuit of individual strivings. More than one neophyte social worker has been perplexed about why members of a family cannot muster much exuberance about the education of their children when, at the time, they are caught up with the fact that the children are suffering from poor nutrition.

In that the family is composed of distinct individuals, each with his own set of needs, it is essential that existing disparities be appraised both in relation to their meanings for the individual and in their implications for the family as a whole. What the family may label as deviant or delinquent may, in fact, represent the attempt of one member to fulfill certain healthy strivings for autonomy that run counter to the essential values of the family as a unit. Hence, the constraints or permissions that the family sets forth need to be noted.

Finally, the social worker needs to evaluate whether there are sources available either within the family itself or in the social environment for the gratification of the specified needs.

e. GOALS, VALUES, AND ASPIRATIONS: Again, these issues touch on all of the factors that come within the purview of study and evaluation. To what extent are the family's aims and values articulated and understood by the various members? Are they indicative of the family's true potential, or are they reflective of resignation or compromise? And again we come upon the matter of differentiation, the extent to which the family will permit the pursuit of individual values and goals.

f. SOCIO-ECONOMIC FACTORS: This category corresponds with that described in the study and evaluation of the individual except that here we focus on how certain shared beliefs and matters of heritage and identification provide the essential fabric that gives the family its structure and patternings. Ethnicity, class, or culture may well be the core of the family's stability, the source of control, or the basis of its norms and values. Some families may suffer from the transition from one set of cultural beliefs to another or may be aimless and bereft of any identification.

3. FACTORS IN THE STUDY AND EVALUATION OF SMALL GROUPS: Knowledge of the structure and dynamics of small groups is basic to the understanding of any and all of the other social units encountered in social work practice. As was previously noted, the full appreciation and meaning of the traits and sentiments of individuals cannot be achieved without some apprehension of the individual as an interacting member of his groups. We can also understand the family as a small group that has the added ingredients of primary kinship, need fulfillment, and affiliation. The study of organizations, it will be seen, includes consideration of their inter- and intragroup processes. And similarly, communities can be understood, in part, as a composite of intergroup linkages.

A salient characteristic that distinguishes the typical small group from other social units is the process by which some aggregation of persons begins to form itself into a definable group structure that has purpose, stability, and a sense of direction. It is this phase of group development that will be discussed here by the use of a framework that includes the functional, structural, and interactional characteristics of group formation.

a. FUNCTIONAL CHARACTERISTICS: These are the factors which determine what the group is all about, how it develops its purpose and takes on direction, and consequently, how it operates.

(1) How the group came to be is a major determinant of its function and therefore is an indicator of the social worker's role as its leader. Groups usually form in one of two ways. First, there are the naturally formed groups exemplified by a neighborhood group of adolescents or a special interest or friendship group growing out of affiliations in vocational or organizational settings. These groups can be characterized by an explicit or implicit sharing of common interests, values, and goals.

Second, groups may be formed by the efforts of such outside agents as recreational, psychotherapeutic, or task-oriented settings. These groups tend to have more prescribed functions and, in contrast to the naturally formed groups, have the task of developing and articulating their values, norms, and goals. As can be seen, the role of the social worker would differ considerably with each type of group. In the first type, he would have to gain entry into an existing organism and in some measure adapt to its function and value system. In the second, a major aspect of his role would be to facilitate the emergence and development of that group's properties.

(2) What the group's objectives are has direct meaning for the content it will deal with, the formality with which it is structured, and the quality and intensity of the relationships and interactions within it. The following are broad categorizations of types of groups and their purposes.

(a) AFFILIATIVE, FRIENDSHIP, AND SOCIAL GROUPS: These tend to place the greatest emphasis on their continuity and cohesiveness. The mutuality and satisfaction derived from positive social interaction are the major goals and purposes of these groups. Hence, there is a tendency to avoid conflict and to stress homogeneity and identification.

(b) TASK-ORIENTED GROUPS: Committees and social action or ad hoc groups created to achieve specific ends or to resolve certain problems fall into this category. While personal or interpersonal rewards and satisfactions may accrue from interaction, these outcomes are secondary to the work that has to be done on the task at hand. Consequently, the group's emphasis is on substantive rather than affective content.

(c) PERSONAL CHANGE GROUPS: A broad array of groups is covered here—those which may be loosely termed as psychotherapeutic as well as T-groups and encounter groups. Their purpose is to effect some change in the behavior, perception, attitudes, or ways in which persons typically relate to one another. While it is possible that these changes may evolve out of any group experience, in this instance personal change represents the major thrust of the group's efforts. The tensions and strains that are inherent in change experiences direct the focus of these groups to the dynamics of interpersonal behavior within a context that provides a balance of vulnerability and support. Emphasis, therefore, is on both psychological and social content.

(d) ROLE ENHANCEMENT AND DEVELOPMENT GROUPS: These include recreational, educational, and interest clusters that are designed to increase knowledge, understanding, or performance in certain aspects of a role (e.g., parent education, certain adolescent groups, and prerelease planning groups). While these groups may vary in the degree of explicitness of purpose, they generally are aimed at factors related to role expectations, identifications, and functions. The emphasis here is on the rewards and gratifications derived from participation, observation and learning, and the support for improved performance.

(3) Another factor that determines function is the way in which the group is affected by or is representative of other groups in immediate or contiguous systems. That is, how a group is perceived or perceives itself as conforming to or deviating from outside values will impinge on how it operates. The group that appears to be deviant may quickly develop strong bonds among its members as a defense against outside pressures or, conversely, may suffer some loss of cohesiveness because of a preoccupation with external rather than internal conditions. Examples might include certain social action groups whose attempts at reform run counter to prevailing values, adolescent groups that make their differences visible by styles of dress and behavior, or patient groups which seek change in hospital procedures.

b. STRUCTURAL FACTORS: These are the conditions within a particular group which give it its particular configuration and which bear on how the group operates and carries out its function.

(1) How the membership of a group is selected and how new members gain entry has a great deal to do with the group's form and substance and governs the social worker's role. The readiness of a group to accept new members is indicative of its tolerance for change or its need to maintain rather unyielding boundaries. It is important to ascertain what resistance to new membership might mean in terms of the quality of existing relationships, certain fears, or perhaps some apprehension of the loss of continuity. Finally, there is the question of qualifications, not merely for entry but for assimilation into the group. Does the group put the new member through a period of probation? Are there rituals, formal or implicit, that the group applies? Are these generalized practices or those imposed by certain persons or substructures?

(2) Obviously, the persons who comprise the group will give it its unique character and differentiate that group from all other groups. Of significance, first of all, are the personalities of the individual members and their needs, motivations, and behavior patterns. This underscores the fact that although the individual member makes certain adaptations in order to become an interacting member who identifies with the group, he in no way loses

his individuality and thereby contributes to the peculiar complexion of his group. Another dimension of a group's composition is the extent to which and the areas within which there is homogeneity or heterogeneity. Homogeneous groups tend to achieve cohesiveness more rapidly than those that are marked by sharp differences in attitudes, values, and personality. Yet where differences exist, there is a greater opportunity for exchange, for a contrast of viewpoints and values. Thus a measure of the group's heterogeneity lies in its ability to capitalize on its differences for the benefit of its members and to utilize support and reinforcement for valued similarities.

When the social worker begins to work with an existing group, he will have to contend with values and behaviors that may be well institutionalized within the group's structure. His first task will then be the assessment of the factors of composition, heterogeneity, and homogeneity. When the social worker initiates the formation of the group, membership selection and the balance between similarities and differences becomes a knotty problem. Intelligence is a prime factor in selection because it has much to do with the members' facility in communicating with each other. Where marked disparities exist, the members face a formidable obstacle to gaining real understanding of one another's beliefs, ideas, intentions, and feelings. Knowledge of the prospective members' value systems enables the social worker to make some judgment about the extent to which there can be opposing beliefs within the group and where mutuality is needed. This decision is based on the purposes of the group. For example, a task-oriented group may be constructed on the basis of shared commitments about a certain end whereas a psychotherapy group may profit from the presence of sharply opposed value systems. The age of the members may or may not have bearing on the structure of the group. In an adult group that has a common purpose and value system, age differences may be of minor consequence. In an adolescent group, the interests and activities of, say, a thirteen year old and a seventeen year old would differ markedly and impede mutuality. Factors of sex, social status, culture, and the like need to be taken into consideration in relation to the particular group, its function, and its purpose.

(3) The presence of subgroups—pairs, factions, or cliques—

within a group discloses a great deal about the makeup of that group. These subgroups may persist over time or may be transient affiliations that arise and disappear as the group moves through its various stages.

The composition and nature of the relationships that comprise these subgroups are subject to scrutiny. What is their reason for being? What prompted their emergence? Another question is whether they are in accord with or in opposition to the group's values and purposes. Do they represent an enclave of resistance, a source of security for its members, or a force that can be used to further the group's aims?

(4) The nature and locus of authority and control relates to the issues of leadership, the hierarchy of positions within the group, and the location and use of power as it impinges on the structure of the group.

First, there is the prime matter of the social worker's role as a leader of the group. How he perceives his role, how it is perceived by the members individually and in concert, and the extent to which there is congruence in these perceptions governs how the group works together. Does he see himself and is he seen as one who provides direction, establishes rules, encourages democratic participation, explains, and teaches? Does the group turn to him for decisions, or do they use his expertise in arriving at their own? In short, in which way does the group legitimize his role as a leader, and transactionally, how does he carry out this role as an influential force?

Second, a leadership role that is formally assigned or tacitly accepted and understood will emerge within the group. Whether this role is merited or assumed through power tactics, how it is perceived by the membership, and what it achieves in terms of the group's intent are significant for the structure and operation of that group.

Finally, the matter of how decisions are made, which can also be considered as an interactional factor, symbolizes something about the structure of the group. Who participates in the process, the amount of agreement or disagreement that is generated, how conflict is dealt with, and the kinds of patterns that evolve may reveal a great deal about the hierarchy of power within the group. For example, one group may rely without question on the decisions of certain members whereas another may insist on consensus or equality of participation in all instances.

c. INTERACTIONAL FACTORS: Here we come to the quality, meaning, and nature of the interchanges that take place within the group. These are the vital characteristics of any group, the real expression of its life, purpose and function

(1) Of immense importance are the norms and values, the rules and guiding beliefs that develop out of the transactional process and which serve to maintain the system, provide guidelines for performance, and ease any power differentials. These may be expressed formally as in the rules and procedures of a club or informally as in tacit agreement among the members. Norms may be observed in the constraints that govern what may or may not be discussed, priorities, who takes the lead and who follows, and the apparent rewards for adherence or the sanctions applied in the case of deviance.

(2) The quality, depth, and nature of the relationships that form and grow are measures of the character of the group. How members interact with one another (e.g., whether formally or informally, competitively or cooperatively, with freedom to be intimate or a tendency toward constraint) reveals prevalent attitudes and the type of personal behaviors transferred to the group relationships that nurture or impede healthy social interaction.

(3) The concept of cohesiveness encompasses all of the preceding group characteristics, for it is indicative of the extent of "groupness" that prevails. In more specific terms, cohesiveness refers to the degree to which the members have begun to experience a sense of interdependence as expressed through individual commitments to the group's continuity and value. It is also apparent in the extent to which members tend to share common perceptions of the group's purposes, norms, and goals. In most instances, these attitudes and feelings do not find direct expression; instead, they are manifested in a shift in value hierarchies, in loyalties, and in the tendency to resist threats to the group's continuity from either internal or external sources.

4. FACTORS IN THE STUDY AND EVALUATION OF ORGANIZATIONS: The complexity of organizations would make it possible to study them from a number of vantage points and according to a variety of frameworks. What we will be seeking here is a beginning grasp of the ethos of an

organization, its manifest characteristics and its human components. The intent is to provide the reader with a means of analyzing an organization through the examination of certain specific parts which contribute to its organismic state. Hence, whether the social worker is dealing with the organization that hosts his practice, one that is the target of practice itself, or an organization that in some way bears on his practice, it is essential that he understand it not as an immutable monolith but as a product and composite of human needs, values, and interactions.

a. THE ORGANIZATION AS A SYSTEM WITH A MANDATE

(1) The organizational task, its particular mission within the social structure, gives the organization visibility. Of importance is the clarity with which its task is enunciated, for it takes into account how this task is perceived by the organization's members as well as by its constituents. From this appraisal it is possible to determine the presence of certain discontinuities and misconceptions and whether they are a consequence of inadequate interpretation or the manner in which the organization's mandate is implemented.

In addition, the task of the organization can be measured against the type of social problem or condition with which it was designed to deal. We will consider this point further in the discussion of the competence of the organization.

(2) Individual and group roles are relevant to the task, for beyond the task itself, we are interested in the human element. Who are the persons who have responsibility for carrying out the mandate of the organization? Whether they are designated as administrative, supervisory, professional, paraprofessional, or voluntary personnel, what are the elements and parameters of their respective roles? In addition, is there congruence between expected and actual role behavior and between how these roles are perceived by the role bearer and by others? The significance of these issues comes to our attention when we attempt to locate services or get something done by an organization and, with increasing frustration, find ourselves being passed about because some of the staff are confused about who is to do what despite a profusion of titles and ranks.

At times it is possible to cut through this confusion if we come to understand which roles are appointed and which are delegated, assumed, or earned. Thus it is not uncommon to find that a particular clerical worker who has assumed the responsibility can provide the needed information or services more readily than the professional or administrator for whom she works.

(3) The location of the organization within a system of organizations is also important. How the particular organization fulfills its function depends, in part, on where it stands within the network of relevant organizations. This takes into account, first, the definition of the population group it is designed to serve and the kind of problem or task for which it is accountable.

Second is the question of the organization's isolation from or cohesion with other pertinent organizations. Is the organization an anomaly within its community, or does it correspond with the efforts of other organizations? Consider the different statuses of the store front setting that treats such residual problems as addiction and runaways and a community-sponsored child guidance center. The former may find itself having to be totally self-sufficient because it is dealing with a deviant population, whereas the latter may have easy access to the resources of other organizations. Consequently, the quality of interorganizational communication is a significant point, as is the way the organization manages the input from external sources.

b. THE CULTURE OF THE ORGANIZATION: By definition, these are the shared characteristics that give the organization its identity.

(1) The style with which the organization operates and its goal direction are governed by the explicitly or implicitly shared persuasions of its members. These governing beliefs may be derived from formal sources or may come forth somewhat adventitiously.

In the former case, the beliefs may be a direct consequence of the legal mandate of the organization which defines its purpose and/or its founding ideologies. Why the organization came to be may be the basis of a pervasive doctrine or conviction. Other formal sources are the prevailing theories that guide organizational action. These may include theories about social disorganization, personality, or technology. Finally the source of a governing ideology may be a manual of operations that serves to spell out in definitive terms how the organization is to operate.

The more adventitious sources of belief may be a consequence of many factors. Over a period of time the expectations and attitudes of the members of an organization may change, or the value system of the social structure may undergo transition. The substitution of professionally trained for previously untrained staff, the emergence of new explanations of personal or social disorganization, shifts in attitudes about families and sex, or changes in the demographic nature of the community are examples of factors that can contribute to the modulation of previous beliefs.

(2) The modes of interaction that are typically used with either external supporting groups or within and among groups and individuals in the organization gives that organization its peculiar character. Whether interaction takes the form of ritual, deference to authority and the hierarchical structure, and the use of formal channels of communication or persons or groups tend to interact in more informal ways reveals a great deal about the perceptions of its members and its structure.

(3) Culture is also determined by the typical resources, methods, and procedures that are used to accomplish tasks—the organization's technologies. It can be seen that organizations that provide commodities and such material needs as financial aid, housing, and health care will differ in their generally shared beliefs from those that provide such services as counseling, institutional care, education, and information. Both will also diverge from the beliefs held by organizations that have other functions—investigation, social control, and planning and coordination, for example.

(4) The importance of the technology of the organization as a cultural factor is evident in the distinctive ways in which its tasks and functions are implemented. The particular jargon that is employed tends to characterize its membership. New entrants into the organization, whether employees or constituents, find themselves needing to learn proper modes of communication. The routine and protocol that are followed become ingrained types of organizational behavior. The techniques and skills that are used to accomplish the task also become part of the culture. These and other factors coalesce into a style of action that typifies the organization as perhaps client centered versus organization centered, as creative versus routinized, or as formal versus informal.

c. THE COMPETENCE OF THE ORGANIZATION: A critical element in the assessment process is the capability of the organization to carry out its mission. The following are more evident factors that serve as measures of competence.

(1) Such material items as the availability and adequacy of funds, a suitable physical plant, and necessary equipment comprise one aspect of the organization's resources. Others that make the preceding resources viable are the human resources—the expertise, knowledge, motivation, and morale of the persons who carry out the purpose of the organization.

(2) The organization's special scope of authority is another important factor. Here we are not only concerned with the particular forms of knowledge and ability that are contained within the organization but with how the community and the organization's constituents ascribe authority to it and thereby legitimize the organization's competence.

(3) The special status, force, and control held by the organization in relation to its position within the larger system affects how it can bring its influence to bear in fulfilling its purpose. One variable is the kind of power that is delegated to it by the system or its supporting body. Another variable is its status among other organizations in terms of its prestige and its ability to get its share of available resources.

(4) Inevitably, the competence of an organization is linked with the effectiveness of its plans and programs. This includes, first, the merit of guiding policies as well as their flexibility and responsiveness to the changing nature of the task. Second is the efficiency of internal decision-making processes as they affect how the problem is attacked. Finally, there is the question of whether the organization has available or has access to the information required for planning as well as the planners who can design effective programs and procedures.

(5) Again, in relation to the human factor, the level of morale of the organization's members, their depth of commitment to the task, and the cohesiveness of their attitudes and beliefs about the worth of the organization's mission will determine, in the end, how its purpose is executed.

(6) We have dealt, thus far, with the individual factors that build into the evaluation of the organization as a whole. An overriding issue is synergism, the degree to which these factors combine

or the extent to which there is coperative effort between organizations that produces more than the sum of the parts. While a committee made up of representatives of various organizations may meet to resolve, say, problems about referral procedures, other results may accrue from this meeting in addition to the resolution of the problem. For example, the meeting may establish a clearer understanding of the objectives and purposes of the respective organizations as well as the impetus for further forms of communication.

5. FACTORS IN THE STUDY AND EVALUATION OF A COMMUNITY: We again approach a system of such magnitude that we must select only those factors for assessment which are most pertinent to typical social work tasks. There are many fascinating ways to study the community—geographically, politically, economically, and institutionally, for instance. Our orientation here is to the human, organismic properties of the community. The following outline is designed to develop some appreciation of the community in these terms, whether the social worker is engaged in a problem-solving endeavor with certain community groups or whether he is attempting to understand how conditions within the community impinge on his practice with other social units.

a. THE COMMUNITY AS A SOCIAL SYSTEM: A systems approach to the community enhances the possibility of sorting out and making more visible particular elements of the community and how these elements are related to one another as they bear on the problem or task.

(1) The category that includes the community's salient organizations, institutions, and groups is designed to factor out which units affect the existing condition and how they are linked with other pertinent units. Recalling the Wright family, we found that the school, the court, and industry had some direct bearing on the presenting problem. In this regard, any of these units can be studied as a possible target for change or solely as a source of influence to which some kind of adaptation would need to be made. The determination of this factor then leads logically to the following categories.

(2) The location of the problem must be determined. Given the identification of the particular units in their relation to the problem or task, what is the most efficient and economical point of intervention?

(3) Individuals, groups, or other systems may be participants in the problem-solving process. Either within the target system or in contiguous systems, are there units that can be engaged to deal with the problem? To what extent are they accessible, and what stake do they have in the possibility for change?

(4) In accord with a systems orientation, the concept of resonance alerts the social worker to the effects of anticipated change. That is, how will change in any one of the relevant systems affect the others? What kind of feedback, resistance, or cooperation can be anticipated?

b. THE COMMUNITY AS AN ORGANIC ENTITY: This touches on the vital aspects of community life—the intrinsic values, beliefs, and behaviors relative to the social work task which disclose the particular ambience within which the practitioner must work.

(1) Social values are the predominant beliefs and preferences that create a social climate which can enhance or deter the achievement of professional objectives. The following are a few examples.

How the community insists upon or is permissive about social control and conformity will determine, first, the degree of deviancy that is imputed to the client system and, second, the constraints within which the change process must operate. Attitudes about abortion, divorce, minorities, mental illness, and illegitimacy are but a few illustrations of this factor.

Opportunities for social mobility (or their lack) will govern the nature of practice, particularly with clients who fall into class, ethnic, or racial groupings which are considered as separate from the values of the dominant community.

How the community defines success or failure and how these notions are assimilated by the client system has at least a subtle influence. Whether the dominant systems in the community value monetary gain or education or the virtues of hard work may seep into the setting of goals and the consideration of possible outcomes.

(2) At this point we will deal only briefly with the important concept of the power structure and its sanctions, leaving its elaboration for the core phase. We do need some beginning appraisal of the character of the power structure, how it imposes controls, and where it is located within the community. The issue of how power is manifested takes into account its explicit and implicit characteristics—whether one who defies control experiences particular penalties in direct or devious ways.

How power is achieved within the community is equally significant. Is it ascribed on the basis of status or position, earned as a
result of achievement, or delegated by superordinates? Or is its
attainment assumed as a consequence of certain imbalances within
the community?

(3) While the major social problems and issues need to be
identified as characteristics of the community, the following factors
qualify their significance to the community.

How the prevailing problems are defined and by whom governs
how they are to be attacked and resolved. Similarly, the beliefs
that are held about their causes are directly linked to the remedies
or controls that will be proposed. Thus one group will define
poverty in terms of shiftlessness and dependency and will see
forced employment as the solution. Another group will attribute
the cause to cultural defects and will encourage the upgrading
of the poor through education, better housing, and so forth. Still
another will stress the psychological causes and propose forms of
treatment.

Finally, how the community labels the victims of its social problems can be seen in relation to these definitions. Whether one is
labeled sick, incompetent, culturally inferior, or just different
governs his actions and attitudes and how he may or may not
approach the opportunity for problem resolution.

(4) The problem-solving capability, which is linked with the
preceding factors, points to the resources available within the
community that are designed to cope with the defined social problems or forms of social disorganization. This would include the
competence of the social welfare system, the accessibility and
breadth of services, and their viability and responsiveness to the
problem.

c. INTER-COMMUNITY STRUCTURES AND PROCESSES: These are
the relationships and negotiations within governmental and non-
governmental sectors and the resulting capabilities and power that
enhances or deters the social work task.

## E. Intentions and Interventions with Client Systems

As previously noted, these two factors in interrelation constitute the
aims and actions of the social worker. They are predicated on a set of
assumptions derived bilaterally from knowledge about the system with
which he is working as well as about related systems. They are directed

toward providing a context for social learning and change in which capabilities for problem solving are modified, sustained, augmented, or enhanced.

The categories of interventive activity that follow describe general forms of influence and management rather than the application of specific techniques. How these interventions are put into action will tend to reflect the particular practitioner's own style and mode of operation. For example, a particular distortion may be clarified by giving explicit information or by indirect or analagous means. Either may be effective; each is a different expression of the same interventive intent. In addition, the specific characteristics of each system obviate any universal type of intervention. Passive individuals or lethargic groups might well require more assertive forms of intervention than those which are more active, although in either instance the practitioner's intent could be the same. Thus the following types of intervention are to be viewed as general strategies responsive to the particular task and used to afford the least ambiguous and most economic approach to problem solving.

To avoid redundancy, it is necessary to shift the focus from the specific social units analyzed previously to the two major forms of human association that are typical of social work practice—the interview and the group meeting. Irrespective of whether the target of service is the individual, family, group, organization, or community, the context of intervention is either the one-to-one relationship or the group setting. While it is apparent that certain differences exist between practice with, say, a group of adolescents and a task-oriented group of citizens, for our purposes the definition of a common base of interventive activity will permit the translation of this knowledge into its specific forms in response to the specific requirements of practice. In this and in the following phases, the delineation of interventive activity will be organized according to the variables that are typical of practice in general and those that are appropriate for interviews or group meetings. In addition, interventions that are particularly significant for special tasks or problems will be specified. The use of a framework of structural, functional, and content-related interventions will assist in ordering them in accord with their purposes.

1. STRUCTURAL INTERVENTIONS: These are the actions that have as their intent the establishment of a system within which effective problem solving can take place.

a. PREPARATION FOR THE INTERVIEW OR GROUP MEETING: Included here are the intentions and actions that precede contact and are aimed at enhancing the use and value of the planned encounter.

(1) Pertinent data is collected and reviewed. To achieve some initial impressions and possible directions or alternatives for action, various sources might be consulted. Previous records, application forms and letters, or conferences with other professionals or persons knowledgeable about the system or problem are helpful in preparation. In other instances, the assembly and analysis of statistical data or research material may be essential.

(2) Planning for the meeting includes doing all that is necessary to reduce unnecessary obstacles. That there is understanding about the time and place is essential, as is arranging that the meeting will be as comfortable, private, and free from interruptions as possible. When the meeting is more goal directed, an agenda or program may need to be constructed.

(3) Consideration needs to be given to the appropriateness and value of some contact with those persons whose interest and/or participation impinge on the change endeavor. The following are offered as examples.

The decision to discuss the impending visit of an adolescent with his parents would depend on factors of emancipation or their support of or participation in the change process. Similarly, at this or at a later point, the practitioner may want to involve the mate or the family of an adult to gain cooperation and to expand his evaluation of the problem.

Referral sources should be informed both to gain needed information and to maintain necessary connections and mutuality in the endeavor. When the intent is to resolve certain community-based problems, other organizations and groups might need to be alerted.

When the plan involves the entry of a new member into an ongoing group, some thought should be given to the information that the group needs in order to deal with the event effectively.

b. STABILIZING THE POINT OF ENTRY: At the very outset of the interview or group meeting the social worker's activity can reduce uncertainty and confusion and thereby ease strains that block the use of the experience.

(1) The social worker provides essential directions and information. Here he provides what the client system needs to know in order to adapt to a foreign situation.

(2) Apprehension about an unknown, new experience is in-

evitable. Hence, the social worker's sensitivity to these conditions and his ability to deal with conflict and emotional states is invaluable.

(3) In the case of the group meeting, a bridge to the development of relationships is made by the practitioner's assumption or delegation of the responsibility for introducing the new member and dealing with the usual social amenities.

c. CLARIFICATION OF ROLES AND PURPOSES: The following are the issues that undergird interventive activity aimed at achieving a beginning orientation to the immediate or long-range purpose of the interview or group meeting.

(1) The determination must be made of what the participants seek or anticipate from the change process. As expectations become clarified, the client system is introduced to the nature of the problem-solving process, its continuity, and the attendant roles and responsibilities. For example, the client comes to discover that he is part of a joint endeavor, that certain goals are attainable while others are not, or that there are certain temporal implications.

The expectations of other constituents about the change event also may require activity on the part of the social worker. As he becomes aware of the problem and the needs of the client system, it may be necessary to resolve differences between the policies of the change setting and his own intentions. Or he may have to work out the expectations of other systems related to the task (e.g., referral sources, family members, or other community groups).

(2) A successful initiation of the problem-solving process involves planning and the clarification of procedures and intentions with either immediate or long-range implications. The client system should be involved in determining such structural factors as when and how often subsequent meetings are to be arranged, the kinds of information that will be required, and who will participate in the process.

As has been indicated, planning may also involve the change setting as regards the use of resources, the effect of policies, and the participation of other staff or others related to the problem in such matters as their cooperation or the provision of required information.

(3) Certain actions may be needed to validate, identify, or

reformulate prevailing perceptions about the problems or tasks requiring professional attention. Differential perceptions about the problem need to be worked out to provide a common ground for subsequent activity. The social worker may need to redirect the attention of the client system to other areas, establish certain connections, provide needed information, or deal with affect that blocks understanding. In addition, the determination of where the problem is located within the array of systems clarifies, to some extent, how the problem is to be attacked.

(4) Confidentiality is a factor which will influence how the members of the change system deal with the problem. This factor involves the extent to which data and communications are privileged and if not, to whom the information will be given and for what reasons.

2. FUNCTIONAL INTERVENTIONS: These intentions and actions differ in their quality. Whereas the preceding are designed to set the form of the change process, these serve to establish the process itself. It is good to note that the delineation of structural, functional, or content-related interventions is not intended to suggest that they are applied exclusively of one another. The framework is used only for purposes of analysis; therefore, a particular intervention may have a number of purposes. Clarification of feelings, for example, may tell the client something about the permissibleness of types of behavior, and simultaneously advance the problem-solving process.

a. DISSONANCE REDUCTION: This category includes the many specific actions that are aimed at eliciting and resolving conflicts about assuming the client role. Some approaches to this problem are as follows.

(1) Conflicted feelings must be evoked. As long as feelings remain internalized they will sustain fear and misconceptions about the experience. For example, clients may nurture the idea that their transfer to a group is indicative of second-rate help. Or they may assume that association with a social action group involves particular risks and labels. Consequently, the emergence of these feelings not only reduces their potency but subjects them to scrutiny and clarification.

(2) Rewards and gratifications should be provided. Stressing that these must be realistic and in accord with the developing relationship and the change process, some compensations can be

offered to offset dissonance. The interest and concern of the social worker may provide enough satisfaction at the time to make up for the conflict that the client is experiencing. New learning or needed information may also provide compensation. In any event, the client system should find it possible to take something away from his first encounter with the social worker or group that will, at least, balance the effects of his dissonant feelings.

(3) Realistic hope should be provided. A more exact form of the preceding category is the support for or the offering of hope relative to the resolution of the problem or the completion of the task. The client is most often a client because he as yet cannot envision change. The social worker has a different vantage point, for his separation from the problem enables him to contemplate probable outcomes. How he translates these probabilities can also serve to offset dissonance.

(4) Temporary controls should be provided. Where dissonance is expressed behaviorally in a way that is not immediately subject to change or reduction (e.g., by over-aggressiveness, threat, or manipulation), the extent to which the social worker can bring his influence to bear will permit him to impose certain controls. This action may have the function of reducing anxiety and bypassing behavior which would ordinarily impede the transition into the client role. Forms of control are exemplified by managing the extent and flow of communication in a group and by setting limits for behavior or types of confrontation.

b. SYSTEM AND RELATIONSHIP DEVELOPMENT: The interventive activities in this instance are aimed at establishing a climate which, through its openness and freedom, provides the medium for change. These interventions may be consciously and deliberately employed or may be responsive to interactional conditions.

(1) Taking into account the temper of the relationship or group, the genuineness with which the social worker discloses his concern and interest as well as his potential for and style of responsiveness and relatedness (his presentation of self) sets forth a model for healthy social interaction.

(2) Enhancing functional communication patterns points first to the selective use of language that is free of ambiguity and geared to the client system's maximum level of comprehension. Talking down is not implied here; instead, the aim is to meet the client

system on some ground of mutual understanding. The second element is the practitioner's responsiveness to and use of latent levels of communication.

(3) Interventions that facilitate the emergence of rules and norms are geared to identifying and developing patterns of interaction that help to reduce power strain and set useful boundaries for behavior. The appropriate degree of formality or informality has to be established in order to give the change system a sense of healthy social reality. For example, will first or last names be used? Will the relationship operate according to some protocol or notions about professionalism, or will it be allowed to seek its own level based on the characteristics of the participants?

The question of who will take the initiative around specific matters is important. Within the dyad, family, or group, will the social worker be active in questioning or directing, or will the responsibility fall on the client system?

How will authority be handled? Will it fall primarily within the domain of the practitioner, or will it be delegated? This is significant within the task-oriented group where the social work role may be that of an advisor or consultant, a provider of data, or one who tends to engineer the program.

The social worker is a key figure in determining how much concordance is required, for persons coming into relation need to know the extent to which differences can be tolerated and the sanctions for them. Similarly, persons can speed up their adaptation to the new environment by getting some clarity about what can and cannot be discussed.

Finally, a major task of the social worker in the group is to assist the group in determining and defining its norms. In task-oriented or certain adolescent groups, these norms may need to be made explicit—in the first instance, to specify a way of operating; in the second, to ensure stability. In practice with families, the social worker may find himself confronted by preexisting norms, and he will need to identify and modulate those that interfere with the change process. In still other cases, it may well be the social worker who is aware of the emergence and potency of norms and rules; this makes them no less effective nor the practitioner less responsive to their development.

(4) Guiding and directing involve direct and indirect means of

helping individuals and groups learn how to use the problem-solving experience most effectively. In some respects, this form of teaching precedes change efforts relative to the problem.

The practitioner's teaching role is evident in demonstrating and helping the client system learn the value of the exchange of ideas and information. Above and beyond the content itself, he points to how relationships are strengthened, misconceptions are reduced, or awareness is deepened through interaction.

Cognitive processes are also enhanced when the social worker teaches the client system to observe, search for, and analyze data. Here he helps establish past-present connections in terms of causality, points up blocks to perception, and elicits or provides the information that is needed to clarify the issue at hand. On another level, the value that he places on relationships and his support for their development tends to forestall the continuation or intrusion of debilitating forces.

(5) Interventions that enhance motivation include efforts to bring into the open and to activate both the internal and the external potentialities for problem solving. The first of these forms of intervention deals with setting goals that are in accord with capabilities. While this is a mutual effort, the social worker's judgment can prevail because he has a more objective view of what outcomes are possible. Hence, while the motivation of the client system is related to the extent that attainment of a goal is believed to be possible, that system would tend to set the goal at lower limits than would the social worker.

As goals become more explicit (although still tentative at this stage), motivation is strengthened by the social worker's support for these aims and by the encouragement and reward that he offers for these beginning advances to the problem-solving task.

In practice with families and groups, the social worker can use the forces within the group as a source of persuasion. Tacit appreciation of each member's endeavors can be made more explicit in order to serve as a source of support and encouragement.

Finally, when conditions outside the change system curtail motivation, the practitioner may need to engage others who are related to this effect. This could mean securing certain material needs for the system, interpreting the purposes of the change experience in order to change misconceptions, or directly involving these persons in the change system.

(6) Another intervention involves eliciting and validating commitments or contracts. In the attempt to secure explicit or implict expressions of the client system's investment in the change process, the social worker must gear his expectations to what the client is ready to do at a particular time. First, commitments can only conform to what a person has at stake in the possibility of change. Consequently, some clients may be prepared only to stabilize existing conditions whereas others might be striving for more momentous changes. Second, the extent of the commitment sought needs to be clear in the practitioner's mind. With a more reluctant client system, their agreement may rest on a very limited plan such as continuation for a specified number of interviews or group meetings. With others, the commitment would grant the social worker the right to engage with the client in more intense, long-term attempts at problem solving. But irrespective of the depth or breadth of the commitment, there must be some mutuality about the plan in order to proceed.

3. CONTENT-RELATED INTERVENTIONS: Inasmuch as the preceding categories have to do with content, here we will deal briefly with the actions that manage the major issues, themes, and transactions with which the change system is concerned—those problem-related topics that give substance to the structure and function of the process.

a. BALANCING OF SELECTIVITY AND FOCUS: These are the deliberate and responsive actions that select content for consideration, direct observation, and as a result, set the course and direction of the change process.

(1) Out of the array of information that is available or, on the other hand, because of the paucity of information, the social worker must make certain choices about what data is pertinent to the problem-solving task. This in turn directs the client system in its perception of events, conditions, and experiences relative to the problem.

(2) The strategy of selection of content sets the focus of continuing interventions. Depending on such variables as his own guiding theories, how he comes to understand the problem, and the tentatively set goals, the social worker's activity may converge on one or more of the following vectors.

The immediate task may prescribe the major content areas—for example, the data required to secure certain legislation or what needs to be known relative to changing health care programs. Similarly, the critical nature of the current difficulty may accent those spheres of information that will enable the client system to begin to take action as quickly as possible. When causality is ascribed to past events and relationships, the focus will be more heavily on historical and developmental factors as they affect the present circumstances.

Intra-system dynamics generally is an ongoing point of attention. Within a one-to-one relationship, the social worker-client transactions are subject to study. In a family or small group, its dynamics are the key factors that bear on the problem and govern how help will be used.

(3) Focus and selection ultimately become operationalized in the way that the client begins to learn how to use relevant data for decision making and the construction of alternatives for action.

b. ESTABLISHING THE PARAMETERS OF INTERCHANGE: While the preceding points considered the specification of content areas, here we are concerned with the strategies that maintain the purposeful flow of discussion and exchange. As has already been indicated, the content that is selected must be related to the objectives of the system. This the social worker sustains by indirect or direct means—his silence, disapproval, or lack of response when the discussion strays or the direction that he imposes through elicitation and confrontation. In addition, his content-related interventions are linked with his appraisal of the affect, readiness, and state of individuals, singly or collectively. At the same time, he may need to go beyond the boundaries that the client system has erected or that social convention prescribes based on his judgment and assumptions about the system's level of tolerance.

## F. Appraisal

The third component of strategy in the induction phase is the course of action wherein the social worker withdraws from interaction to review and reevaluate what has transpired. This reflection may occur at intervals during direct contact with the client system (in the interview or group meeting), in seclusion, with other colleagues, and with superiors or other evaluative sources. The following questions are designed to guide the practitioner's appraisal of where the client system is in the phase of practice and its readiness to proceed into the more intensive or specific problem-solving activity of the core phase.

1. THE TARGET

 a. Is there clarity and mutuality about who is the client and/or target for service?

 b. To what extent are the client roles defined and accepted?

2. THE PROBLEM OR TASK

 a. Have the issues been sufficiently identified so as to substantiate and define the purpose and goals of service?

 b. Do the participants understand the nature and meaning of the problem or task with enough explicitness to permit engagement and participation?

 c. Is the problem or task synchronous with the program, resources, and services of the change setting?

 d. Is the problem or task one that fits the practitioner's skill and capability?

3. DATA

 a. With what is known about factors relative to the system, problem, or task, can some preliminary assumptions be made about causality, procedure, and the prediction of possible outcomes?

 b. If further information is needed, are the sources available?

4. EXPECTATIONS

 a. What impressions are held by the client system about its roles and responsibilities and about what the social worker, the group, or the change setting will do or provide?

 b. Is there correspondence between what the change setting requires and can offer as expressed in its policies and culture? How can the client system adapt to and utilize these conditions?

 c. Is there correspondence between what the social worker expects of himself as a change agent and what the client system requires or can achieve?

 d. What implications does the impact of planned services have on the expectations of significant others?

5. MOTIVATION

 a. How well activated is the change system in terms of interest and incentive?

 b. Have resistances been identified either within or external to the system? Are they amenable to modification or reduction?

 c. Can other sources that will enhance motivation be tapped (e.g., the ingenuity of the social worker, potential strengths within the system, or support by outside forces)?

6. ATTITUDES

a. What feelings and perceptions have emerged out of the experience thus far relative to trust, personal investment, hope for change, and continuance?

b. What level of negative feelings can the system tolerate and still remain effective?

c. To what extent are these feelings and attitudes in accord with reality?

7. PLANNING

a. Has it been possible to develop the quality of assumptions about the problem or condition which will permit the development of further strategies on logical and rational grounds?

b. If so, have the next steps been worked out in sufficient depth and detail to permit the most effective and economic use of the problem-solving process?

(1) What themes and topics need to be pursued?

(2) Which theories will best explain the phenomena under consideration?

(3) What methods, techniques, and skills will best lend themselves to the attainment of the desired outcomes?

(4) What persons or systems should be included in or excluded from the problem-solving process?

(5) What resources are required for the task?

8. LEGITIMIZATION OF THE SOCIAL WORK ROLE

a. To what extent does the client system ascribe confidence and authority to the professional role and to the change setting?

b. In what terms does the client system grant the social worker the right to influence and intervene?

9. OTHER FACTORS INCLUDE THE PARTICULAR DEMANDS AND NEEDS RELATIVE TO THE UNIQUE CHARACTERISTICS OF THE INDIVIDUAL, GROUP, OR PROBLEM. THESE FACTORS INCLUDE:

a. Needed policy or procedural changes;

b. A need for special studies or data; and

c. A need for additional members for a group to achieve the desired balance.

# 2

## THE CORE PHASE

### A. *Characteristics*

As a corollary to the preceding phase, the core phase is distinguished by the decrease in questions and activity about role responsibilities and behavior and an increase in the energies directed toward the essential problem or task and its means of resolution. Although attention to system regulating needs continues, increasing responsibility for this process shifts from the social worker to the members of the system. As norms and regulative behaviors become built into the system, it develops unique adaptive techniques for dealing with regressions, external intrusions, and disruptions.

A working unanimity about the change process unfolds. The participants move toward concordance in their understanding of the nature and order of problems or tasks requiring attention, the delegation or assumption of responsibilities, the locus of authority, and conceptions about possible goals and ends. At the same time, some role differentiation takes place wherein each individual can begin to pursue his respective task in his own style.

Resources available to the problem-solving task become more visible. A more ordered and systematic awareness of the need or problem permits a more incisive search for potentialities and resources either inside or external to the system. Similarly, obstacles blocking their achievement become open to examination and possible resolution.

Greater clarity about the professional's role accrues. A more penetrating awareness of the problem-client configuration enables the practitioner to use his repertoire of skill and knowledge in more creative, precise, and planful ways.

Similarly, other resources can be utilized more selectively. Those within the change setting may be used, or when there is a disparity between program and actual services, this situation may give rise to specific incentives to modify policies that impede the achievement of the design and purpose of the setting. In the same way, the practices of other organizations or community subgroups and systems may be studied to learn their value or hindrance for the change process.

Within the core phase, new patterns of behavior and refined problem-solving techniques can be developed, rehearsed, tested, and evaluated. The change system itself may be the source of new approaches that can be transferred and tested in other systems. Or experiments taking place in other systems may be reported in the change system for examination and validation of their interactional potential and relevance for projected ends and goals.

## B. Study and Evaluation in the Core Phase

### 1. PURPOSES

a. The fundamental purpose of study and evaluation persists—namely, the selection and processing of data for problem analysis, goal setting, and the determination and refinement of interventive methods. In the core phase, assessment aims at more precise and purposeful understanding. An analogy with the skilled student of jigsaw puzzles is pertinent. When he completes the difficult task of building the outer borders of the puzzle, the interior pieces begin to fit together more readily as he begins to recognize form, color, and the relatedness of the individual shapes.

b. These fundamental purposes also include searching retrospectively for the meaning and effect of prior knowledge and interventions on the current state of the change system as well as their implications for subsequent planning and action.

c. Finally, the purposes include inducing members of the client system into the search for knowledge and awareness. While study and evaluation in the initial phase tended to be a function of the practitioner's need to comprehend and plan, the client system now is involved in the process. Its members are taught to make connections between formerly disparate pieces of knowledge so as to promote more orderly, thoughtful, and autonomous approaches to problem solving.

### 2. FACTORS IN THE STUDY AND EVALUATION OF THE INDIVIDUAL IN ANY SYSTEM: In addition to the continuing refinement and study of the factors covered in the induction phase, the following points need to be considered.

a. SYSTEM AND RELATIONSHIP FACTORS: As an ongoing target of inquiry and as a basis for effective systems maintenance and relationship development, the following points require assessment.

(1) Role ease is the measure of the extent to which the individual internalizes, understands, and acts out his status and responsibility in the change system. This also takes into account how the individual's role complements or conflicts with others' roles in the system. Thus while a group member might feel quite comfortable in his client role, other members may be threatened by his security. This situation would place him in a conflicted or ambivalent state relative to the worth of his role.

Finally, how the client role is in or out of accord with other roles carried by the individual may become an issue. The demands of participation in the change process may detract from such role responsibilities as work or family. Or psychological and social implications may arise out of the stigma that others append to the client role.

(2) According to how the individual perceives and reacts, the climate of the change system depends on the qualities of the system that enhance or inhibit the opportunity for open expression. Does he see certain risks or threats? Do maladaptive patterns which impede the development of the system persist?

(3) As the individual assumes his role within the system, it can be inferred that he will employ certain behavioral patterns (system regulating behaviors) in order to sustain the continuity and stability of that system. How he operates along the continuums of conformity and opposition, autonomy and over-identification, and dependence and independence can reveal how he perceives the system and his role within it. This is a transactional observation of behavior that is more apparent in family and group systems. In those instances, his behavior will tend to complement that of others. It is evident in the person who breaks silences when others can tolerate them, in the peacemaker who mollifies others' aggressive tendencies, or in the comedian who reduces tension and anxiety when it becomes overwhelming.

(4) The impact and meaning of the relationship involves how the individual sees and uses the change relationship as a source of or adjunct to change.

First, it can serve as a corrective experience in which old patterns are subjected to evaluation and testing and new patterns can be risked. Second, the healthy nature of interpersonal behavior may be seen as a model for other relationships. What is learned about social relationships may be transferred to other social experiences outside the change setting. Third, existing relationships may provide an opportunity for observing how others relate and the penalties and rewards for their behavior. Here vicarious learning takes place. Fourth, the strength and import of the relationship may offer the support and incentive for change. The individual may find it possible to take some risks if he can return to the security of the relationship. Finally, the relationship provides a basis for identification with others' values, beliefs, and styles of behaving. This is more than observation; it involves the assimilation of characteristics he prefers in others.

b. COMMUNICATION FACTORS: As the change system and its internal styles of relating become stabilized, patterns of communication and their purposes become accessible to study.

(1) Verbal and nonverbal patternings refer to the emergence of distinctive styles of communication that give the relationship its particular coherence and character. In a sense, how the participants communicate with one another also reveals the normative features in how they agree to relate to one another. In work with larger systems it is also interesting to note how the individual communicates with different members as an indication of his feelings about himself in relation to others. Finally, the patterns evoked by the immediate relationship may provide some clues about the individual's effectiveness in his communications with others outside the system.

(2) On another level, adaptive techniques are the patterns of communication that the personality uses to accommodate to the situation. The client may need to use seductive or manipulative patterns in order to retain control over others. His words may be used to stir hostility or rejection as a means of justifying his own hostility or his belief that he is undesirable. He may attempt to convey feelings of helplessness and thereby cling to a position of dependency. Or through devious means, his intent may be to diminish the status or authority of others within the system. In many instances, the intensity of these patterns can be measured by the inner reactions of the social worker in terms of the discomfort that he comes to feel and his impression that he is being moved in an unwanted direction. The social worker's ability to take a reading on his own visceral reactions is, therefore, a means of knowing what is taking place transactionally.

(3) How persons think and manipulate symbols and therefore engage in the problem-solving task is evidenced by their use of language, both latent and overt. One index is the extent to which the individual relies on concrete terms to explain his thoughts or uses abstractions. Consider the limitations of the person who can express his ideas, emotions, threats, and desires only concrete terms in contrast with another who can employ metaphors and analogies to convey the nature of his inner world. How one sees and understands his universe depends on the richness of the language that he has available to explain it.

(4) Not dissimilar from the preceding category, communication difficulties include discernible problems that interfere with how the individual conveys his messages. The lack of an adequate vocabulary is one example; the individual may just not have the proper words at his disposal to adequately report on his thoughts or experiences. There may also be a discrepancy between language and affect. In this instance, a literal expression of terms may be devoid of meaning because the appropriate affect is lacking or because the feelings that are expressed are incongruous. For example, if a client said, "I felt like killing my kids last night," we would not know whether he meant this literally, whether it was an expression of frustration, or whether something else was troubling him unless the statement was accompanied by feelings that qualified what he meant.

Finally, there may be a discrepancy between the idea and the word. When using such loaded terms as "love" and "hate," persons may append meanings that, at first, are beyond the comprehension of the listener. "Hate" may connote murderous impulses, total rejection, or other meanings that are repulsive to some people, whereas other persons may use the term loosely (for example, the little boy who casually says that he hates girls).

c. ROLE ADEQUACY: We return briefly to this factor because it affects the individual's capability for assuming new role behaviors consonant with the problem or task. Two questions arise here; first, the flexibility or rigidity with which one deals with or clings to his various roles both within and outside the change system; and second, the conditions within the milieu which enhance or constrain role change.

d. DEVELOPMENTAL FACTORS: Although historical and background data remain useful for gaining an appreciation of the uniqueness of the individual, in the core phase the refinement and interpretation of this data also points to how past events contribute to the problem-solving task. One dimension of this factor is the significance of earlier events as they affect the identified problem's presence, continuity, and potential for change. A second is how these events are perceived by the individual as regards his ability to cope with the problem or how he uses past events to distort or rationalize current reality and his behavior within it.

e. PROBLEM-SOLVING CAPABILITY: The key factor in this phase, which is what much of the evaluation of the preceding factors is directed toward, is the individual's ability to engage in the behaviors necessary for problem resolution. The following points are selected aspects of capability.

(1) Motivation is the measure of the extent to which hope, drive, and incentive have been activated and sustained. Subsumed under this factor is, first, the degree of ambivalence or dissonance aroused by the prospects of change and its meaning. Are these feelings reactive to the fear of giving up previous patterns and roles, or are they realistic apprehensions about the untested and unknown? Second, anxiety levels govern the intensity of the individual's involvement and activity in the change process. In some respects, anxiety is the pulse of the endeavor from which the social worker can infer the quality of activation and interest. Third, the forces within the person's social and physical environment require ongoing scrutiny to determine how they contribute to or detract from motivation. Finally, the question of whether the individual can still envision a desirable goal is most important. The original aims may change over time, and what was once seen as feasible may become lost or diffuse.

(2) As knowledge of the person is amassed, a deeper appreciation emerges of his perception, of how he sees and understands his world. Whether he sees himself as being controlled by it or as the master of it will govern the vigor with which he can attack the problem. The preciseness with which he can assess his own strengths and limitations is also significant, as is how he comes to understand the helping experience—as a symbol of his weakness, a sign of dependence, or an opportunity for change. The study of perceptual abilities will reveal, in addition, prior experiences that influence comprehension.

(3) Other abilities and conditions refer, first, to judgment—the individual's capacity to discriminate between effective and ineffective courses of action and their possible consequences. A more nebulous factor is the individual's proclivity for creative thinking and acting, his ability to invent and project possible solutions. Not to be dismissed is the issue of opportunity within the social environment to enact and test out possible solutions to the problem.

(4) Corresponding to the previous points, required input is related to the types of information, guidance, and direction needed to enhance and support the assessed problem-solving potential. Data may be needed to broaden perception, experiences may be constructed, or the person may be directed to certain areas of his environment where he can best try out new roles and behaviors.

3. FACTORS IN THE STUDY AND EVALUATION OF THE FAMILY: The thrust of assessment strategies in the core phase is directed toward the way in which the family begins and continues to engage in problem-solving mechanisms and the implications of these endeavors for the stability and continuity of the family as a unit. Change has potent implications for the type of social unit that comes to the change setting with a preexisting set of patterns. Whether or not these patterns are labeled dysfunctional, in the final analysis they represent the method of adaptation that the family has chosen in accord with what its members believe is essential to the unit's survival. As a result, the prospect of change holds special meaning in terms of how it is perceived as a threat to the state and security of the family.

a. PROBLEM DEFFINITION: How have the family members come to understand the nature and implications of the problem?

(1) Given the fact that the essential problems or needs have been particularized, what is the measure of concordance or agreement among family members concerning their interpretation of a problem's substance or meaning?

(2) Location involves where the family members assign the problem and therefore place the responsibility for change. In optimal instances, they may come to see how they mutually have participated in creating the difficulty and their respective responsibilities or need to cooperate in its resolution. The cause of the problem may be imputed to certain members. Here some complicity may be observed among the members who agree about who the culprit is and among these members and the person who will-

ingly or unwillingly plays the culprit role. This is grossly apparent in the family of the schizophrenic when his bizarre behavior is nurtured by other family members to justify their behavior and the schizophrenic member acts out his sick role in response. A third possibility is the assignment of cause to conditions or sources outside the family. While this may be a valid assumption, it does not necessarily negate the preceding tendencies in terms of the way in which the family has come to deal with external influence.

(3) Following in logical progression is intention, the question of how the family members wish to enact their perception of the difficulty. Assuming that there is some striving for change, what aspects of family life and what relationships need to be considered? Or if existing patterns need to be retained, how can they be modified to reduce their disabling consequences? It should be noted that in most cases this is not an either-or determination. The evolvement of change within any social unit usually entails the strengthening of certain patterns and the modification of others with an eye to the stability of the unit as a whole.

b. ROLE CHANGES: Any shift in the balance of a family will result in a role change. The significance of one's role has already been stressed; therefore, the following implications require consideration.

(1) Role status involves changes that have occurred in the assigned or assumed positions within the family relationships. A desirable outcome of the family's attempts to work on the problem is the emergence of a central figure who begins to assume some authority for the problem-solving experience. This is a beginning indication that the social worker's role as a prime mover is decreasing and a sign that the family is competent to deal with its conflicts and problems.

Changes in role status are inevitably accompanied by alterations in self-conception and self-esteem. Confusion and self-doubt may arise as one's position becomes threatened by changes in others' role behavior. The child who has dominated the family by tantrums, for example, finds himself stripped of coping behavior when his parents no longer fall into the trap.

(2) Balance involves the implications of a steady state for the family as a unit when their internal roles change. An example is the threat posed to the family when a formerly inhibited and compliant adolescent begins to express aggression.

(3) Because families strive for constancy and invariability, resistances to role change are inescapable. The tendency itself need not be viewed as deleterious; the modes that are employed are important. Typical resistances include the rigidification of roles, withdrawal from interaction, or forms of pseudocompliance to change expectations.

c. NORMS AND RULE PATTERNS: This point involves the amenability of regulatory patterns to modification. Because the social worker can now understand the family in retrospective terms, he achieves a more profound understanding of the implications of the norms that the family has used.

The term emerging patterns refers to new forms of rule setting which point to the ways in which control is imposed and maintained, affection is given, and needs are fulfilled. For example, parents may give up the practice of giving or withholding affection as a means of maintaining control. These patterns may also indicate the extent to which some decentralization of authority is allowed, where greater autonomy and self-responsibility are afforded and assumed, and if differentiation is permitted. That is, are individual members allowed to act as individuals according to their own predilections and values, or does a need for conformity to a single set of values persist?

d. PROBLEM-SOLVING CAPABILITY: In addition to the factors covered under the "Individual," the following points pertain to the family.

(1) Efficiency, as indicated, points to the latitude for change permitted by the family structure, composition, and expectations. The quality of leadership within the family is significant, both as it is actually carried out and as it is perceived and interpreted by family members. This assessment aids the social worker in determining what kind of input is needed to make problem solving more efficient (e.g., supporting current efforts, supplying required information, or giving guidance about how to manage certain tasks).

(2) Attention should also be given to how the family maintains or alters the communication patterns and networks through which problem solving is effected. Are messages clearly conveyed and understood? Have there been changes in the networks that are used to convey control, discipline, order, and the like?

(3) Differentiation of problem-solving tasks is vital. Irrespective of the breadth or specificity of the problem, each member needs to

be clear about his function in the endeavor. Thus there are actions that can be taken by subunits (parents, siblings) and by certain individuals (father, mother, older and younger children).

(4) The role of the social worker vis-à-vis the family refers to how his function and presence is understood by the family. What qualifies his role, first of all, is the extent to which he has been permitted to enter the family and to become an influential force. As this is established, the determination of how he is perceived and used by the family follows. The following are typical roles ascribed to the practitioner.

He may be seen as a role model of an adequate adult or parent. From observing his values, attitudes, and behaviors, parents may draw certain conclusions about how they should act; and children may revise their views about the expectations held by their parents.

Members of the family may attempt to use the social worker as a mediator, as one who will resolve differences, act as a referee, or settle arguments.

When the social worker is seen as an influence, the family permits him to enter the interactional scheme and exert his authority in effecting change. In this instance, he is assigned as much or more status as other family members.

As an observer, the social worker is only permitted to stand on the periphery of the family and may or may not be called upon to express his views. Although in some cases this can be seen as resistance, in others the family may only need the presence of the professional in order to work out their difficulties.

The family may perceive the social worker as being on the side of a particular member. Here he is seen as acting on behalf of another, possibly in opposition to the perceiver's needs.

The specification of these perceptions does not mean that they operate exclusively of one another. For example, as an influence and observer of interaction, the social worker may act as an advocate of one of the weaker members.

(5) A risk in practice with families and groups is the possibility of losing sight of the individual members as entities with special needs that can be met only outside the unit. This might include helping the individual to deal with the demands of family treatment or other external conditions, giving vocational or educational counseling, or supplying marital counseling for parents.

4. FACTORS IN THE STUDY AND EVALUATION OF SMALL GROUPS: While the induction phase focused on the processes by which an aggregation of individuals formed itself into what could be called a group according to the criteria that were used, we now are interested in how this organism functions to achieve its purposes and reason for being.

a. COHESIVENESS: It is appropriate that we pick up our assessment of the group using the last factor discussed in the preceding phase. As noted, the extent to which the members have moved toward a state of concordance and identification with the group's value and purpose is the overriding measure of its coherence as a unit. Cohesiveness takes the following factors into account.

(1) Rewards and gratifications—the positives that accrue to the group's members—are salient issues, for they act as the glue that holds members in relation. This is not intended to suggest that positives are always pleasurable or self-centered; the confirmation of one's realness may be a gratification that results from caring for or fulfilling another's needs.

(2) "Trade-offs" take into account the individual needs, goals, or values that have had to be abridged in order to achieve cohesion. The strength of a member's affiliation with the group must be measured in relation to what has been given up to make that affiliation possible. In addition, this assessment points to those conditions which may potentially reappear and reduce cohesion.

b. PROBLEM, TASK, AND GOAL FORMULATION: This task involves where the group is at any point in time relative to its objectives.

(1) Determining the original purpose involves questioning whether the reasons for the group's formation still prevail. If not, what are the implications for the structure, membership, and continuity of the group?

(2) The current purpose alludes to the question of whether the membership shares a common view of the problem, objective, or goal.

(3) Based on his knowledge of and experience with the group, can the social worker make some assumptions about the group's potential and future purposes? For example, does he predict that it will disband once current goals are achieved, or will it go on because of the social gratifications it provides or because it intends to deal with other problems or objectives?

c. GROUP DYNAMICS: This factor concerns the unique styles of interaction that evolve within a group to give it its own identity and structure.

(1) The patterns of interaction through which the group transacts its business include:

(a) PARTICIPATION: Are most members generally involved, or do only a selected few take part?

(b) ACTIVITY: Does the group generally operate at a high pitch of interaction or in more phlegmatic ways?

(c) FORMALITY: Does the group tend to follow rituals or rely on spontaneous expression?

(d) CONCORDANCE: To what extent does the group permit a differentiation of ideas and actions?

(e) DEMOCRACY: Are rights and responsibilities equally shared, or does a hierarchy of power control interaction?

(f) INTIMACY: Does the group foster or restrain the development of relationships and personal expression?

(2) Communication patterns reveal forms of interaction as expressed in the way members communicate and the evolving styles that are typical of the group. On one level, the peculiar character of the group is evident in its vocabulary and language patterns. Similarly, the verbal and nonverbal modes used to express affect, ideas, and attitudes reveal how members understand one another. Frequently, groups produce their own idioms. And as they develop a history, particular events serve as reference points for subsequent communication (an outsider, of course, would fail to comprehend these references). The facility of the group's communication patterns also reveals how they deal with problems and whether they gravitate toward or pull back from one another. Finally, silence needs to be considered as a manifestation of the group's way of operating or as indicative of some block.

(3) Autonomy, in this case, refers to the degree to which the group takes responsibility for its operation. The social work role activities are contingent on this factor, for the measure of autonomy affects the amount he must structure, guide, and teach in order for the group to function optimally.

(4) System maintenance refers to the patterns that have evolved to promote the group's survival and continuity. These include, first, the modes of socialization used to adapt members to preferred

ways of acting and relating. Second, the strength of norms and sanctions used to preserve control and order. Last is the question of whether the existing roles within the group provide models for desired behavior and attitudes. These patterns may emerge around the group's operations as a whole and in relation to specific conditions. In the first instance, the group may be discernible by its own ethos. In the latter, an array of norms may apply to lateness, the order of discussion, taboo topics, and the like. Or role models may be visible for such issues as how to be aggressive, self-revelation, and decision making.

(5) The implications of the group for individual members, another aspect of assessment, again calls attention to the fact that the group is composed of distinct individuals. Hence, it is equally important to study how the individual accommodates to and participates in the dynamics of the group and what meaning this process holds for his adaptation. For example, does participation imply increased self-actualization, or does it reflect mere conformity in the face of group pressures?

(6) Given the current state of the group process and dynamics, how do these conditions contribute to or, on the other extreme, stalemate the group's aims and purposes, its tasks and goals?

d. AUTHORITY AND CONTROL: It is important to observe changes in leadership functions over time in relation to the role itself or the emergence and decline of specific leaders within the membership. Whether and how leadership is assigned, assumed, or merited and in response to what kinds of conditions is indicative of the state of the group and how it functions. The groups's values, goals, and identity are reflected here, as are implications for the social worker's role and responsibilities.

e. SUBSYSTEMS: This point involves evaluating whether any change in previous subgroups have occurred and whether they show the intensification, realignment, or dispersion of prior associations. What is the meaning of these changes for the structure of the group?

(1) What is the quality and nature of the emotional ties between specific persons? Relationships and affiliations have purpose and may reveal that they serve to protect a member from involvement or attack, provide a positive identification, or enable him to learn about intimacy, trust, and sharing.

(2) It is also important to appraise role behaviors in order to

see the differences in how individual members act as entities and how they interact in their subgroups and with the group as a whole.
f. CONTENT: This refers to the group's major areas of interest and concern.

(1) Over a period of time the particular and recurring themes to which the group addresses itself and their relevance for the group's purposes constitute group focus. Whether the group tends to center on intragroup or external content may, in some instances, be a measure of the group's strength. We would expect a task-oriented group to emphasize ways of getting the job done and to place less emphasis on what is taking place within the group. Conversely, a psychotherapeutically oriented group would be preoccupied with relationships and transactions among the members. In the former case, an absorption in intragroup matters may point to problems that interfere with task resolution; in the latter, preoccupation with events outside the group may reveal some reluctance about interpersonal involvement within the group.

(2) Individual focus refers to the concerns and interests of individual members and involves their consonance with the group's focus. Are there opportunities for the expression and consideration of individual needs?

g. CONFLICT: Dissension and factionalism are certain consequences of group interaction unless conditions subvert or regiment their expression. The issue is not the presence of conflict but the methods used to resolve it.

(1) The dissonance arising out of conditions within the group may, first, reflect the heterogeneity of the group and resulting divergences of ideas and attitudes. Other sources of intragroup conflict may be confusion about aims, the absence or inadequacy of leadership, or the group's level of tolerance for conflict.

Denial or avoidance of the problem, compromise, the application of control, conformity to the majority, discussion, and mediation are typical modes of conflict resolution at various points in time. Or if the conflict is irreconcilable, disintegration and dissolution of the group may result.

(2) Extragroup conflicts arise when dissonance intrudes into the group from pressures outside the group. Illustrations include demands for change and conformity from other persons or groups, discord within the systems represented by individual group mem-

bers (e.g., families, organizations, and elements of the community), and conflict with the change setting's policies and program.

Such external pressures may serve to strengthen the group's solidarity and vigor about its purposes, encourage the development of new strategies, bring about capitulation, or cause the group to disperse.

h. THE ROLE OF THE SOCIAL WORKER: This point involves the implications of the preceding factors for the activity of the practitioner.

(1) Of importance is the social worker's position within the group as it is mutually understood. For example, as a leader and enabler, he is responsible in some measure for helping the group to use its potential. As a model, his behavior and values provide the members with an exemplar of healthy social interaction. As a control, he provides limits and sets the boundaries for behavior. Finally, as a source of guidance and information, he is used for consultive purposes as required.

(2) The social worker's clarity about his role in relation to the group assists in determining his behavior—when, for example, he should inform, guide or interpret, or when certain members can assume these functions.

(3) In addition to the social worker's relationship with the group as a whole (as revealed through his role and status), the quality and character of his relationships with individual members requires study.

5. FACTORS IN THE STUDY AND EVALUATION OF ORGANIZATIONS: The assessment of organizations in the core phase will deal in greater depth with their organismic characteristics. This design attempts to apprehend the vital and operational qualities of an organization that are subject to change through social work interventions. This assessment is directly linked with the prior analysis of groups which offered an understanding of the interactional component of organizational behavior.

a. THE ORGANIZATION'S GOALS: A primary means for understanding the particular character of an organization and its effectiveness is the assessment of its aims in relation to its accomplishments. Following are three orders of goals.

(1) Primary goals are the explicit objectives of the organization. These may be articulated in its mandate, title, or statement of intentions.

(2) Secondary goals derive from the primary aim of the or-

ganization. They may be planned as a consequence of observing the outcome of primary goals, or they may emerge serendipitously.

(3) Clientele goals are what the consumers of organization's services believe its objectives should be.

Obviously, a disparity between the first two goals and the last will create a state of disconnectedness between the providers and users of services. For an example of this goal concept, let us suppose that an organization has as its primary aim the provision of educational services to mentally retarded children. Over a period of time, staff members come to find that full use of these services is precluded because of poor attendance. Further inquiry reveals that the parents of the children do not fully understand the purpose of the program, partially because they lack understanding of their own role in the endeavor. In addition, these parents expected the organization to accomplish more than it was producing. As a result, the secondary goal of parent education was created and set into motion as an adjunct to the primary goal.

b. EVALUATION OF GOAL PURSUIT: This factor provides a measure of the organization's efficacy, including its operation and structure.

(1) Consensus refers to the extent to which there is agreement and commonness of purpose about the value and viability of the set goals and their relation to the needs they are designed to meet. Consensus takes into account the following bodies: the members of the organization, as expressed in their commitment to the task; related systems (supporting or cooperating organizations), as expressed in their support and teamwork; and clientele, as expressed in how services are used.

(2) Normative influences include the standards, criteria, and guidelines that are available and are used to ensure control and to measure the validity of goal pursuit. The clientele's access to the organization and the existence of feedback channels are primary mechanisms of control. Another is the opportunity for line personnel to document their observations and direct them to appropriate bodies. A final influence is the presence of a system within which the organization can review and reevaluate its operation. Statistical and research techniques may be employed in the last instance.

(3) Resources include the ways and means relative to goal achievement, their availability, and the efficiency with which they are used. In addition to the adequacy and quality of personnel and the financial

and physical resources previously mentioned, the capability of established procedures and programs to function smoothly is also a resource.

(4) A future orientation is a more nebulous factor that refers to the extent to which current goals are constructed so that they will be responsive to anticipated changes in the conditions they were designed to meet. The ability of the organization to perceive coming events tells something about its flexibility and versatility.

(5) The final measure of goal pursuit is the empirically observable or quantifiable evaluation of its accomplishments in relation to the preceding factors. The organization's accomplishments may be gauged by its impact on particular issues and problems and/or on sectors of the population. In addition, goal achievement may affect the programs or services of related organizations and systems either as its intent or as a consequence of how systems in relation affect one another.

c. ORGANIZATIONAL POWER STRUCTURE: The concept of power is one that deserves extentive elaboration. For our purposes, we are concerned here with the distribution of power within the organization so as to be able to identify the key persons or units that influence how the organization carries out its task.

(1) In considering administration, we are concerned with the characteristics of persons or groups of persons who can be identified as wielding control relative to the organization's strategies. This refers to the typical styles of operation, the techniques and modes that are used and the systems and channels over which control is held. Qualifying the performance of these factors are accessibility and responsiveness.

(2) The preceding factors also apply to supervisory and line personnel who can be identified as wielding influence and authority relative to the processes and tactics of the organization. The study of the two independent units of power cannot be complete without some appraisal of how they complement one another.

(3) In some instances, the organization's clientele, either as a body or by representation, may act as a power force and may influence the organization's policy, program, and delivery of services. A case in point is the Welfare Rights Organization and the pressure that it has been able to bring to bear on public welfare organizations. Assessment of this unit would include the characteristics of its key

persons, its own power structure, whether it acts as a cohort or adversary in relation to the organization, the leverage it can apply, and the channels by which it has access to the organization.

(4) The operational aspects of power encompass some of the processes by which power is effected. The hierarchical structure of the organization defines where power is located and the rights, roles, and responsibilities attendant to it. The ways in which power is delegated, assumed, or merited (with respect to specific duties) informs the observer about the person in a power position. Power that is earned tends to be more stable than power that has been granted or seized. Finally, the many ways in which power is employed is significant. For example, is it used to cut through protocol, to get a job done, for personal gain, to sustain programs, to maintain a separation between superordinate and subordinate positions, or to maintain the stability of the organization?

d. DYNAMICS OF THE ORGANIZATION: Because of the complexities in and differences among various types of organizations, we will only briefly consider some manifest qualities that illuminate the inner mechanism or operation.

(1) An organization's communication systems involve its prevailing networks, channels, and feedback systems and their effectiveness, formality, and style in processing information. For example, at first glance an organization may seem to have a well-defined system by which information is handled or persons are instructed and directed. But on closer scrutiny, it may become apparent that an informal network is in operation. Such a network may be pervasive throughout the organization, or it may be the closed channel of a selected few. What this points to is the need to observe the human as well as the procedural components of message exchange.

(2) Concordance, in this case, refers to the extent to which the organization requires adherence to its stated procedures and aims or directly or tacitly permits deviation. In addition to clarifying its members' parameters of activity, this factor takes into account the rewards and compensations that are given for compliance and the constraints and warrants for departure from the norms.

(3) The factor of tolerance for strain refers to the amount of tension and imbalance that the organization can endure, the con-

flict and attempts at differentiation with which it can deal. How tension is managed is equally significant. Is it by arbitration, sharing of ideas, paternalistic control, or autocratic power?

(4) Perpetuation refers to those patterns, practices, and rules that are designed primarily to ensure the stability and continuity of the organization. While these may be expressed in terms of culture, identification, ritual, or regulation, their significance (beyond their value for the continuity of the organization) lies in the extent to which they impede the delivery of services or tend to rigidify the setting.

6. FACTORS IN THE STUDY AND EVALUATION OF THE COMMUNITY: The assessment of the community in the core phase of practice is designed to achieve a more precise and incisive understanding of the special forces and processes, the elements of community life that impinge on the social work task. Again, this reflects a dual intent; one to identify salient conditions that affect the problem-solving activities of other social units using professional services; the other to illuminate conditions within the community to determine their modifiableness through social work intervention.

a. SOCIAL VALUES: Continuing with the appraisal of values, the following issues are subject to examination as regulating forces on the behaviors of community members.

(1) Value sources are important, for the origins of dominant beliefs and preferences, to the extent that this can be judged, indicate their potency.

The embedded cultural beliefs of a community may be the source of persistent and unyielding values. The relatively homogeneous community with a stable population that has a stake in the continuity of a set of social conditions offers itself as an example.

Values in transition or conflict are more usual. Here the community experiencing change, say, as a result of a shift from an agricultural to an industrial economy may undergo a period when certain values become dim or fragmented. Or another community that is sustaining changes in its population or is facing the emergence of new power groups may find itself coping with sets of opposing values.

As will be noted, the orientations of a community may also result from its institutions, special groups, or other sources. The essential point here is that the strength of any dominant value is in proportion to its source's investment in its continuity, a fact which holds a clue to its impact or amenability to change.

(2) This brings us to the identification of institutional forces, the major establishments that impinge on existing value systems. Included are those that both articulate and enforce these value systems. Most apparent are the agencies of social control and those in conflict with these systems—for example, political groups that are bent on reform or religious groups that have broken away from traditional views. Increasingly, there is a third group that selectively supports certain values but attempts to change others. Certain public welfare organizations, for example, continue to support the notion that aid below the subsistence level will provide incentives to work and simultaneously attempt to alter persistent myths about the corrupt welfare recipient.

(3) Similarly, the category of human influences serves to identify the individuals or groups who stand for and have a stake in the maintenance or change of the value system.

(4) We come now to the question of the integrity and rectitude of existing values. Inasmuch as the study of any value system can only be made by an observer whose perceptions are colored by his own values, this judgment is more or less subjective. One measure of the virtue of particular values lies in the principles for action contained within them. Whether they are employed consistently or hypocritically and for what ends is significant.

Christian principles that are used to justify racial segregation or beliefs about free enterprise that throttle competition are striking examples. Another measure is whether or not existing values are representative of the needs and beliefs of the various populations and groups within the community.

b. SOCIAL FORCES AND CONTROLS: These forces include the discernible elements of the community that have as their function the control and regulation of particular aspects of community life.

(1) Constituting the official forces are the identifiable persons or bodies who by sanction or delegation of authority have the role, status, and means to influence or impose controls or regulations. This group could include elected officials, legislators, and city and county attorneys. Contingent on their domains of influence are the areas or limitations of their responsibilities and the interrelation-

ships with or support from other community forces. In reference
to the latter conditions, a person in office may be relatively isolated
from other sectors of the community, or his influence may extend
into regions beyond the boundaries of his assigned position.

(2) Unofficial forces include the identifiable persons or groups
who, because of charisma or power in other domains, have roles
and statuses that permit them to wield influence. Business leaders,
clergymen, educators, and leaders of minority groups are examples.

(3) Institutional forces involve the identifiable structures in or
outside the community that are capable of imposing forms of social
control. Of consequence are the means that are used—for example,
by education or indoctrination, by socialization, by legal action,
by isolation and labels (as in the case of persons labeled "deviant"),
or by treatment (as in the case of persons labeled "sick").

(4) Symbolic forces include the persistent icons, institutions,
and beliefs that by their very presence serve as forms of control.
These vary from community to community but might include, first,
venerated personalities who have little actual power but who symbolize certain preferred attitudes and behaviors. The heritage of
the community is another influence. Heritage may promote beliefs
about one's honor and rights, the status of women, the privilege of
owning hand guns, and social status. Certain youth, religious, and
ethnic groups also stand for forms of social control, although they
lack official enforcement powers.

(5) The category of perceived controls approaches the issue of
social control from the point of view of the community and its
subgroups. Of importance is how they react to and comprehend
the locus and mechanics of control and the extent to which their
perceptions agree with reality. How informed and interested are
they, and how do they appraise these systems? In practice with
certain citizen groups, it is important to determine the extent to
which these social processes are seen as immutable.

(6) Briefly, decision-making processes refer to the means by
which determinations about community life are made. As one looks
at particular issues, under what aegis are decisions made? Is the
community adequately represented, or are the decisions rendered
by special groups? What persons or groups participate in and influence the kinds of decisions that are made?

C. PROBLEM SOLVING AND THE CHANGE PROCESS: In the core phase, assessment of the major problems of the community involves study in greater depth and precision with regard to how these problems are understood and identified by segments of the community and the solutions that are offered for their resolution.

(1) The term activators refers to the persons or groups that have been legitimized by factions of the community and that are capable of mobilizing and impelling action. Their legitimation implies the presence of power to act and to represent some element of the population, whether small or large. These activators might include organizations that are designed to apprise the community of existing conditions or to set changes in motion (e.g., welfare councils, community action systems, or organizers acting on behalf of other social welfare settings). Or they might represent groups and organizations that have evolved more informally or in reaction to a particular social problem. Examples of such groups or organizations include ethnic, racial, and religious groups as well as the news media and political bodies.

(2) Resisters are the identified individuals, groups, or community substructures that have a stake in maintaining the status quo or that actively oppose change. Of importance are the rationales that are used, the nature of their influence, and the threats or meanings that change implies. Thus it is important to determine whether opposition to a problem-solving scheme is indicative of misinformation about the plan, incongruent with existing values, or a threat to the stability of the system. The array of opposition in some communities to family planning, abortion, or the treatment of offenders illustrates the variety of motives that undergird resistance to change.

## C. Intentions and Interventions in the Core Phase

Interventive activity during this phase is aimed at advancing and fostering the more complex elements of problem solving. Based on the assumptions derived from the compilation of data related to the client system-problem configuration, interventive activity is directed toward the development of possible solutions and alternatives for action and then to their testing and evaluation. Simultaneously, it is the social worker's task to attend to conditions within the change system that would reinforce or impede the change processes.

The avenues leading to problem resolution are diverse and entail a number of types of change on the part of the client system. While it is possible that these changes may in themselves be indicative of the desired goal, they are also the transitions that are prerequisite to goal achievement. Following are the more typical forms of change to which interventive activity is directed.

PLANNING: The casting of a more orderly and effective way of thinking and acting, indivdiually or in concert with others, about the means by which desired ends can be attained.

BEHAVIOR CHANGE: The modification or modulation of maladaptive patterns that impair or the strengthening of productive behaviors that enhance problem solving.

CHANGE IN SELF-PERCEPTION: The attempt to strengthen beliefs and attitudes related to working out the problem by the achievement of a more viable and expansive means of self-appraisal.

ROLE PREPARATION: The acquisition of knowledge and skills that are commensurate with role expectations and status in order to attack the problem with greater authority and mastery.

DEMOCRATIC PARTICIPATION: The enhancement of motivation and the development of skills necessary for citizen participation in the activities of groups and systems concerned with the problem or task.

VALUE ELABORATION: Bringing to a conscious level the more exact nature of beliefs and preferences and arranging them hierarchically so as to support actions that are consistent with significant values. These values are then tested against those of other relevant systems.

PARTICIPATION IN TASK OPERATIONS: Engagement with others in the attempt to devise strategies and actions for task achievement.

CHANGE IN INTERPERSONAL BEHAVIORS: Modification of usual patterns of relating and interacting to maximize the use of immediate human association (dyad or group) or those outside the change system who bear on the problem-solving endeavor (family, other groups).

The following explication of interventions relative to the core phase will comprise, first, those that are pertinent to all social units and, second, those that are particularly relevant to families, small groups, and task-oriented groups.

1. STRUCTURAL INTERVENTIONS

a. MAINTENANCE OF THE CHANGE SYSTEM: In contrast with the effort to foster the development and strength of the change system in the induction phase, here the purpose is to sustain its continuity by giving attention to the stresses that result from disruptions brought about by change.

(1) Internal or external sources of strain are indentified. These might be the discontinuities within the dyad or group that accrue as a consequence of the breakdown of prior patterns, shifts in role relations, or other transitional factors. Or as the members of the system begin to change, their effects might stimulate response in others which tend to disrupt the operation of the change system.

(2) Coping mechanisms are strengthened. With the source of stress identified, it is possible to mobilize potentialities for its resolution. Helpful or supportive role behaviors of key persons may be enlisted—say, those of a father in a family or of dominant persons within a group. Previously norms and patterns that served the system well may be articulated and strengthened. Or persons outside the system may be involved either for interpretation of what is happening or for more direct participation.

(3) The social worker lends hope and motivation. Whether or not the strains affecting the system are accessible to management, the social worker's ability to envision possible outcomes may be a source of needed support.

b. MODULATION OF THE CHANGE PROCESS: This stage involves actions that manage the maladaptive behaviors and interactions which interfere with the flow and progress of the change process. These actions could include the maintenance of direction and focus in response to attempts at diversion and the redirection of responsibility as a reaction to members' attempts to reduce their part in the endeavor.

c. MAINTENANCE OF AND SUPPORT FOR INITIAL COMMITMENTS: With disruptions that accompany change, some confusion or uncertainty might well arise about the client's involvement. He may wonder whether the discomfort is worthwhile or if the desired goals are really achievable or even desirable. At this point the social worker needs to identify what is at stake and the costs of the unresolved problem.

2. FUNCTIONAL INTERVENTIONS

a. ADVANCING EXPECTATIONS: This refers to the social worker's attempts to block the client system's tendency to settle for less. Here he clarifies goals that are beyond the system's expectations and encourages and supports the endeavor to achieve them.

b. COUNTERACTING TENDENCIES TOWARD INERTIA: The functioning of the change system may be impaired by the client's desire to regress or maintain the status quo. Here the social worker's felt presence and influence can be used to offer direction, point up costs, inject his own concern, or give inspiration.

c. DEMONSTRATION: In many instances, the client system may be oblivious to its own capabilities or gains. Or it may lose sight of the practitioner's role and effectiveness. Here the social worker can use what has transpired thus far or the nature of the transactions to demonstrate his ability to help and to illuminate the client's strengths and capabilities.

d. IDENTIFICATION AND MANAGEMENT OF PERSISTENT BEHAVIORS: As behaviors come to take on meaning relative to how the client system and its members adapt to their social world, the ways in which these behaviors enhance or impede the change process can be taken into account. As these behaviors are brought to awareness (e.g., through interpretation by the social worker or confrontation by peers), they become subject to modification or control.

e. PATTERNING: These are the many means by which the social worker or the group reinforces the use of the more productive behavioral patterns that have begun to take the place of the old ones. For example, approval and confirmation by the valued group may encourage the continuation of attempts to take on a new role or to give up provocative behaviors. Conversely, the disapprobation of the group or social worker, expressed directly or symbolically, serves to deter regression.

f. GUIDANCE, DIRECTION, AND INFORMATION GIVING: These interventions maintain the course of the change experience. The input of data is required to enable the system to deal more rationally with the problem at hand. Setting limits and a focus will provide boundaries and determine areas for concentration.

g. ELICITING AFFECT AND PERCEPTIONS: Latent or disguised feelings and thoughts are major targets of professional activity in all phases of practice. In this phase, their implications for problem-solving activity become more important. The social worker may wish to deal with how feelings or distortions block growth and change, impede the development and use of relationships, or sustain negative attitudes about one's self and others. Reality testing is also an objective. The social worker may act on how these feelings are irrationally manifested in behavior, communication, or transactional events.

h. CLARIFICATION OF INTERPERSONAL BEHAVIORS AND ATTITUDES: drawing from his observation of or reports about human relationships, the practitioner is able to identify, reveal, and deal with the consequences of interaction. He may directly intervene in transactions that perpetuate dysfunction (e.g., scapegoating in families). He may demonstrate how past patterns of relating deny the possibility of change or how current relationships serve to correct previous distortions. Or he may bring to consciousness how existing relationships can serve as models for others.

i. REFINEMENT AND ENHANCEMENT OF COMMUNICATIONAL MODES: The meaning of particular communication styles should become manifestly clear in this phase. A greater degree of affinity and correspondence should be possible as a result of the social worker's ability to speak the client system's language and thereby deal with the idioms and metaphors that are peculiar to the system's way of functioning. In this regard, he is able to deal with problem-solving endeavors in the system's terms; in addition, he can manage those dysfunctional patterns that interfere (e.g., self-disqualification, double messages) or the inability to get thoughts and ideas across.

3. CONTENT-RELATED INTERVENTIONS: These are the ongoing actions that deal with the substance of change transactions.

a. INQUIRY AND CLARIFICATION: Here we are concerned with the search for pertinent data from within or outside the system, the analysis and interpretation of their meanings, and their application in problem solving. Included are the collection of data to determine alternatives for prior patterns or procedures, the consideration of past events as they influence current functioning, and the urgency of conditions in the immediate social or physical environment.

b. SEARCH FOR ALTERNATIVES: What we know about the components of the problem-client system configuration creates a foundation for the consideration of alternative possibilities for action.

(1) Engagement of the client system involves reinforcing the system's ability to move from a preoccupation with the past to the contemplation of possible alternatives in the present.

(2) Assisting with analysis, the group's or the social worker's perceptions and judgments can be used as a reality base against which alternative actions can be tested. Creative thinking and en-

visioning the widest range of possible solutions are encouraged and measured against estimations of possible outcomes. In that the notion of reality is, in essence, a subjective estimate which is usually based on consensus, the widest latitude should be offered for imagery and enterprise.

c. EXPERIMENTATION AND REHEARSAL: This stage involves the use of all available resources to enable the client system to test out and examine proposed forms of action. These may be deliberate, thoughtful endeavors or the logical product of the change experience thus far.

(1) Use of the transactional process indicates how new behaviors and alternatives for action are manifested within the immediate system. Examples include the deliberate use of role playing, brainstorming sessions, the member who gathers up his courage and attempts a new behavioral approach to a problem, and ruminations about value choices.

(2) The use of extrasystem events refers to the use of immediate relationships to study the outcome of experimental attempts in other social environments so as to evaluate problem-solving techniques, capabilities, and consequences.

d. ATTENTION TO DISSONANCE: Here we are concerned with the actions which bring to awareness or provide compensation for the ambivalence, anxiety, or confusion resulting from attempts at change.

4. INTERVENTIONS WITH FAMILIES AND SMALL GROUPS

a. MAINTAINING COHESIVENESS AND CONTINUITY: These interventions pay special attention to the value and use of the group's potentials.

(1) Clarification of commonalities refers to the reinforcement of characteristics held in common (attitudes, intentions, goals). It also involves how they function to create identity and mutuality. At times of stress, group and family members may lose sight of their common purpose, particularly as they become preoccupied with individual needs and threats.

(2) Clarification of disparities and disjunctions refers to the direction of attention to conditions which impede the group's movement. The particular group may be engaged in the exploration of these conditions and possible solutions, and group forces and dynamics may be used to resolve the difficulty. Strengthening the

status of key members, enhancing certain norms, and using the force of the majority are examples.

b. MAINTENANCE OF THE STRUCTURE: Similar to the preceding category, this factor takes into account the viability of the group or family as a unit. Role changes may cause certain dislocations requiring the support and participation of the practitioner. Attention needs to be given to the difficulties of persons whose self-esteem has been damaged by the loss of status. Changes in structure may disrupt the balance of the group, and the social worker may have to be the force who undergirds incentive and direction.

c. CULTIVATING THE GROUP'S CAPABILITY FOR MANAGING CONFLICT AND DECISION MAKING

(1) An essential responsibility of the interventive role is to provide the data that the group needs in order to make workable decisions.

(2) Universalizing involves enabling the group to understand the inevitably of conflict and to find means for its resolution.

(3) Through guidance and direction, the social worker manages the group's processes in the following ways.

(a) CLARIFICATION: Bringing the range of alternatives for action into the open;

(b) INTERPRETATION: The social worker's impression and analysis of the problem with which he sees the group struggling; and

(c) REFLECTING AND SUMMING UP: In a sense, packaging the group's various thoughts, plans, and endeavors into a cohesive unit as a cognitive base for action.

(4) The social worker uses group dynamics. To effect positive action, he may delegate or rely on authority figures in the group to manage conflict or initiate decisions; bring into the open covert attitudes and purposes; and estabilsh heretofore unrecognized linkages between the thoughts, values, and motivations of particular members.

d. MEMBER-ORIENTED INTERVENTIONS: Here actions are aimed at the needs, status, and participation of individual members.

(1) When they negatively affect individual members, certain group processes may have to be managed and the group's intentions modulated. Merely bringing these needs into the open may be sufficient; in other instances, the social worker may have to impose controls or slow down the group's activity.

(2) Advocating involves the social worker's actions on behalf of group members who are blocked or incapacitated by the group experience. The social worker's action is predicated on his assessment of the validity of taking this stand in terms of the member's role and position within the group.

(3) Supporting, another form of intervention, involves undergirding the individual's ability to deal with group demands and pressures. In some instances, individual interviews may be in order to work with personal fears or confusions that are not accessible within the group itself.

(4) The social worker may need to clarify distortions. There are times when the majority of the group can proceed with full clarity and mutuality about their plans and intentions, but certain members, for a host of reasons, may be perplexed about what is taking place. Hence, it is essential for the social worker to see to it that all members are to some extent part of the flow. Helping these members understand the reality of these events blocks hostility, apathy, or withdrawal.

5. INTERVENTIONS WITH TASK-ORIENTED GROUPS: Although the preceding interventive considerations also apply here, certain other activities are peculiar to groups that have a specific mission.

a. ASSISTING WITH THE PROGRAM DEVELOPMENT: Depending on the sophistication and capability of the group, the social worker may need to intervene to provide system and order to the endeavor. The following actions might be included.

(1) Defining purpose refers to helping the group to think through with some precision the particular means and goals to which they wish to give their attention. Ordering priorities is the major area of concern.

(2) Managing realities involves bringing to awareness the limitations of time, finances, and resources and the implications of these limitations for the task.

(3) In setting up procedures, the social worker helps to develop the means by which the task will be approached (e.g., constructing a program, setting up an agenda).

b. PROVIDING DATA: If the client system is to consider possible alternatives in the most informed way, the social worker may need to provide the following kinds of data.

(1) Demographic data concerning certain populations.

(2) He may provide pragmatic and conceptual knowledge. This information may concern other efforts to deal with the problem, or it may be a schema or framework for organizing what is known.

(3) He may give presentations (reports, research findings).

c. STRUCTURING COMMUNICATION WITH OTHER SYSTEMS: The social worker may assist with the preparation of reports, findings, and budgets that are comprehensible to supporting or allied bodies.

d. TRAINING: The social worker may guide or teach members for purposes of maximizing participation or in order that members may assume leadership roles. This activity could include, for example, delegating and supporting an authority role, enhancing indigenous leadership, or setting up leadership training sessions.

e. MOBILIZING POWER AND AUTHORITY: Here the social worker enables the group to recognize and utilize its realm of influence and power while he manages tendencies toward the abdication of authority.

f. ESTABLISHING CONNECTIONS: These activities facilitate cooperation with other groups or systems which are relevant to the task.

## D. Appraisal

The review of the content and processes of the core phase has as its purpose the estimation of the efficiency and capability with which the change system is accomplishing its problem-solving intent. Following are the major questions relative to the appraisal of this phase and its stages.

1. THE TARGET

a. Has the change process included all of the salient members of systems related to the task for adjunctive, supportive, or consultive purposes? Included, for example, are other family members, referral or other interested sources, and other organizations or groups related to the task.

b. How will the addition of or contact with other members of the system influence the balance and structure of the change system? What consequences need to be taken into account?

2. DATA: Has sufficient data been secured, or are there still major gaps and uncertainties that interfere with the development of cognition or the expansion of alternatives?

3. PROBLEM OF TASK

a. Does developing awareness of the problem, alternatives, and goals lie primarily within the knowledge domain of the social worker, or is it adequately shared by the client system?

b. Has responsibility for problem solving shifted to the client system? Are its members taking hold of the task?

c. Are there adequate opportunities for the client to experiment and test out new ways of problem solving? Are these opportunities within the change system itself, within significant groups, or in other aspects of the social environment? If they do not exist, can they be developed?

d. What resistances to change can be identified? What meanings do they have in terms of adaptive techniques and patterns? What are their meanings in terms of the change experience? For example, are they indicative of fear, ambivalence, confusion, or uncertainty about outcomes? Do they reveal a lack of knowledge needed to grapple with the problem or ambiguity resulting from the social worker's own uncertainty about goals?

4. CONSEQUENCES OF THE CHANGE EXPERIENCE

a. What rewards, gratifications, and securities within the experience sustain participation?

b. What strains and tensions derived from the experience need attention, and what are their sources? For example, do anxieties result from transitions in adaptation, from intimacy and relational problems, or from intra- or extragroup pressures?

c. What is the survival potential of the change system as it engages in the strains of problem solving? Can intrusions or risks be identified and met?

d. Is there clarity about the implications and consequences of newly developed behaviors and tactics for the client system and for other relevant systems?

e. What are the implications of change within the immediate system for the change setting's existing policies and programs? For example, are they validated in terms of their usefulness and purpose, or are deficiencies and inconsistencies revealed?

f. What implications do various aspects of change on the part of the client system have for the values and beliefs of the change setting, the community, or other dominant systems?

(1) What are the costs? Should the client conform with or resist current value demands?

(2) To what extent can the client and the social worker deal with negative consequences when change is antithetical to expected values and behaviors?

5. THE SOCIAL WORKER'S ROLE

a. Has the role and function of the social worker achieved a level of clarity that permits effective professional action and a departure from ritual?

b. How does the social worker define his role, and how does the client system define it?

c. Does there need to be a reconsideration of the social worker's stance, activity, and direction because the client system needs to see him differently?

# 3

## THE ENDING PHASE

### A. Characteristics

The completion and termination of the change process is an aspect of professional practice that resists precise definition. In part, this is due to the fact that contemplation of separation and termination in any social relationship stirs some amount of discord, uncertainty, and unpredictable behavior. The same type of disengagement may effect tears, fright, or despair in some persons and stoicism, denial, or hostility in others. Termination of the professional relationship, which is immensely important to its members, is not excepted from these emotional reactions. A number of other reasons contribute to making termination difficult to pin down.

First, in the termination process the social worker lacks the amount of control that was evident in the preceding phases. While he can use his influence and authority to induce persons into the client role and can set problem solving into motion, he has less opportunity to manage the termination process once some amount of change has been achieved and rewarded in action. At these times, motivation, interest, and anxiety may decrease in unpredictable ways. Although the social worker may still hold more ambitious aspirations and goals which are in line with potentials, the client system is the final arbiter of the nature and amount of change needed. This is not to say that the client's estimate should be taken at face value; other motives need to be considered. Yet it is possible that what appears to be premature in the professional's estimation may be quite appropriate for the client system's current needs or definition of the problem.

Unforeseen events occurring beyond the control of either the practitioner or the client may prematurely bring the change experience to a close. Spontaneous resolutions to preexisting problems, modifications in the change setting's policies and programs, the effects of vacations, and the loss of a project's funding are examples of conditions that might attenuate services.

There is also the question of whether relationships do, in fact, come to an end with the physical separation of the participants. That is, when persons are able to work out some difficulty that has meaning for their existence and their relationships with others, and when it is accomplished in relation with another caring and committed human being, the vital meaning of that relationship would tend to persist. Thus the image of the helping person would continue in the same way that we carry with us the images, the living materiality of others who have entered our lives.

In this regard, we may also question whether termination is a viable concept for the profession. It applies to a notion of practice that constructs "openings" and "closings" as the parameters of the practitioner's affiliation with his clients. In contrast, can professional services be thought of as ongoing processes to be used at times of stress and need in the existence of individuals, families, groups, and communities? This approach is analogous to the flow of a stream and the attempts to unblock or hasten its course at critical points.

Finally, we need to ask if the terms "ending" or "termination" adequately convey the import of the entire change experience. Ending refers only to the fact that a certain stage has been completed; it also denotes *beginning,* for it marks the start of more fully autonomous and productive management of a person's life and tasks. With these considerations in mind, let us return to the model of practice in order to integrate logically the process of departure from the change experience.

Other primary characteristics of this phase include, first, its aim to consciously and deliberately deal with the issues and problems of separation so as to facilitate and make useful the disengagement from service. In many respects this phase is the culmination of all the energies and efforts previously applied; it therefore demands the use of acuity and judgment to ensure that what has been learned and enacted may be maximized.

Termination involves planning and preparation, the selection of the next steps in accord with the situation's needs. These might include arrangements for follow-up or return contacts, transfer to other resources within the setting or referral to another setting, taking care of administrative factors (e.g., fees, reports, procedures), or the exigencies of ending when other services are needed but are not available.

The ending phase is also a period of review, summary, and evaluation. This endeavor enables the practitioner to understand his role, function, and contribution and the change setting to evaluate the merit of its program, policies, and services. But most important, it helps the client system come to understand what has occurred, how it came to be, its meanings, and its implications for future planning and action.

### B. *Study and Evaluation in the Ending Phase*

1. PURPOSE

a. The assessment of the nature and degree of learning and change that has occurred leads to a number of observations about the experience in toto. Review of the initial and ongoing goals reveals their relationship to the final outcome and helps to determine whether the services were effective in achieving these aims or whether the goals were realistic in relation to what was achievable.

b. Study and evaluation brings the roles of the participants into sharper focus. Members of the client system can learn more about their strengths and potentials as well as about their lacks and needs as they are revealed in the outcomes of their problem-solving experience. Likewise, the social worker can achieve some self-conscious evaluation of his capability and effectiveness and can realize new-found abilities generated by the unique characteristics of the particular change experience. These, in addition to what he has learned from errors or misjudgments, then become applicable to other change situations.

c. The prospect of separation may disclose certain attitudes, feelings, and beliefs never before revealed. Further, they indicate the extent to which there is agreement about readiness to terminate. This knowledge assists in determining the nature and timing of interventions used to obviate either premature closure or the extension of services beyond the point of maximum value.

d. Not the least of the purposes of assessment is determination of whether there are additional or unanticipated tasks or difficulties that need professional attention and provision of the necessary planning and resources.

2. FACTORS IN THE STUDY AND EVALUATION OF THE INDIVIDUAL IN ANY SYSTEM: The following factors are useful for both review and appraisal.

a. THE PROBLEM OR TASK: Through retrospection, the definition of the initial difficulty that precipitated and sustained service is refined, and the methods and processes by which a solution was achieved are identified. Following are the major implications and factors.

(1) Internalization refers to the extent to which newly learned problem-solving techniques have become an integral part of the individual's repertoire. Given this evaluation, are forms of reinforcement and support or opportunities for testing still required?

(2) Testing is the means by which task achievement or problem resolution is enacted and verified in the social environment. The kind of feedback and confirmation that follow are also important.

(3) Social implications include the interpretations and reactions of significant persons or systems to the changes. What is the expected affect of these reactions on immediate or future plans? How will these reactions support or impede changes in the individual?

(4) Transferability is the extent to which new problem-solving techniques and capabilities can be expanded and extended to other problems, issues, or tasks.

b. SYSTEMS AND RELATIONSHIP FACTORS

(1) Past significance involves what was learned and applied from membership in the affiliation with the system. How did the members of the system (including the social worker) participate in relationships and contribute to the support and climate of the experience?

(2) Present significance refers to how the structure of the system or the strength of relationship sustains and stabilizes the individual during this period of transition. It may also involve how the importance of or need for the relationship stands in the way of readiness to terminate.

(3) Future significance involves speculation about the extent to which the relational experience will serve as a model, a source of strength, or a value in the individual's life.

c. READINESS FACTORS: These are the conditions which contribute to the individual's inclination to terminate.

(1) The level of anxiety is the measure of concern about the implications of the problem or task. The form of anxiety must be carefully delineated, for it may be residual, an appropriate remnant of past feelings that cannot be fully diminished; responsive to ambivalence about the anticipated separation; or indicative of still unresolved, perhaps masked problems.

(2) Taking into account the level of anxiety, what is the level

of motivation, the degree of impetus and desire relative to pursuit of the problem-solving task? Does a decrease in motivation indicate that essential needs and objectives have been adequately met, a willingness to compromise, or an appropriate recognition and acceptance of what can realistically be achieved?

(3) The potential for change refers to the appraisal and judgment of whether the extent of change which has been achieved is fairly coincident with capabilities.

(4) Use of one's own resources is evidenced by the individual moving to a more pronounced use of his own strengths and autonomy and away from an undue dependence on the change system.

(5) Cognition involves the individual's awareness of the events that led or contributed to change. This may include how he has come to understand the problem and put it into some perspective relative to his own life, what he has invested in and achieved from the change experience, and the experiences and problems that still lie ahead.

d. THE MEANING OF TERMINATION: Here we are concerned with the individual's interpretation of the event.

(1) It is not unusual for the social worker and the client to be out of accord with one another in terms of their understanding of this critical phase. Thus any misconceptions or distortions held about the social worker's intentions (e.g., rejection, indifference) need to be understood.

(2) Turning to expectations, we are concerned with the evidence of question or apprehension that the prospect of termination has stirred in the individual. He may feel uncertain about his ability to manage other problems alone. A very pertinent question has to do with the availability, conditions, and location of further help, if needed.

3. FACTORS IN THE STUDY AND EVALUATION OF FAMILIES: It is timely to note at this point that the assessment of change in family operations, relationships, and structure needs to be qualified because certain elements differentiate the family from other social units. A major assumption is that the degrees of freedom for change are more limited for family groups than for the other units studied.

This limitation is a product of the survival requirements of the family as a structure. Frequently, much of family life is built around demands, usually covert, that its members comply with established rules and norms that are designed to ensure the status quo and continuity. Any changes in attitudes, any differentiation of behavior carries possible threats to the status and security of its members and, hence, to the continuity of the family itself. To some extent, these issues are not as critical for individuals, groups, or organizations. Individuals who are somewhat independent of family ties are freer to make a number of choices for action that therefore have less impact on the needs and feelings of others. A groups' survival, on the other hand, is of great importance, but it is not as critical as it is in a family. The demise of a group may create serious disturbances; yet freedom to move into other groups is more pronounced than the opportunities for family members to switch families. Thus group members can face greater risks in their strivings for change. Similarly, organizations usually can endure some degree of internal change and displacement. Because they generally are well-entrenched, organizations can cope with differentiations within their structure without undue risks to their continuity.

Thus, in some instances, "change" in a family may mean that its members have come to grips with the fact that no change is possible, that, in fact, the family structure and rules are fixed and rigid. The positives in this case should not be deprecated. This recognition can dilute unrealistic hopes or reduce scapegoating. Decisions then can become more realistic and explicit. While this is not to say that major shifts and changes cannot be accomplished, these points may serve to temper the meanings and implications of the following factors.

a. THE PROBLEM OR DIFFICULTY: Here we are concerned with the assessment of changes and conditions relative to the conflict that initiated or sustained the change experience.

(1) Capability refers to the extent to which the family unit's problem-solving abilities have emerged as a means of coping with internal and/or external strains. These may be evidenced in the behavior of an individual whose change and assumption of responsibility in relation to the problem has effected change within the unit as a whole, the way members of a subgroup have been able to work out their relationships within the subgroup and with the family as a whole (e.g., mutuality between parents about parental roles), and the healthier ways in which family members handle transactions with one another.

(2) Realignments are apparent shifts in role relations and responsibilities. They include the emergence of new roles of authority

and responsibility which can be counted on to sustain the changes that have been achieved and the implications of these changes for the family members' roles and statuses.

(3) Goals and values may provide indications of change, reordering, or the assimilation of new standards and aspirations. Of importance here is how the fit the needs of individual members and the family as a whole and what amount of differentiation they permit.

(4) New or modified patternings may be apparent in the way individual members and the family as a whole now provide for their own and each other's affectional, personal, material, and confirmatory needs.

(5) Continuity involves the estimation of the family's ability to survive as a unit. It may then be determined, that the family needs other types of assistance (e.g., material needs and commodities, services provided by other community groups or other forms of counseling).

b. READINESS FACTORS

(1) Levels of anxiety are measured by the extent to which there is consonance of feelings about current conditions and the preparations for termination.

(2) Motivation involves the extent to which the family as a whole or dominant forces within it wish to invest more energy in the change process.

(3) How has the family come to understand its problems, modes of functioning, relationships, or the needs and behaviors of its members? What family members have learned about one another and about their respective personalities will serve the family as it contends with the stresses of family life.

(4) Individual needs are central in the consideration of other forms of service for selected family members when there is not consensus about terminating.

4. FACTORS IN THE STUDY AND EVALUATION OF THE SMALL GROUP: Plans for termination with small groups raise special considerations that are peculiar to the group experience. Despite the degree of identification and oneness that a group may develop, it remains somewhat heterogeneous. Its members have unique needs relative to their life situations outside the group and, in addition, entered the group and will depart from it as distinct individuals. Hence, consensus about the readi-

ness to terminate may not be readily achieved. Even task groups that formed to achieve specific goals may resist ending because social benefits or affiliations have developed. Groups that meet to effect personal and interpersonal change would be expected to view termination as a rather unappealing event. This is a natural consequence because intense relationships have evolved out of the interaction in such a group, and the members have become interdependent. These factors, then, become contingencies that need to be studied as integral parts of this phase.

a. PROBLEM OR TASK

(1) First, we are concerned with the extent to which the group has succeeded in achieving the objectives for which it was formed. This also takes into account the estimation of the original purposes as they related to final outcomes.

(2) Capability refers to the effectiveness of group processes as they have impinged on the problem-solving process. This factor includes how individual members have operated as well as the functioning of subgroups and the group as a whole.

(3) Determining consequences involves assessing the particular contingencies that have resulted from the change experience and have stemmed from the diversities of its membership. These could include, for example, the emergence of the nucleus of a new group with a different purpose, the identification of another set of problems or tasks, or the emergence of some unanticipated problems or needs on the part of certain members.

b. READINESS

(1) In this case, the level of anxiety refers to the dominant feelings and attitudes, particularly those evidenced in group interaction relative to the anticipated disbanding. For example, we could include concerns about unresolved problems or unfinished business, concerns about the possible dissolution of existing relationships, or the unresolved needs of individual members.

(2) Motivation involves the extent to which the group is still absorbed with the problem or task. A decrease in motivation is frequently apparent when attendance drops, the level of interaction diminishes, or attention shifts from intragroup to extragroup issues. Motivation is also related to how the group defines and identifies its success in problem resolution.

(3) Cognition refers to the group's awareness of the processes and gains that made this social experience beneficial. Examples might include the extent to which the group's members have come to share similar perceptions of the experience, their awareness of the kinds of social learning that have accrued, and each member's comprehension of his own gains and how they have affected the changes in others.

5. FACTORS IN THE STUDY AND EVALUATION OF THE ORGANIZATION AND THE COMMUNITY: Here we are concerned with various aspects of problem resolution and planning.

a. THE OFFICIAL ASSESSMENT OF THE IMPACT OF CHANGE ON THE ORGANIZATION, ITS PARTS, OR THE SEGMENT OF THE COMMUNITY TO WHICH IT WAS DIRECTED: Such an assessment would include the preparation and submission of coherent reports dealing with the current implications of change, implications for the next steps or contingencies related to the task, and the effect of the immediate outcome of the change process on existing decision-making processes.

In short, because of the general perpetuity of organizations or communities, the immediate change needs to be viewed and understood in terms of its meaning for subsequent conditions. Simple examples are the successful culmination of an organization's attempts to revise certain prohibitive policies and the creation of a new service designed to combat a particular social problem in a community. Have these plans been studied in relation to how potential conditions would influence their implementation?

b. OFFICIAL ASSESSMENT OF THE IMPACT OF CHANGE ON CLIENTELE OR CITIZEN GROUPS DIRECTLY OR INDIRECTLY AFFECTED: This might include consideration of the need for a follow-up evaluation of the consequences.

c. OTHER IMPLICATIONS: Because of the diversity of tasks and problems falling within the purview of organizations and communities, the following examples are offered. The meaning of change may affect the need to modify other existing programs, policies, and services; or the definition of new tasks and objectives may arise from the immediate changes. Also, a consideration of resources may be required to carry out the product of the problem-solving experience; or plans may be made to transfer leadership functions to other individuals and groups or to retain the present leadership. Finally other residual tensions or discords may require attention.

## C. Interventions with Various Client Systems

The following points include the broad array of interventions that are typical of the termination of practice.

1. REINFORCEMENT OF CHANGE: Through these activities the social worker attempts to stabilize the problem-solving patterns that have evolved.

a. ENACTMENT AND EVALUATION: These interventions enable the client system to put into practice that which has been gained and learned.

(1) Validating capabilities involves providing rewards and reinforcement to support and strengthen desired behavior.

(2) Clarifying differentials enables the client system to understand the varied implications of particular problem-solving techniques. For example, consider the client who has learned to assert himself and now needs to test out these forms of self-expression according to the requirements of his different roles.

(3) Blocking tendencies toward regression involves anticipating or dealing with the inclination to return to previous modes of behavior.

(4) Identifying opportunities refers to helping the system to find the occasion to implement plans and techniques.

(5) Dealing with the implications of change takes into account the feedback that the client system is receiving as well as the impact of change on significant others.

b. ENHANCING THE POTENTIAL FOR THE TRANSFER OF LEARNING: These are interventions that enable the client system to utilize what has been learned for other problems or conditions. This may include identifying and clarifying other situations subject to the newly found problem-solving skills (e.g., how more adequate marital roles carry over into parent-child relationships or how a citizen group can move on to the completion of more complex tasks).

2. INTERVENTIONS RELATED TO THE POSSIBILITY OF UNPLANNED TERMINATION: When, according to the social worker's appraisal, premature termination seems possible or imminent, the following interventions typically apply.

a. TESTING FOR MOTIVATION: These interventions focus on or clarify the diminution of intent and its meanings. When motivation cannot be activated, consideration needs to be given to alternatives for action or to the provision of channels for reentry into the change setting at another time.

b. MANAGING RESISTANCES: As was previously noted, these interventions attempt to bring to conscious awareness the expectations, disappointments, misconceptions, or apprehensions that militate against continuance.

c. MANAGING IMPEDIMENTS: These activities are concerned with the structural and functional factors that block interaction, participation, and change. The following interventions might be included.

(1) Modifying imbalances in group structure is applicable when the obstacle does not reside within the particular member but rather is the consequence of an unworkable group composition (e.g., an overabundance of members who dominate discussion).

(2) Policies and procedures that impair the change system's operation may be modified.

(3) The impediment may be inequities or deprivations in the client's environment (extrasystem problems) that block his participation in the otherwise desirable change experience.

(4) Managing forces outside the change system may require the involvement of relevant persons, groups, or organizations, or when they are not accessible, helping the client to mobilize his capabilities to deal with these conditions.

3. PREPARATION FOR PLANNED TERMINATION

a. APPRISING: This factor involves determining the appropriate timing and bringing to the client system's awareness the impending reality of termination. These interventions also include clarifying the system's actions and attitudes about the readiness for termination and setting aside sufficient time to deal with contingencies.

b. INVOLVING: Those actions serve to engage the members of the system in planning for the contingencies of ending. This approach involves helping the client system to make a formal or informal evaluation of the meaning of the change experience.

c. MAINTAINING: These interventions support and hold constant the change system during movement out of services. The object is to strengthen the system's use in managing tensions and apprehensions, supporting appropriate leadership roles, and preventing premature departure.

d. PLANNING: These interventions are geared to postservice needs and conditions. Many actions are possible here. For instance, the social worker may make preparations for transferring clients to other persons within the change setting (including arranging for introductions, making records available, and preparing reports), or he may provide channels for entry into services elsewhere. He may clarify, if appropriate, the future availability of his help, the setting's services, or other resources; and he may, in fact, arrange for follow-up contacts. He often assists with the preparation of reports and findings. Finally, he manages the contingencies arising from goal achievement (e.g., identifying emerging problems and the individuals or groups requiring further service).

## D. Appraisal

The ending phase is in itself a period of appraisal and a process of estimating the outcome of service and identifying the factors which contributed to or detracted from the achievement of the desired goal. The following issues and questions, indicative of the broader ramifications of the change experience, also require attention.

### 1. PRACTICE FACTORS

a. What has been learned from the experience that has meaning for the professional knowledge of the social worker and other related professionals?

(1) Can conceptualizations or assumptions be made that will expand awareness or help unravel the complexities of the particular social problem that was treated?

(2) Can what has been learned be transferred to similar situations?

b. What has been learned as a result of using certain methods, techniques, and skills with particular social units or population groups that can enhance the capability of the social worker or other professionals? Is it possible to sort out orientations to problem solving that have proved to be efficient and helpful?

c. What contingencies or issues have arisen from the experience that have implications for similar endeavors? These might include the value of reaching-out services, preventive work to anticipate certain problems, the need for specific types of information, and the value of engaging other resources or organizations.

d. What are the implications of the outcome for further study and research?

2. ADMINISTRATIVE FACTORS

a. What implications arising from the change experience bear on the effectiveness and utility of existing policies, programs, and services? Are there indications for change or for strengthening or maintaining current policies?

b. Has the change event been sufficiently documented to inform the administration of the nature of the problems treated, the population groups served, and the implications and otucomes of service?

3. ACCOUNTABILITY

a. Are adequate records, reports, findings, or recommendations prepared in the event that there is later contact with the client system, for transfer to other professionals or resources, for statistical and accounting purposes, or to specify the outcome and consequences of service?

b. Have others related to the problem or task (referral sources, other organizations) been appropriately informed?

# BIBLIOGRAPHY

Allport, G. W. "Social Science in Perspective," *Personality and Social Encounter*. Boston: Beacon Press, 1960.

American Association of Social Workers. *Social Casework: Generic and Specific*. A report of the Milford Conference. New York: American Association of Social Workers, 1929.

Aptekar, H. "New Trends in Social Work Practice." Unpublished seminar presentation, San Diego State College, 1967.

Arkava, M. L. "Social Work Practice and Knowledge: An Examination of Their Relationship," *Journal of Education for Social Work*, Vol. 5, No. 2 (1967), 10–12.

Bartlett, H. "Social Work Fields of Practice." In *Encyclopedia of Social Work*, ed. by R. Morris, Vol. 2. New York: National Association of Social Workers, 1971.

Berenson, B. G., and R. R. Carkhuff. *Sources of Gain in Counseling and Psychotherapy*. New York: Holt, Rinehart and Winston, 1967.

Bergson, H. "Intuitionism," *An Introduction to Metaphysics*. New York: Putnam, 1912.

Bertalanffy, L. von. *General Systems Theory*. New York: George Braziller, 1968.

Blau, P. M. *Exchange and Power in Social Life*. New York: John Wiley and Sons, 1964.

Boehm, W. W. "Common and Specific Learnings for a Graduate School of Social Work," *Journal of Education for Social Work*, Vol. 4, No. 2 (1966), 15–26.

————, dir. *Social Work Curriculum Study*. 13 vols. New York: Council on Social Work Education, 1959.

Bruner, J. *The Process of Education*. New York: Vintage Books, 1960.

Bruno, F. J. *Trends in Social Work Practice: 1874–1956*. New York: Columbia University Press, 1957.

Buckley, W. *Sociology and Modern Systems Theory.* Englewood Cliffs, N.J.: Prentice-Hall, 1967.

Burns, M., and P. Glazer. "Similarities and Differences in Casework and Group Work Practice," *Social Service Review,* No. 4 (1963), 416–28.

Campbell, D. T. "Methodological Suggestions from a Comparative Psychology of Knowledge Processes," *Inquiry,* No. 2 (1959), 152–82.

Carson, R. C. *Interactional Concepts of Personality.* Chicago: Aldine Publishing Co., 1969.

Coleman, H. "The Importance of Helping Person Characteristics in Social Work Treatment and Their Implication for Social Work Education." Master's thesis, San Diego State College, 1967.

Council on Social Work Education. *Statistics on Social Work Education, 1968–69.* New York: Council on Social Work Education, 1970.

Deutsch, K. W. "Mechanism, Teleology and Mind," *Philosophy and Phenomenological Research,* Vol. 12 (1951), 198.

Ellenberger, H. *The Discovery of the Unconscious.* New York: Basic Books, 1970.

Eron, L. D., and R. Callahan. *The Relation of Theory to Practice in Psychotherapy.* Chicago: Aldine Publishing Co., 1969.

Etzioni, A. *Modern Organizations.* Englewood Cliffs, N.J.: Prentice-Hall, 1964.

French, L. *Psychiatric Social Work.* New York: Commonwealth Fund, 1940.

Goldstein, A. *Therapist-Patient Expectancies in Psychotherapy.* New York: Pergamon Press, 1962.

Goldstein, A.; K. Heller; and L. Sechrest. *Psychotherapy and the Psychology of Behavior Change.* New York: John Wiley and Sons, 1966.

Goldstein, H. "A Search for the Primary Content and Nature of Social Work Practice in Family Casework." Doctoral dissertation, University of Southern California, 1970.

Gordon, W. E. "A Critique of the Working Definition," *Social Work,* No. 4 (1962), 7.

Gouldner, A. W. *The Coming Crisis of Western Sociology.* New York: Basic Books, 1970.

Guilford, J. P. *The Nature of Human Intelligence.* New York: McGraw-Hill, 1967.

Hamilton, G. *Theory and Practice of Social Case Work.* New York: Columbia University Press, 1951.

Hartman, A. "But What Is Social Casework?" *Social Casework*, No. 7 (1971), 411–19.

Hearn, G. "Toward a Unitary Conception of Social Work Practice." Address to the 4th Annual Student Social Work Conference, University of Washington, 1963.

Henry, W.; V. Sims; and S. Spray. *The Fifth Profession*. San Francisco: Jossey-Bass, 1971.

Hill, Octavia. *Life of Octavia Hill,* Ed. by C. E. Maurice. London: Mac-Millan Co., 1913.

Hinsie, Leland E., M.D., and Robert Jean Campbell, M.D., eds. *Psychiatric Dictionary,* "Socialization." New York: Oxford University Press, 1960.

Hollis, E. V., and A. L. Taylor. *Social Work Education in the United States*. New York: Columbia University Press, 1951.

Jehu, D. *Learning Theory and Social Work*. London: Routledge and Kegan Paul, 1967.

Kadushin, A. "The Knowledge Base of Social Work." In *Issues in American Social Work,* ed. by A. J. Kahn, 39–41. New York: Columbia University Press, 1959.

Kasius, C., ed. *A Comparison of Diagnostic and Functional Case Work Concepts*. New York: Family Service Association of America, 1950.

Katz, R. L. *Empathy*. New York: Free Press of Glencoe, 1963.

Kelso, R. W. "Changing Fundamentals in Social Work." In *Readings in Social Casework,* ed. by Fern Lowry. New York: Columbia University Press, 1939.

Klein, P. *From Philanthropy to Social Welfare*. San Francisco: Jossey-Bass, 1968.

Kohs, S. C. *Roots of Social Work*. New York: Association Press, 1966.

Konopka, G. *Social Group Work: A Helping Process*. Englewood Cliffs, N.J.: Prentice-Hall, 1963.

Laing, R. D. *The Self and Others*. New York: Pantheon Books, 1969.

Lennard, H., and A. Bernstein. *The Anatomy of Psychotherapy*. New York: Columbia University Press, 1960.

————. *Patterns in Human Interaction*. San Francisco: Jossey-Bass, 1969.

Levine, S. "Psychotherapy as Socialization," *International Journal of Psychiatry,* No. 3 (1969), 645–55.

Lide, P. "Dynamic Mental Representation: An Analysis of the Empathic Process," *Social Casework,* No. 3 (1966), 146–51.

London, P. *The Modes and Morals of Psychotherapy.* New York: Holt, Rinehart and Winston, 1964.

Lurie, H. L., ed. *Encyclopedia of Social Work.* New York: National Association of Social Workers, 1965.

McCormick, M. J. "Social Advocacy: A New Dimension in Social Work," *Social Casework,* No. 1 (1970), 3–11.

MacIver, R. M. *The Web of Government.* New York: Macmillan, 1947.

Mullen, E. J. "Differences in Worker Styles in Casework," *Social Casework,* No. 6 (1969), 347–53.

Perlman, H. H. "Social Work Method: A Review of the Past Decade," *Social Work,* No. 4 (1965), 166–78.

Picardie, M. "Learning Theory and Casework," *Social Work* (London), No. 1 (1967), 10–15.

Pincus, A., and A. Minahan. "Toward a Model for Teaching a Basic First Year Course in Methods of Social Work Practice." In *Innovations in Teaching Social Work Practice,* ed. by L. Ripple. New York: Council on Social Work Education, 1970.

Plotnick, H. "The Attitudinal Orientation of the Worker and Accuracy in Predicting Client Behavior," *Social Service Review,* No. 1 (1965), 23–30.

Prosch, H. *The Genesis of Twentieth Century Philosophy.* Garden City: Doubleday and Co., 1964.

Reid, W. "Characteristics of Casework Intervention," *Welfare in Review,* No. 8 (1967), 11–19.

———. "A Study of Caseworkers' Use of Insight-Oriented Techniques," *Social Casework,* No. 1 (1967), 3–9.

Reynolds, B. C. "The Social Casework of an Uncharted Journey," *Social Work,* No. 4 (1964), 13–15.

Richmond, M. *Social Diagnosis.* New York: Russell Sage Foundation, 1917.

———. *What Is Social Casework?* New York: Russell Sage Foundation, 1922.

Robinson, V. *A Changing Psychology in Social Case Work.* Chapel Hill: University of North Carolina Press, 1930.

Robinson, V., and J. Taft. *A Functional Approach to Family Casework.* Philadelphia: University of Pennsylvania Press, 1944.

Rogers, C. "Client-Centered Therapy." In *Theories of Counseling and Psychotherapy,* ed. by C. H. Patterson. New York: Harper and Row, 1966.

Ross, M. G. *Community Organization: Theory and Principles*. New York: Harper and Brothers, 1955.

Ruesch, J. "General Theory of Communication." In *American Handbook of Psychiatry*, ed. by S. Arieti, Vol. 2. New York: Basic Books, 1959.

Schmidt, J. "The Use of Purpose in Casework," *Social Work*, No. 1 (1969), 77–84.

Schneiderman, L. "Social Welfare, Social Functioning and Social Work: An Effort at Integration." Mimeographed. Ohio State University, 1969.

Sloan, R. B. "The Converging Paths of Behavior Therapy and Psychotherapy," *International Journal of Psychiatry*, No. 7 (1969), 493–500.

Smith, H. C. *Sensitivity to People*. New York: McGraw-Hill, 1966.

Strupp, H., and A. Bergin. "Some Empirical and Conceptual Bases for Coordinated Research in Psychotherapy: A Critical Review of the Issues, Trends and Evidence," *International Journal of Psychiatry*, No. 2 (1969), 18–80.

Strupp, H.; R. Fox; and K. Lessler. *Patients View Their Psychotherapy*. Baltimore: Johns Hopkins University Press, 1969.

Studt, E. "An Outline for the Study of Social Authority Factors in Casework," *Social Casework*, No. 6 (1954), 233–36.

———. "Worker-Client Authority Relationships in Social Work," *Social Work*, No. 1 (1959), 23–26.

Stumpf, J. "Teaching an Integrated Approach to Social Work Practice." In *Innovations in Teaching Social Work Practice*, ed. by L. Ripple. New York: Council on Social Work Education, 1970.

Taber, M., and A. Vattano. "Clinical and Social Orientations in Social Work: An Empirical Study," *Social Service Review*, No. 1 (1970), 34–43.

Taft, J. *Dynamics of Therapy in a Controlled Relationship*. New York: MacMillan, 1935.

Thibaut, J. W., and H. H. Kelly. *The Social Psychology of Groups*. New York: John Wiley, 1959.

Thomas, E. J., and R. A. Feldman. "Concepts of Role Theory." In *Behavioral Science for Social Workers*, ed. by E. J. Thomas. New York: The Free Press, 1967.

Watzlawick, P.; J. Beavin; and D. Jackson. *Pragmatics of Human Communication*. New York: W. W. Norton, 1967.

Westcott, M. *Toward a Contemporary Psychology of Intuition*. New York: Holt, Rinehart and Winston, 1968.

Witte, E. F. "The Curriculum Study: Some Personal Observations," *Social Work*, No. 3 (1959), 3–15.

Zanger, A. "A Study of Factors Related to Clinical Empathy," *Social Casework*, No. 2 (1968), 11–32.

# INDEX

Acceptance, 135–36; social worker's ability for, 70–73; stages of, 72
Adaptive functions: in study of the individual, 199–201
Addams, Jane, 26
Agency. *See* Change Environment
Allport, G. W., 117
American Association of Social Workers. *See* Professional organizations
American Social Science Association, 23
Appraisal of practice, 189; administrative factors in, 275; in core phase, 260–62; in ending phase, 274–75; in induction phase, 228–30
Authority: definition of, 83–84; derivations of, 84–85; in groups, 211–12, 243; in organizations, 216; in social worker-client system, 132. *See also* Power

Bartlett, H., 186
Beavin, J., 61, 163
Berenson, B. G., 170
Bergin, A., 59, 170
Bergson, Henri, 69
Bernstein, A., 111, 113, 120–21, 131
Bertalanffy, L. von, 105, 111, 114, 187
Black Box concept, 164
Blau, P. M., 84
Boehm, W., 50
Bruner, J., 69
Bruno, F., 22, 24, 25, 26, 27, 28, 37

Buckley, W., 110, 111, 116
Bureaucratic protocol, 97–98

Cabot, R., 25
Callahan, R., 166
Campbell, D. T., 166
Canon, I., 25
Carkhuff, R. R., 170
Carson, R. C., 80, 137, 171
Casework. *See* Individuals, practice with, and Social Casework
Causality, 159–60; in early practice, 26; changes in conception of, 114–15
Change: in community, 252; concepts of, 159–60; consequences of, 261; definition of, 159–60; enactment and evaluation of, 272; reinforcement of, 272; social learning and, 169; types of, 253
Change environment, 121–30; culture of, 124–25; communication in, 128; definition of, 121–22; output of, 127–28; purpose and function of, 125–26; structural properties of, 124–25; as a symbolic influence, 97–98
Change system, 120–53; maintenance of, 253–54
Charity Organization Society, 24
Client (system): ability to relate, 140–41; attitudes and expectations of, 132–33; characteristics of, 111–17; definition of, 18, 117; involuntary, 86–87, 133–34; role of, 129–30, 233; role induction of, 131; role strain in,

**SOCIAL WORK PRACTICE:**
**A Unitary Approach**

Composition, offset lithography, and binding by the Kingsport Press, Kingsport, Tennessee. The typeface is Times Roman, the paper Warren's University Text watermarked with the emblem of the University of South Carolina Press, and the binding is in Roxite vellum manufactured by Holliston Mills.